THE YOUNG PEOPLE'S
ENCYCLOPEDIA
OF THE
UNITED STATES

General Editor: William E. Shapiro

I

ABERNATHY / FOLSOM CULTURE

KINGSBROOK

First published in 1992 by The Millbrook Press Inc.,
2 Old New Milford Road, Brookfield, Connecticut 06804

© Grisewood & Dempsey Ltd. and The Millbrook Press Inc., 1992

LIBRARY OF CONGRESS CATALOGING-IN-PUBLICATION DATA

The Young People's Encyclopedia of the United States
p. cm.
Includes index.
Summary: A multivolume encyclopedia with over 1200 alphabetically-
arranged entries covering such topics as the history,
physical features, festivals, and music of the United States
and its neighbors, Mexico and Canada.
ISBN 1–56294–054–6
1. The United States—Encyclopedias. Juvenile.
2. North America—Encyclopedias. Juvenile.
[1. United States—Encyclopedias. 2. North America—Encyclopedias.]
E156.Y68 1992
970.003—dc 20   91–4141
CIP
AC

Printed and bound in the United States

THE SUBJECT SYMBOLS

Each entry in this encyclopedia has its own easily recognized symbol opposite the heading. This symbol tells you at a glance which area of interest the entry falls into. Below are the 12 subject areas we have used.

HISTORY Events from before colonial times to the present day.

LITERATURE AND THE ARTS Novelists, playwrights, folklore, folk art and crafts, theater, dance, painting, sculpture, architecture of the United States.

PEOPLE AND CULTURE Native and immigrant peoples of North America, their languages and customs, education, health and welfare, social issues.

GEOGRAPHY The land and climate of North America: geographic regions, mountain ranges, rivers and lakes, coastlines, national parks.

SCIENCE AND SPACE Explorations into fields of science and astronomy, famous scientists and innovators.

INDUSTRY AND TECHNOLOGY Transportation, natural resources, manufacturing — industries of yesterday and today.

GOVERNMENT AND LAW The U.S. government, its branches and how it works; the armed services and other governmental organizations; political parties; laws and treaties.

RELIGION, PHILOSOPHY, AND MYTH The wide variety of religious denominations, philosophers and their ideas, myths and legends.

SPORTS AND PASTIMES Baseball, football, basketball, and other sports, sports heroes, plus many hobbies.

COUNTRIES AND PLACES Our neighbors in North and Central America and places of interest.

ANIMALS, PLANTS, AND FOOD North American animals and their habitats, North American plants, agriculture and food, including regional specialities.

STATES AND CITIES Descriptions of each U.S. state, major cities, and sites within and around the country.

Products of American AGRICULTURE are exported around the world.

ABERNATHY, Ralph David

The Reverend Ralph David Abernathy (1926–1990) was a leader of the CIVIL RIGHTS movement. Born into a poor farming family in Alabama, he graduated from college and became a Baptist minister. Abernathy became friends with Dr. Martin Luther KING, Jr., in Montgomery, Alabama. The two of them led the successful protest against segregation on the buses there. Abernathy and King worked together in many other civil rights demonstrations and sometimes were arrested and went to jail together. After King was murdered in 1968, Abernathy succeeded him as president of the Southern Christian Leadership Conference. He held this position until 1977. Abernathy told the story of his role in the civil rights movement in the book *The Walls Came Tumbling Down*.

ABOLITIONISTS

Abolitionists was the name given to people in 19th-century America who urged that SLAVERY be ended, or abolished. In 1808 the importation of slaves was outlawed in the United States. But slavery itself continued to be legal in 11 southern states, where plantation owners depended on it to make a profit. When abolitionists began to condemn slavery more severely, some states responded by passing harsher laws against runaway slaves. They even made it unlawful for masters to free their slaves.

Such actions won more people to the abolitionist cause. By 1840 more than 150,000 people were members of abolitionist societies. It was still not a popular

▼ Many abolitionists were Quakers or New Englanders, but freed slaves such as Frederick Douglass also joined the movement. William Lloyd Garrison founded a newspaper, The Liberator, which tried to make more people aware of the fight against slavery. Lucretia Mott was a Quaker who helped to found the American Anti-Slavery Society. Wendell Phillips, a New England orator, gave up his law practice to join the abolitionist cause.

Wendell Phillips **Lucretia Coffin Mott** **William Lloyd Garrison** **Frederick Douglass**

▲ Rain Man *stars Tom Cruise and Dustin Hoffman hold two of the four Oscars won by the 1988 film at the Academy Awards. Rain Man was named best film, and Hoffman won the best actor award.*

▼ *The Oscar was named accidentally in 1931 by an academy librarian, Margaret Hickman. When she saw the statuette she exclaimed, "Why, it looks like my Uncle Oscar!"*

cause, however, even in the North. Abolitionists' meetings were often broken up by mobs, and their printing presses were sometimes destroyed.

The abolitionists themselves did not agree about how slavery should be abolished. One group, led by William Lloyd GARRISON, demanded an immediate end to slavery without any payment, or compensation, to the owners. Others wanted a gradual program of freedom, or emancipation, with compensation. Still another group, who came to be called "anti-slavery men," simply opposed the spread of slavery into the new states. Some abolitionists, such as Harriet TUBMAN, an escaped slave, helped other slaves flee to the North by way of the UNDERGROUND RAILROAD.

Among the abolitionists were several famous writers. They included John Greenleaf WHITTIER, Julia Ward HOWE, Harriet Beecher STOWE and the poet and essayist James Russell LOWELL. Their works helped to awaken the public's conscience to the evils of slavery.

ACADEMY AWARDS

The Academy Awards are special tributes to MOTION PICTURES released in the previous year and to those involved in making them, including film actors, actresses, writers, and directors. These awards have been presented each year since 1929.

The awards themselves, statuettes called Oscars, are given by the Academy of Motion Picture Arts and

Academy Award Winners: Best Film 1960–1990

Year		Year	
1990	Dances with Wolves	1974	The Godfather, Part II
1989	Driving Miss Daisy	1973	The Sting
1988	Rain Man	1972	The Godfather
1987	The Last Emperor	1971	The French Connection
1986	Platoon	1970	Patton
1985	Out of Africa	1969	Midnight Cowboy
1984	Amadeus	1968	Oliver!
1983	Terms of Endearment	1967	In the Heat of the Night
1982	Gandhi	1966	A Man for All Seasons
1981	Chariots of Fire	1965	The Sound of Music
1980	Ordinary People	1964	My Fair Lady
1979	Kramer vs. Kramer	1963	Tom Jones
1978	The Deer Hunter	1962	Lawrence of Arabia
1977	Annie Hall	1961	West Side Story
1976	Rocky	1960	The Apartment
1975	One Flew Over the Cuckoo's Nest		

Sciences. All members of the academy are people who actually work as professionals in the film industry. Oscar winners are chosen by a vote among all the members.

Some famous winners of the Best Picture Award include *Gone With the Wind* (1939), *Casablanca* (1943), *Lawrence of Arabia* (1962), and *Rain Man* (1988). People may win an Oscar more than once in a lifetime. Jane Fonda won the Best Actress Award for *Klute* (1971) and for *Coming Home* (1978). Marlon Brando won the Best Actor Award for *On the Waterfront* (1954) and for *The Godfather* (1972).

ACHESON, Dean

Dean Acheson (1893–1971) was secretary of state from 1949 to 1953, under President Harry TRUMAN. Before that, from 1945 to 1947, he served as undersecretary. Acheson set U.S. foreign policy during the early years of the period known as the COLD WAR, including the U.S. government's refusal to recognize Communist China. In 1947 he helped Secretary of State George C. MARSHALL devise the Truman Doctrine—economic aid aimed at keeping Greece and Turkey free of Soviet domination. He also played a part in setting up the Marshall Plan in 1947. In 1949 he helped create the NORTH ATLANTIC TREATY ORGANIZATION (NATO).

▲ *Dean Acheson's book,* Present at the Creation: My Years in the State Department, *won a Pulitzer Prize for history.*

ADAMS, Ansel

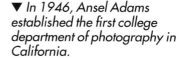

▼ *In 1946, Ansel Adams established the first college department of photography in California.*

The work of the photographer Ansel Adams (1902–1984) expresses his love of the American landscape. Adams worked almost entirely in black and white. By carefully controlling the black and white tones, he produced powerful, haunting images, especially of the American West. His work helped to establish photography as an art form in its own right—not just a poor relation of painting. The photographs also awakened the public to the need to conserve America's unspoiled land. Adams was a campaigner for conservation, and his photographs helped to persuade people of the rightness of his cause. Adams also wrote a number of books on photography.

In 1940, Adams helped to set up a department of photography at New York City's Museum of Modern Art. Six years later, he founded a photography department at what is now the San Francisco Art Institute.

John Adams
Born: October 30, 1735, in Braintree (now Quincy), Massachusetts
Education: Harvard College
Political party: Federalist
Term of office: 1797–1801
Married: 1764 to Abigail Smith
Died: July 4, 1826, in Quincy

▼ A drawing of the White House made in the early 1800s. The White House was not yet completed when President John Adams and his wife, Abigail, moved into it.

John Adams was the first vice president of the United States and the second president. Adams was born in Massachusetts and studied to be a lawyer. He later became a leader in opposing British policies in the American colonies.

Adams was elected to the Massachusetts House of Representatives in 1771 and to the CONTINENTAL CONGRESS in 1774. In Congress he argued for American independence. In 1776 he helped draft the DECLARATION OF INDEPENDENCE.

In 1780, Adams helped draw up the state constitution of Massachusetts. He served as a minister to France, the Netherlands, and Britain. He helped to negotiate the treaty with Britain that ended the American REVOLUTION. In 1789 he became America's first vice president, under George WASHINGTON, the first president.

Two political parties were emerging at this time: the more conservative FEDERALISTS and the liberal Democratic-Republicans. Adams, a Federalist, believed in a strong federal government.

In 1796, Adams was elected president. Thomas JEFFERSON, a Democratic-Republican, became vice president. In office, Adams supported the Alien and Sedition Acts. The aim of these acts was supposedly to curb French revolutionaries who were trying to stir up feeling in the United States. Many people wanted to go to war with France, but Adams avoided it. He was criticized, however, by many people who believed that the Sedition Act was an attack on Americans' basic rights. In the election of 1800, Adams was defeated by Thomas Jefferson. Twenty-five years later he saw his son, John Quincy ADAMS, become president.

John Quincy Adams was the sixth president of the United States. He was the son of John ADAMS, the second president. Trained as a lawyer, he served abroad as a minister and was then elected U.S. senator from Massachusetts in 1803. Adams was a FEDERALIST, but his party forced him to resign his seat because he supported many Democratic-Republican goals.

President James MADISON appointed Adams minister to Russia and Britain, and Adams negotiated the treaty that ended the WAR OF 1812 with Britain. From 1817 to 1825, Adams was President James MONROE's secretary of state. In 1818 he negotiated the treaty with Britain that placed the portion of the U.S.–Canadian border that lies west of the Great Lakes along the 49th parallel.

The next year Adams negotiated a treaty with Spain that gave Florida to the United States. Adams also

▼ The Erie Canal was opened at the beginning of President John Quincy Adams's term of office. It enabled ships to pass between New York City and the Great Lakes.

helped draw up the MONROE DOCTRINE. It stated that the United States would no longer allow European countries to colonize the Americas.

In the 1824 presidential election, Adams beat Andrew JACKSON by gaining the support of Henry CLAY. Jackson was very bitter and opposed Adams for his entire term of office. Many roads and canals were built during this period, and the country prospered. But for Adams the time was a political failure. In 1828 he lost the election to Jackson. From 1831 until his death in 1848, Adams served in the House of Representatives. There he fought for the protection of Indian tribes and against slavery. For years he argued against the "gag rules," which prevented any discussion of slavery. Finally, in 1844, Adams succeeded in getting them repealed.

John Quincy Adams
Born: July 11, 1767, in Braintree (now Quincy), Massachusetts
Education: Harvard College
Political party: National Republican
Term of office: 1825–1829
Married: 1797 to Louisa Catherine Johnson
Died: February 23, 1848, in Washington, D.C.

▲ *The cousin of President John Adams, Samuel Adams was committed to the cause of American independence.*

ADAMS, Samuel

Samuel Adams (1722–1803) was one of the driving forces in the American colonists' fight for independence from Great Britain. After his graduation from Harvard and several brief and unsuccessful careers, Adams turned to Massachusetts politics. He soon became convinced that the British Parliament had no right to pass laws for the American colonies, since the colonists had no representatives there. Parliament's power to tax the colonists was especially resented, and Adams was one of the first Americans to protest against this "taxation without representation." His activities ranged from writing articles against Britain to stirring up riots, such as the ones that broke out in Boston in 1765 against the hated STAMP ACT. Adams was also a leader of the BOSTON TEA PARTY. Like his more moderate cousin John ADAMS he was a delegate to the CONTINENTAL CONGRESS and a signer of the DECLARATION OF INDEPENDENCE. From 1794 to 1797, he was governor of Massachusetts.

ADDAMS, Jane

Jane Addams's visit to a *settlement house* in London's East End while on a visit to Europe gave her the idea of setting up a similar refuge in Chicago. In its first year, more than 5,000 of Chicago's poor, many of them recent immigrants, passed through the doors of Hull House. Volunteers gave them practical lessons in English and other subjects.

Born into a prosperous family, Jane Addams (1860–1935) became an outstanding social reformer. Concern about Chicago's large and poor immigrant population led her and a friend, Ellen Gates Starr, to establish Hull House in 1889. This was America's first settlement house, providing services to the poor. Among the facilities at Hull House were a day nursery, lodging for working girls, a community kitchen, and vocational training. Jane Addams also worked for many other causes, including world peace, factory inspections, an eight-hour working day for women, and women's suffrage (voting rights). In 1931 she was awarded the Nobel Peace Prize.

ADIRONDACK MOUNTAINS

The Adirondack Mountains are in northeastern NEW YORK State. They cover about 5,000 square miles (13,000 km²). The region has hundreds of peaks. The highest is Mount Marcy, at 5,344 feet (1,629 m) above sea level.

There are more than 200 lakes, including lakes George

and Placid. Lake Tear of the Clouds, on Mount Marcy, is the highest source of the HUDSON RIVER. There are many gorges, waterfalls, streams, ponds, and swamps in the Adirondacks, and the region is noted for its beautiful scenery. There are a number of parks and resorts. Adirondack Park covers a large portion of the region, and within it is the Adirondack Forest Preserve.

In 1858 this wilderness inspired a poem, "The Adirondacks," by Ralph Waldo EMERSON. The mountains were named after a local Indian tribe in 1609. The word meant "tree eaters." People's activities in the mountains since colonial times can be studied at the Adirondack Museum, near Blue Mountain Lake.

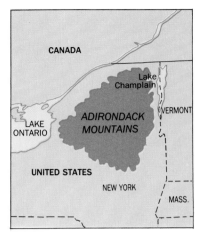

▲ The Adirondack Mountains of upstate New York are a northern branch of the Appalachian range.

◄ Some of the rocks that make up the Adirondack Mountains are more than 1 billion years old.

▼ Posters such as this one, printed in 1895, attract attention from passersby and are still an effective form of advertising.

ADOBE *See* Pueblos

ADVERTISING

The United States has the world's largest advertising industry, with more than 6,500 agencies. Over $100 billion is spent on advertising every year. The center of the industry is New York City, and many of the largest agencies are based there. The term "Madison Avenue" is often used to refer to the advertising business because that is the New York street where most of the agencies were originally located.

The agencies compete with one another to handle advertising for many different businesses. The largest agency is Young & Rubicam. The largest advertiser is the Philip Morris Company, which is involved in the

▶ *The bright lights of Broadway in New York City advertise everything from movies to new technology.*

The Top 10 Advertisers in the U.S. (by spending)
1. Philip Morris Co.
2. Procter & Gamble Co.
3. General Motors Corp.
4. Sears, Roebuck & Co.
5. RJR Nabisco
6. Grand Metropolitan PLC
7. Eastman Kodak Co.
8. McDonald's Corp.
9. PepsiCo Inc.
10. Kellogg Co.

tobacco and food industries. It spends over $2 billion a year. Procter & Gamble, which makes many of the soaps and detergents used in American homes, General Motors, and Sears, Roebuck all spend over $1 billion.

NEWSPAPERS get the biggest share of the nation's advertising budget. More than $31 billion is spent on newspaper ads each year. TELEVISION advertising costs more than $25 billion.

Advertising laws, both state and federal, protect the public from false advertising. Federal laws are enforced by the Federal Trade Commission. It supervises all types of advertising and tries to make sure that advertising claims are not misleading.

▼ *Engineers use computers to create advanced aircraft designs.*

AEROSPACE INDUSTRY

The aerospace industry builds and looks after aircraft, missiles, and space vehicles. The term *aerospace* was coined in the 1950s by the U.S. Air Force. It described the first airplanes that could fly outside the Earth's atmosphere. Since then aerospace has become the country's most advanced industry. Aerospace projects cost millions, and sometimes billions, of dollars.

Some aerospace companies, such as Lockheed and BOEING, make complete aircraft. Others, such as General Dynamics and Northrop, specialize in landing gear, in-flight computers, and other instruments. Much of their work is for the armed forces and the government's space program. The 1989 budget of the National

Aeronautics and Space Administration (NASA) was more than $11 billion. In 1989 the top ten aerospace companies in the United States did over $118 billion worth of business.

Major events affect the aerospace industry directly. The triumphant moon landing in 1969 was a success for the whole industry. But aerospace firms were hurt by the *Challenger* space shuttle disaster in 1986. (See also AVIATION; AIR TRANSPORTATION.)

▶ Aerospace companies have already produced aircraft and spacecraft. Today research is being conducted to create a plane that will travel both in the Earth's atmosphere and in space.

The Top 10 Aerospace Companies in the U.S. (by sales)
1. Boeing
2. United Technologies
3. McDonnell Douglas
4. Rockwell International
5. Allied-Signal
6. General Dynamics
7. Lockheed
8. Textron
9. Martin Marietta
10. Northrop

AGASSIZ, Louis

▼ Louis Agassiz believed that at one time much of the Earth's surface was covered by glaciers. Lake Agassiz, a glacial lake that once covered North Dakota, Minnesota, and southern Manitoba, was named in his honor.

Jean Louis Agassiz (1807–1873) was a Swiss-born naturalist and geologist. He spent two years in Paris doing research and became a professor in 1832.

Agassiz's great interest was the study of fish (ichthyology). He wrote his first major work on them when he was only 22. Shortly after this, he wrote a *History of the Fresh Water Fishes of Central Europe*.

Agassiz became fascinated by extinct fish—fish that now exist only in fossil form. He wrote a great work on fossil fish which described more than 1,700 species. Agassiz also showed that vast glaciers once covered much of the Northern Hemisphere.

In 1846, Agassiz came to the United States, and became a professor of geology and zoology (the study of animals) at Harvard two years later. Agassiz was an important popularizer of science, and has been called the "best friend that students ever had."

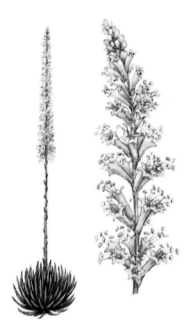

▲ *The agave, or century plant, and its flowers. Mexicans use the sap of some agave plants to make alcoholic drinks such as tequila.*

▼ *Dairy farms, such as this one in Pennsylvania, keep Holstein cows because they are the best producers of milk.*

AGAVE

Agave is the name of a family of desert plants. In the United States agaves grow in the South and the West. They have thick, sharp-edged leaves, and flowers borne on a tall stalk up to 40 feet (12 m) high. Some varieties live for 60 years before they flower. A common type of agave was once thought to flower only once every 100 years and then die—thus it has also come to be called the century plant.

The leaves of the agave die after the plant has produced flowers, but the base does not die and will produce new plants.

AGRICULTURE

Agriculture means cultivating the land. It includes not only growing crops but also raising livestock. In the United States more land—over 1 billion acres (400 million ha)—is used for farming than for anything else. Agriculture accounts for only about 2 percent of the total national income, but U.S. produce feeds not only Americans but people in other countries as well. The United States exports about $30 billion worth of food each year.

Many of the more than 2 million farms in the United States have been family farms ever since the days of the pioneers and the HOMESTEAD ACT. The pioneers set the agricultural pattern for the country as they moved

◄ Combine harvesters are used to cut and separate the grain (seeds) from the rest of the wheat. On large midwestern farms, a combine harvester operated by one person can harvest in a day what it once took many workers weeks to do.

west. By the early 1900s, different regions, or belts, were specializing in different crops. Many of these belts still specialize today in the same way. Over the last 50 years the number of farms has steadily decreased, while the size of farms has increased. This is largely because of improved farming methods and laborsaving machines that make farm work faster and much more efficient.

CORN is the most important crop grown in the United States. It is grown in most states, but especially in the fertile region known as the Corn Belt, stretching from Indiana to Nebraska. The United States grows 44 percent of the world's corn. The soybean is now the second most important crop, and in several states it is the main crop. The United States grows more than half

U.S. CONTRIBUTION TO WORLD PRODUCTION OF SOME MAJOR CROPS

U.S. production 28.6%

World production 71.4%

($ millions)

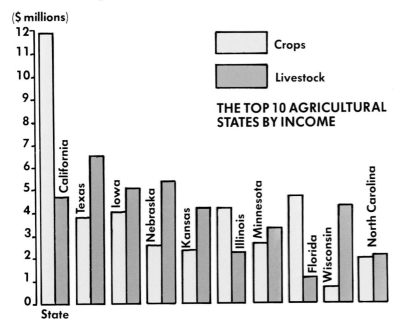

Crops

Livestock

THE TOP 10 AGRICULTURAL STATES BY INCOME

State

California, Texas, Iowa, Nebraska, Kansas, Illinois, Minnesota, Florida, Wisconsin, North Carolina

U.S. PRODUCTION OF SOME MAJOR CROPS

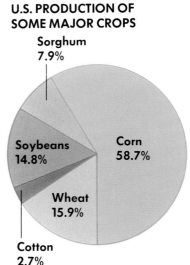

Sorghum 7.9%

Soybeans 14.8%

Corn 58.7%

Wheat 15.9%

Cotton 2.7%

▶ *Colonial farmers used a homemade plow to prepare their fields for planting. An iron spade on the bottom cut and lifted the soil.*

of all the soybeans in the world.

Many farmers join marketing cooperatives, which help them to find the best markets for their products. Farm organizations lend support to farmers, and federal and state laws set such things as minimum farm prices and standards of quality for farm products.

Over the last 150 years, new technology has made farming much more productive. In 1850 the average farmer could grow only enough food to feed five people; today the average farmer can produce enough to feed almost 80 people.

AILEY, Alvin

The Alvin Ailey American Dance Theater, formed in New York in 1958, is one of the most exciting and popular DANCE companies performing today. Its founder, Alvin Ailey (1931–1989), studied modern dance under such great names as Doris Humphrey and Martha GRAHAM. But he also danced in Broadway shows, and the dances he created for his own company are generally livelier and more colorful than most modern dance. Although the company is now multiracial, many of its dances are about the experiences of black people. The most famous of these is *Revelations*. Basically about religion, it is set to the music of spirituals. Ailey often chose jazz and blues for his dances.

The Alvin Ailey American Dance Theater has been the starting point for at least one successful career. The pop star Madonna began her career in New York City as a dancer with Ailey's company.

▶ *Caverna Magica, one of Alvin Ailey's spectacular dances, is performed here by April Berry and Company. In 1987, Alvin Ailey received the Scripps Dance Award for his lifetime contribution to dance.*

The U.S. Air Force is the youngest branch of the armed forces. Its responsibilities are large and call for a huge number of different types of aircraft (over 9,000 in all) and more than 600,000 airmen and women.

The Air Force has three major jobs. One is to defend the United States and its allies against attack from enemies. A network of radar stations, backed up by airborne radar planes called AWACS, can detect enemy missile or aircraft attacks. Fighter planes can then be called up to destroy them. The second and most important job during war is to attack enemies. Long-range bombers can drop nuclear and other bombs far behind

▲ The Air Force was originally a branch of the U.S. Army. It was not until 1947 that it became an independent branch of the armed forces.

World War I   World War II   Modern security police officer   Modern B52 pilot

◄ Air Force uniforms have not changed dramatically in the corps' brief history.

▼ The F-15 jet fighter can break through the sound barrier within 19 seconds.

enemy lines, and fighters can attack enemy troops and planes and support U.S. troops. The Air Force also transports U.S. troops to battle zones.

Perhaps its most important role, however, is that of a deterrent force—that is, to prevent the outbreak of war. It does this mainly by possessing large numbers of strategic nuclear weapons on land bases in the United States. Because their destructive power is so great, no enemy wants to risk the possibility that it will be destroyed by them. Originally the Army Air Corps, the Air Force became a separate service in 1947.

AIR TRANSPORTATION

Air transportation is the fastest way of traveling within the United States. Airline networks connect all major cities with regular flights. There are more than 100 scheduled passenger airlines in the United States. In 1989 alone, airlines carried more than 450 million passengers in the United States. Nearly half of those passengers were traveling along the "Northeast Corridor," the stretch of the East Coast from Washington, D.C., to Boston. This is the world's busiest air route.

Remote areas, such as most of Alaska, rely on airplanes to deliver food and medicine. Some "flying doctors" cover thousands of square miles just to make house calls. Their small planes are adapted to landing where there is no airport. Skis or pontoons are put over the wheels so the plane can land on snow or water.

▶ Commercial airliners carry passengers and cargo all over the world. Some, such as this TriStar, can carry between 250 and 400 passengers.

Airports in large cities are very busy. Chicago's O'Hare Airport is the world's busiest. More than 50 million people pass through it every year. Some airports are so big that buses are needed to connect the terminals. The biggest airport in the United States, Dallas–Fort Worth, covers 17,500 acres (7,082 ha). Atlanta has the fastest growing airport in the United States. All larger airports have one or more additional terminals for handling cargo only. Air transportation in the United States is regulated by the Federal Aviation Administration, a government body. The FAA establishes safety standards for airports, qualifications for pilots, and licenses for aircraft. (See also AEROSPACE INDUSTRY; AVIATION.)

The 10 Busiest Airports in the U.S. (by number of passengers)
1. O'Hare International, Chicago
2. Dallas–Fort Worth Regional
3. Los Angeles International
4. Hartsfield International, Atlanta
5. John F. Kennedy International, NYC
6. San Francisco International
7. Stapleton International, Denver
8. Miami International
9. La Guardia, NYC
10. Logan International, Boston

▶ An aircraft ground crewman wears earmuffs to protect his ears from the noise as he refuels an airliner.

▼ A plan of Hartsfield International Airport, Atlanta, which has more airplanes taking off and landing on its runways than any other airport in the world. Passengers move between its huge terminals on an underground transit system.

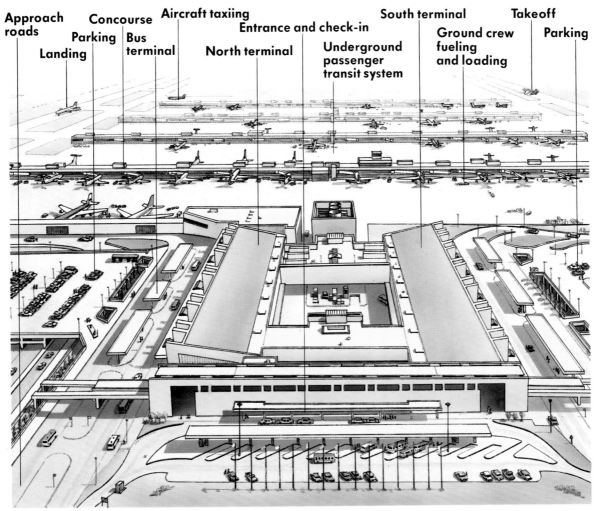

Approach roads

Landing

Parking

Concourse

Bus terminal

Aircraft taxiing

Entrance and check-in

North terminal

Underground passenger transit system

South terminal

Ground crew fueling and loading

Takeoff

Parking

ALABAMA

Yellowhammer

Southern pine

Camellia

Alabama is one of the most historic of the southern states. It was in Montgomery, the capital, that the Confederate States of America was set up in 1861. And it was in Alabama that many of the most important events in the CIVIL RIGHTS campaigns of the 1950s and 1960s took place. In those historic years, blacks successfully demanded an end to discrimination in voter registration, education, and transportation.

Traditionally, Alabama has been a major farming region of the South. In the 1800s, when Alabama was a slave state, cotton was the most important crop. Right up to the early years of this century, cotton was still the state's major product. When a series of poor harvests struck Alabama, farmers began to plant different types of crops, becoming much more prosperous in the process. Cotton is still important to Alabama, but today crops such as corn, peanuts, and soybeans are also grown, and poultry and livestock are raised. Alabama is

Alabama
Capital: Montgomery
Area: 50,767 sq mi (131,476 km²). Rank: 29th
Population: 4,062,608 (1990). Rank: 22nd
Statehood: December 14, 1819
Principal rivers: Tombigbee, Alabama, Tennessee
Highest point: Cheaha Mountain, 2,407 ft (734 m)
Motto: *Audemus Jura Nostra Defendere* (We Dare Defend Our Rights)
Song: ''Alabama''

Florence Russell Cave Nat. Monument
Huntsville
Wilson Lake
Decatur
Tennessee R.
65
Guntersville Lake
Lewis Smith Lake
Gadsden
59
Anniston
20
Birmingham
Cheaha Mtn. 2,407 ft (734 m)
Tuscaloosa
Black Warrior R.
Martin Lake
West Point Lake
20 59
Moundville
85
Phenix City
Selma
Tuskegee
Montgomery
Tombigbee R.
Alabama R.
Chattahoochee R.
65
Dothan
Mobile
10
0   50 miles
0   50 kilometers
GULF OF MEXICO

also one of the most important industrial states in the South. It has huge reserves of the three most important raw materials used in steel-making—coal, limestone, and iron ore.

The southern part of Alabama, especially toward the Gulf of Mexico, is fertile and low lying. This is where most of the state's farms are located. The north is hilly and forested, with many rivers and lakes. Many of Alabama's rivers have been dammed to provide power for hydroelectric power stations. The largest city in Alabama is Birmingham, the center of the state's flourishing steel-making industry.

▲ *Paddle-wheel steamboats on the Tennessee River in northern Alabama. These steamboats were a common sight on rivers throughout the United States during the 1800s. They gradually disappeared as railroads and other more efficient methods of transportation took over.*

▶ *White Hall, at Tuskegee University, the nation's oldest seat of learning for black Americans.*

Places of Interest
● Alabama Space and Rocket Center, Huntsville, houses the world's biggest collection of missiles.
● Mound State Monument, near Moundville, site of 20 Indian burial mounds.
● Jefferson Davis House, Montgomery, was home to the President of the Confederacy for the first few months of his term.

Alaska is the largest state in the United States and the most northerly. It is at the northwest corner of North America. Almost a third of the state lies north of the Arctic Circle. Wilderness, glaciers, and mountains cover much of Alaska, and its unspoiled natural beauty attracts hundreds of thousands of visitors every year. MOUNT MCKINLEY, at 20,320 feet (6,194 m), is the highest peak in North America.

Much of Alaska has short summers and long, cold winters. Most Alaskans live along the southern coast, where the climate is mildest. Anchorage, the largest city, and Juneau, the capital, are located here. In the southwest the Aleutian Islands stretch westward for 1,100 miles (1,800 km).

The ancestors of the ALEUT people, the Inuit (ESKIMOS), and the American INDIANS were the first people to settle in the Western Hemisphere. More than 12,000 years ago, they traveled across a land bridge that connected Alaska and Asia. The Russians were the first

Forget-me-not

Sitka spruce

Willow ptarmigan

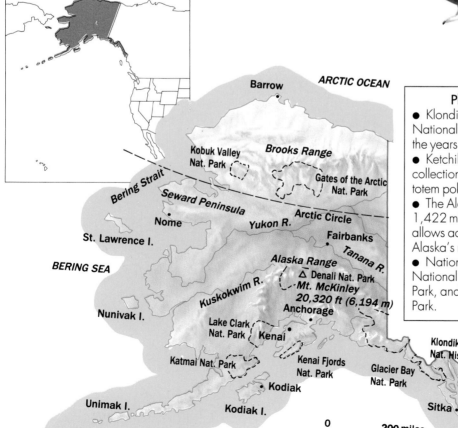

Places of Interest
- Klondike Gold Rush National Park commemorates the years of the gold rush.
- Ketchikan is famous for its collection of potlatch houses and totem poles.
- The Alaska Highway covers 1,422 mi (2,288 km) and allows access to much of Alaska's magnificent scenery.
- National parks include Denali National Park, Katmai National Park, and Glacier Bay National Park.

Europeans to settle Alaska. They came in search of furs in the 1700s. In 1867, U.S. Secretary of State William H. Seward bought Alaska from Russia for $7.2 million. Because it was so cold and desolate, many people called Alaska "Seward's Folly." But when gold was discovered in the late 1800s, thousands of Americans flocked there. Alaska became the 49th state in 1959, and less than ten years later oil was discovered along the Arctic coast. Today oil is the state's main source of income.

Alaska's population is just over half a million. It has fewer people than any other state except Wyoming. But between 1980 and 1990, many people moved to the United States' "last frontier," and its population increased by more than a third.

◄ *Cotton grass flowers during Alaska's brief summer, while in the background Mount McKinley remains covered in snow.*

◄ *Most of the 700 million barrels of petroleum produced in Alaska each year are shipped out through the Trans-Alaska Pipeline, which is 800 miles (1,300 km) long.*

▼ *A ride in a dogsled is a good way of enjoying Alaska's magnificent scenery.*

Alaska	
Capital: Juneau, since 1900 (Sitka, 1884–1900)	
Area: 570,833 sq mi (1,478,456 km²). Rank: 1st	
Population: 551,947 (1990). Rank: 49th	
Statehood: January 3, 1959	
Principal rivers: Yukon, Kuskokwim.	
Highest point: Mt. McKinley, 20,320 ft (6,194 m)	
Motto: North to the Future	
Song: "Alaska's Flag"	

Alberta is one of CANADA's three Prairie Provinces. In the south, huge farms and cattle ranches stretch across the rolling prairie lands. Alberta is one of the most ruggedly beautiful regions of North America. Many visitors come to the Canadian Rockies in the south-western part of the province. Here they ski in the winter and walk, swim, and admire the scenery in the summer. Others visit the mountains and forests of the north to hunt and fish.

Alberta produces more than 80 percent of Canada's oil and natural gas and 50 percent of its coal. It is also an important farming area, growing more oats and barley than any other province. Wheat and potatoes are also important crops. Many ranches raise cattle for beef.

EDMONTON is the capital of Alberta, but CALGARY, which is farther south, is the largest city. More than half of all Albertans live in and around these cities. Calgary is famous for its annual rodeo, the Calgary Stampede, which is held every June.

Europeans first settled Alberta during the 1700s. They were mostly fur traders. The building of the Canadian Pacific Railway in the 1800s and the discovery of oil in the 1940s drew many settlers to Alberta. Today it is one of Canada's richest and fastest growing provinces.

▲ Moraine Lake in Banff National Park, established in 1885.

Wild rose

Alberta
Capital: Edmonton
Area: 248,800 sq mi (644,390 km²). Rank: 4th
Population: 2,423,200 (1989). Rank: 4th
Entry into Confederation: September 1, 1905 (with Saskatchewan, 8th and 9th provinces)
Highest point: Mt. Columbia 12,293 ft (3,747 m)

ALBUQUERQUE

Albuquerque, with 384,736 people, is the largest city in NEW MEXICO and one of the most important cities in the Southwest. It was founded by Spanish settlers in 1706, and named for the Duke of Alburquerque, a governor of New Spain. Its Spanish and Indian heritage is still obvious in its low, flat-roofed buildings. In 1848, after the MEXICAN WAR, Albuquerque became part of the United States. Before 1945 it was a small city, depending on local farms for its prosperity. Since then it has become a major center for nuclear research and its population has quadrupled. The climate is warm and dry, with sun almost all year round.

ALCOTT, Louisa May

Louisa May Alcott (1832–1888) is best known as the author of *Little Women*, a novel about a family of four sisters at the time of the CIVIL WAR. The story is partly based on her own life.

The Alcotts lived in Concord, Massachusetts, where their friends included such famous writers as Ralph Waldo EMERSON, Henry David THOREAU, and Nathaniel HAWTHORNE. Louisa's father was a teacher and philosopher who tried his hand, unsuccessfully, at several ventures, including a communal farm. Louisa worked from an early age to help support the family. During the Civil War she served as an army nurse, an experience described in *Hospital Sketches*. After the success of *Little Women*, she wrote other books for children, including the sequels *Little Men* and *Jo's Boys*.

ALDRIN, Edwin, Jr.

Edwin "Buzz" Aldrin (1930–   ) was the second man to walk on the moon. Born in New Jersey, Aldrin graduated from the U.S. Military Academy in 1951. After a career as a pilot he joined the SPACE PROGRAM as an astronaut. In 1966 he set a record with his 5½-hour space walk on the Gemini 12 flight. On July 20, 1969, the Apollo 11 lunar module landed on the moon, carrying Aldrin and Neil ARMSTRONG. Later, the two flew the lunar module back to the command module, and the mission splashed down safely in the Pacific Ocean four days later.

▲ *The Church of San Felipe de Nerí, built in 1706 by Spanish missionaries, is one of Albuquerque's landmarks.*

▼ *"Buzz" Aldrin stepped onto the moon 18 minutes after Neil Armstrong. Together they set up scientific experiments and collected rock samples.*

▼ The United States produces about 85 million tons of alfalfa every year, more than any other country in the world.

ALEUTS

The Aleuts are the native inhabitants of the Aleutian Islands, about 70 islands that extend in a curved line from the southwestern corner of ALASKA. They are related to the ESKIMOS and speak a similar language. When Russia began colonizing the islands in the 1700s, about 25,000 Aleuts lived there. They lived by hunting and fishing and were skilled in basketwork and in carving stone, bone, and ivory. Each village had its own chief, an office that was usually hereditary—that is, passed on from father to son. By the mid-1900s the Aleut population had declined to about 1,300.

ALFALFA

Alfalfa is a plant that is used to feed many types of animals, especially dairy cows and beef cattle. It is rich in the nutrients they need. Because there are many different types of alfalfa and because it is easy to grow, alfalfa is farmed all across the United States. Most farmers feed it to animals as hay; this is alfalfa that has been cut and allowed to dry. Others store it in silos without drying it; this is called silage. Some farmers let their animals graze on alfalfa where it grows.

ALGER, Horatio

The "rags-to-riches" stories of Horatio Alger (1832–1899) are generally thought to express the "American Dream." Many people apply the term "Horatio Alger story" to the lives of millionaires who have achieved success through hard work and cleverness. In fact, in Alger's books, virtue and good luck are the main ingredients. The typical Alger hero is a poor, fatherless boy who performs some act of kindness for a rich man, who then gives the boy a fortune. Alger himself was not a success. He earned a modest income as chaplain in a boys' lodging house and sold his books for small fees to publishers who made a fortune from them.

ALGONQUINS

Algonquin, or Algonkin, is a name that refers to American INDIANS who originally lived in the eastern provinces of CANADA. They included more than one tribe.

▼ The Algonquins were farmers as well as hunters and fishermen. They grew beans, squash, and corn. The corn was then ground with a wooden mortar and pestle.

The term "Algonquian" (Algonkian) refers to the group of related languages that these tribes spoke. The first Bible that was printed in the American colonies used one of the Algonquian languages called "Natick." During the FRENCH AND INDIAN WAR the Algonquins fought on the side of the French.

ALI, Muhammad

Muhammad Ali (1942–) was the only boxer to win the world heavyweight title three times. Born Cassius Clay in Lexington, Kentucky, he won an Olympic gold medal in 1960. After turning professional, he defeated Sonny Liston to win the heavyweight title in 1964. In 1967 he joined the Nation of Islam (Black Muslims). When he refused to go into the armed forces for religious reasons, Ali was stripped of his title. The U.S. Supreme Court reversed this decision four years later. Ali regained his title in 1974. He lost it to Leon Spinks in 1978 but regained it later that year. He retired in 1979 but fought again, unsuccessfully in 1980 and 1981.

▲ Muhammad Ali combined speed with sudden attacks. He said he could "float like a butterfly but sting like a bee."

▲ In the early hours of May 10, 1775, Ethan Allen and a band of 83 men attacked the British garrison at Fort Ticonderoga.

ALLEN, Ethan

Ethan Allen (1738–1789) was a great patriot during the American REVOLUTION. He gained his first military experience fighting for the British in the FRENCH AND INDIAN WAR. After this he settled in the New Hamp-

Neither American nor British casualties resulted from the attack on the garrison at Fort Ticonderoga. Ethan Allen's troops surprised the occupants of the garrison during a night raid. Allen is said to have confronted the sleepy British lieutenant Jocelyn Feltham shouting, "Come out of there, you damned old rat." When asked on whose authority he was acting, Allen replied, "In the name of the Great Jehova and the Continental Congress." Lieutenant Feltham surrendered immediately.

shire Grants, land that became part of Vermont. In the early 1770s the ownership of this land was given by the British to New York. Allen formed the Green Mountain Boys to fight against New York's claim.

In 1775, in one of the first battles of the American Revolution, Allen and his Green Mountain Boys took Fort Ticonderoga from the British. After the war, he continued his fight for Vermont's statehood and eventually retired to the Vermont town of Burlington.

ALLIGATOR

The American alligator is a large REPTILE that lives in rivers, lakes, and swamps in the southeastern United States. It grows up to 19 feet (5.8 m) long, but most are shorter. Alligators eat fish, frogs, snakes, birds, small mammals, and even young deer. They are strong swimmers and will wait for hours for their prey.

The female alligator lays 20 to 70 eggs in a nest of grass, leaves, and mud. She covers them up and guards them ferociously for about two months until they hatch. Alligators are a protected species, and hunting them is carefully controlled.

▼ Adult alligators hiss, and males also make bellowing noises. Young alligators croak like frogs.

The skin on an alligator's back is tough and ridged with many small bones. The skin on its belly, however, is smooth. Skin from the bellies of farmed alligators is still popular as a material for handbags and other goods.

ALVAREZ, Luis

Luis Alvarez (1911–1988) was a physicist who did much important research into the atom. To learn more about *subatomic* particles—particles inside the nucleus of the atom—Alvarez used a device called a bubble chamber in which the tracks of the tiny particles could be identified. He discovered a number of new particles. Some of these existed for only a short time, one for less than a second. In 1968, Alvarez was honored with the Nobel Prize for physics.

◀ A 17th-century map of Virginia. The first permanent European settlement was founded at Jamestown in 1607, more than 100 years after Columbus first reached the Americas.

AMERICA

The term "America" refers to all the land and islands of the Western Hemisphere. The word comes from *Americus*, the Latin form of the name of the Italian navigator Amerigo VESPUCCI. From the Arctic coast in the north to the southern tip of Argentina in the south, America extends more than 9,500 miles (15,300 km). Together, these lands cover about 28 percent of the Earth's land surface.

America includes the continents of NORTH AMERICA and South America. Central America, which is geographically part of North America, lies between them. The narrowest point in Central America, the Isthmus of Panama, links the continents of North and South America. North and South America are sometimes referred to together as "the Americas."

Another way of dividing up the continent is on a cultural basis. North America includes CANADA and the UNITED STATES. Latin America, so-called because most people there speak the Latin-based languages Spanish or Portuguese, includes all the land and islands to the south of the United States.

Many scientists believe that millions of years ago America was joined to Africa and Eurasia, forming one big landmass called Pangaea. About 200 million years ago this huge landmass broke up, and the continents began to drift to their present positions. This theory that the continents are moving slowly over the Earth's surface is called the *Continental Drift Theory*. Scientists predict that in about 50 million years the California coast will have broken away and drifted northward toward Alaska.

AMERICAN HISTORY
A Timetable

1

18,000 B.C.	Ancestors of the American INDIANS from Asia are the first people to settle in North America.

A.D.

1000	Vikings led by Leif ERICSSON land on the coast of North America.
1492	Christopher COLUMBUS lands in the New World.
1607	English settlers found JAMESTOWN SETTLEMENT in Virginia.
1619	Ships arrive in Jamestown with the first black slaves.
1620	Pilgrims found PLYMOUTH COLONY, Massachusetts.
1681	William PENN is granted a royal charter to set up a colony in what is now Pennsylvania.
1754– 1763	The French and Indian War between France and Great Britain leads to British control of most of eastern North America.

The history of America starts with the history of the Indians. Indians of the Pacific Northwest carved this bird's head (1). In the early 1600s people like the Pilgrims settled in America hoping to build a better life for themselves (2). The painting The Spirit of '76 by Gilbert Stuart (3) captures the feeling that united the colonists in their fight for independence. Pioneers faced many dangers to open up the West in the early 1800s (4). The Civil War split the young nation in two, causing massive casualties (5). The Great Depression of the 1930s left many people starving and homeless (6). About 58,000 American soldiers lost their lives in the Vietnam War before U.S. troops pulled out in 1973 (7). When George Bush was sworn in as the 41st president of the U.S. in 1989 (8), he became the leader of one of the superpowers of the world.

2

1770	British troops kill five colonists and injure six others during the BOSTON MASSACRE.
1773	The BOSTON TEA PARTY takes place.
1774	The First CONTINENTAL CONGRESS meets in Philadelphia.
1775	The battles of LEXINGTON AND CONCORD mark the beginning of the American REVOLUTION.
1776	The DECLARATION OF INDEPENDENCE is adopted at Philadelphia on July 4.
1781	American forces defeat the British at Yorktown, Virginia.
1783	Britain recognizes U.S. independence in the Treaty of Paris.
1788	The U.S. CONSTITUTION comes into effect.
1789	George WASHINGTON and John ADAMS are elected first president and vice president of the new nation.
1791	The BILL OF RIGHTS becomes part of the Constitution.
1803	The United States buys the vast French territory between the Mississippi River and the Rocky Mountains under the terms of the LOUISIANA PURCHASE.
1812– 1815	The United States and Great Britain fight the WAR OF 1812.
1819	Spain cedes Florida to the United States.
1823	The MONROE DOCTRINE warns European countries against interference in the Americas.
1825	The ERIE CANAL is completed.
1836	Texan revolutionaries defeat the Mexican army and declare Texas an independent republic.

3

4

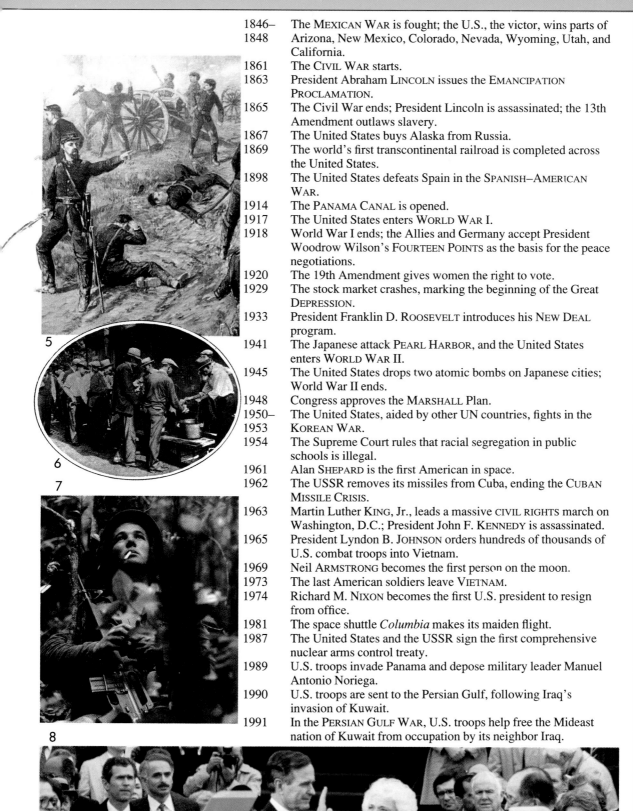

1846–1848	The MEXICAN WAR is fought; the U.S., the victor, wins parts of Arizona, New Mexico, Colorado, Nevada, Wyoming, Utah, and California.
1861	The CIVIL WAR starts.
1863	President Abraham LINCOLN issues the EMANCIPATION PROCLAMATION.
1865	The Civil War ends; President Lincoln is assassinated; the 13th Amendment outlaws slavery.
1867	The United States buys Alaska from Russia.
1869	The world's first transcontinental railroad is completed across the United States.
1898	The United States defeats Spain in the SPANISH–AMERICAN WAR.
1914	The PANAMA CANAL is opened.
1917	The United States enters WORLD WAR I.
1918	World War I ends; the Allies and Germany accept President Woodrow Wilson's FOURTEEN POINTS as the basis for the peace negotiations.
1920	The 19th Amendment gives women the right to vote.
1929	The stock market crashes, marking the beginning of the Great DEPRESSION.
1933	President Franklin D. ROOSEVELT introduces his NEW DEAL program.
1941	The Japanese attack PEARL HARBOR, and the United States enters WORLD WAR II.
1945	The United States drops two atomic bombs on Japanese cities; World War II ends.
1948	Congress approves the MARSHALL Plan.
1950–1953	The United States, aided by other UN countries, fights in the KOREAN WAR.
1954	The Supreme Court rules that racial segregation in public schools is illegal.
1961	Alan SHEPARD is the first American in space.
1962	The USSR removes its missiles from Cuba, ending the CUBAN MISSILE CRISIS.
1963	Martin Luther KING, Jr., leads a massive CIVIL RIGHTS march on Washington, D.C.; President John F. KENNEDY is assassinated.
1965	President Lyndon B. JOHNSON orders hundreds of thousands of U.S. combat troops into Vietnam.
1969	Neil ARMSTRONG becomes the first person on the moon.
1973	The last American soldiers leave VIETNAM.
1974	Richard M. NIXON becomes the first U.S. president to resign from office.
1981	The space shuttle *Columbia* makes its maiden flight.
1987	The United States and the USSR sign the first comprehensive nuclear arms control treaty.
1989	U.S. troops invade Panama and depose military leader Manuel Antonio Noriega.
1990	U.S. troops are sent to the Persian Gulf, following Iraq's invasion of Kuwait.
1991	In the PERSIAN GULF WAR, U.S. troops help free the Mideast nation of Kuwait from occupation by its neighbor Iraq.

5

6

7

8

The American Legion is one of the sponsors of American Education Week, which it founded in 1921. Every year, for a week during the fall, there are special exhibitions, television programs, and conferences that aim to inform the public about the work of education, its problems, and achievements. The idea of Education Week has now been taken up by a number of other countries.

AMERICAN INDIANS *See* Indians, American

AMERICAN LEGION

The American Legion is an organization of veterans of the armed forces—the U.S. Army, Navy, Marine Corps, and Air Force—who served during wartime. It was founded in 1919. Today the Legion has almost 3 million members. There are branches nationwide.

The American Legion provides a meeting place for men and women who are wartime veterans. There are many social activities in which members and their families can take part. But the Legion also tries to help veterans, assisting them with education, housing, or medical care. Some veterans have suffered injuries that make it difficult or impossible for them to go back to their normal lives. To help them, the Legion supports many long-stay hospitals and training programs.

AMERICAN REVOLUTION *See* Revolution, American

▼ *In 1987, Stars and Stripes beat Australia's* Kookaburra III *to win back the America's Cup — the oldest trophy in international sport.*

AMERICA'S CUP

The America's Cup is the world's most important yacht race. It is named after the yacht *America*, which in 1851 won a sailboat race around the Isle of Wight, England, beating 14 British yachts. Between that year and 1983, many attempts were made by British and other yachts to win back the Cup. But the races were always won by American boats. Then in 1983 an Australian boat, *Australia II*, won the Cup. It was the first time in 132 years that an American boat had been defeated. But in Australia in 1987 an American boat, *Stars and Stripes*, won the Cup back. The race is always held off the defending nation's coast.

AMPHIBIANS

Amphibians are animals that have moist skin with no scales. Nearly all live part of their lives in the water and part on land. FROGS AND TOADS are amphibians, as are salamanders. One of the most common salamanders in the United States is the spotted salamander.

Most North American salamanders are 4 to 6 inches (10 to 15 cm) long. The hellbender, however, found in the eastern and central United States, is about 30 inches (75 cm) long. It lives in streams and under nearby rocks.

Some salamanders, known as sirens, look like eels. They are found mainly in the Southeast. The greater siren is 20 to 35 inches (50 to 90 cm) long. Salamanders called congo eels also look like eels. The most common species is up to 30 inches (75 cm) long and is found from Virginia to Louisiana. Unlike most other salamanders, congo eels have a vicious bite.

Mud puppies are a type of salamander found in eastern North America. In the South they are called water dogs. The arboreal salamander is found in Oregon, California, and New Mexico. It breathes only through its skin. Up to 30 live together in tree hollows.

▲ The tiger salamander belongs to the mole salamander family, one of the seven salamander families that live in North America. North America has more species, or kinds, of salamanders than any other continent.

▼ Although she is best known for her beautiful voice, Marian Anderson was also a delegate to the United Nations.

ANDERSON, Marian

Marian Anderson (1902–) was the first black singer to perform at the Metropolitan Opera House in New York City. Her talent was discovered when she was only six, while she was singing in her church choir in Philadelphia. The church raised money for her singing lessons. Her voice developed into a rich contralto, and in her twenties she began a successful concert career. In 1939, Marian Anderson was prevented from singing in Washington's Constitution Hall because of her race. Eleanor ROOSEVELT, the wife of President Franklin D. ROOSEVELT, arranged for her to sing at the Lincoln Memorial instead; 75,000 people came to hear her. In 1955 she made her first appearance at New York City's Metropolitan Opera House in Verdi's *A Masked Ball*.

▲ A young prairie dog keeps an eye open for any sign of danger as it feeds.

ANIMAL LIFE OF NORTH AMERICA

North America has a rich variety of animals. Some, such as the PRONGHORN, American BISON, and PRAIRIE DOG, exist nowhere else in the world. North America is the home of the world's smallest flesh eater, the least WEASEL, and the largest flesh eater on land, the Kodiak BEAR. Each species lives in the habitat that suits it best. The frozen north is home to very few animals during the winter. But during the brief summer many animals, including the CARIBOU and WOLF, migrate there.

South of the Arctic region are the evergreen forests. Farther south are deciduous forests with broad-leaved trees. Animals of the forests include the elk, MOOSE, white-tailed DEER, wolf, COUGAR, wolverine, bear, FOX, BOBCAT, GROUNDHOG, SKUNK, PORCUPINE, SQUIRREL, CHIPMUNK, and OPOSSUM. Rivers and meadows attract such animals as the RACCOON, BEAVER, OTTER, and MUSKRAT. In the mountains are the Rocky Mountain GOAT and BIGHORN SHEEP.

In the center of the continent are the wide prairies. Here live animals that burrow into the ground, such as the prairie dog and the GOPHER. The BADGER, COYOTE, pronghorn, and even the bison roam the prairies.

Life in the hot, dry deserts includes LIZARDS, RATTLESNAKES, and mammals such as the JACKRABBIT and small RODENTS. And a rich variety of animals, including SEALS and SEA LIONS, WHALES, and sea OTTERS, lives around the coasts. (See also AMPHIBIANS; BIRDS; CRUSTACEANS; FISH; INSECTS; MOLLUSKS; REPTILES; see Index for other animal entries.)

The cougar is one of North America's largest predators. It is also known as the puma, mountain lion, panther, and catamount.

▲ The cougar is one of North America's largest predators. It is also known as the puma, mountain lion, panther, and catamount.

▶ In 1889 only 540 bison remained of the vast herds that once roamed the American prairies. Today about 15,000 live protected on game preserves.

ANNAPOLIS

Annapolis, the capital of MARYLAND, is located on the Severn River near the western shore of CHESAPEAKE BAY. It was founded in 1649 by English settlers and today it has a population of 31,740. Annapolis is one of the oldest and most historic cities in the United States. In 1708 its name was changed from Providence to Annapolis in honor of Queen Anne of England. The suffix *polis* is Greek for "city," so *Annapolis* means "Anne's city." Today, Annapolis is famous as the home of the U.S. Naval Academy and as a sailing base. The city still has many colonial buildings—its State House is the oldest state capitol in the nation. The treaty that ended the American REVOLUTION was signed in Annapolis, and the city was the capital of the United States from 1783 to 1784.

▲ Students stand to attention at the U.S. Naval Academy, founded in Annapolis in 1845.

ANTHONY, Susan B.

The fact that American women can vote owes a great deal to the work of Susan B. Anthony (1820–1906). She was born into a Quaker family in Massachusetts that believed firmly in the abolition of SLAVERY. As an adult she worked for the American Anti-Slavery Society. With the end of slavery during the Civil War, she began to fight for WOMEN'S RIGHTS. She was a leader of the National Woman Suffrage Association. She also fought for another cause, that of temperance (abstaining from alcoholic beverages). Anthony's work on behalf of women's rights won her international admiration. Fourteen years after her death Congress passed the Nineteenth Amendment giving women the vote.

ANTS

Ants are INSECTS that live in groups called colonies. Some, such as thief ants and pharaoh's ants, are household pests, invading buildings in search of food. Carpenter ants chew holes in timber. The fire ant is a serious pest in the South. It builds large nests that get in the way of hay cutting. It also feeds on seeds and young plants and has a painful sting. Legionary ants live in warm parts of the United States and in Latin America. They travel in armies of thousands, devouring any insects that stray into their path.

▲ Susan B. Anthony was arrested and fined $100 for voting in the 1872 presidential elections, held long before women won the right to vote.

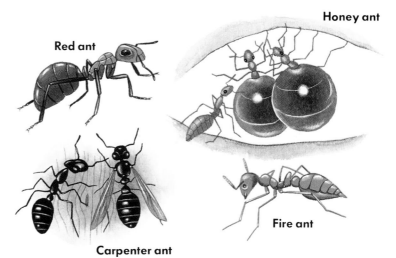

Red ant

Honey ant

Fire ant

Carpenter ant

▶ Four kinds of ants that are found in North America. Carpenter ants damage buildings by tunneling into wooden beams to make nesting space. Honey ant workers called repletes act as storage jars for the honeydew the ants gather. The back part of each replete's body, called the gaster, swells up as the honeydew fills it. Fire ants have a poisonous stinger that can pierce the skin. They have been known to attack baby birds and sting them to death. Red ants are also aggressive in defending their nests.

Harvester ants collect and store seeds in their nests. They are found mainly on the Great Plains. Some ants tend small insects known as aphids, rather as people tend cows. They "milk" the aphids for their sweet liquid, or honeydew. Honey ants, found in the western United States, collect honeydew and store it inside certain worker ants called *repletes*. When an ant wants some honeydew, it taps the replete, which regurgitates (throws up) some of the liquid.

Leaf-cutting ants, found in Texas and Louisiana, strip leaves from plants. In their nests the ants use the leaves to grow a fungus that is used as food. There are no fungus-growing ants outside the New World.

Some ants use "slaves" to help with their work. They kidnap the young of a closely related species from a different nest. Many of the red ants and black ants found in North America are slave-maker ants.

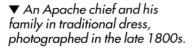

▼ An Apache chief and his family in traditional dress, photographed in the late 1800s.

APACHES

The Apaches are a southwestern INDIAN tribe that originally came from Canada over 1,100 years ago. They were nomads, with no fixed settlements. The Apaches were much feared because they raided other tribes, stealing food and captives for use as slave labor. The very name Apache is thought to mean "enemy."

The Apaches stopped the spread of the Spanish from Mexico. Later they resisted the American settlers who opened the western frontier. A long series of wars under such legendary chiefs as COCHISE, Victorio, and GERONIMO finally ended in 1886. About 10,000 Apaches still live in Arizona, New Mexico, and Oklahoma.

APOLLO PROGRAM *See* Space Program

APPALACHIAN MOUNTAINS

The Appalachians form the great eastern MOUNTAIN range that runs for almost 1,600 miles (2,575 km) from Newfoundland in Canada as far south as Alabama. They are the oldest mountains in the United States. Wind and rain over tens of millions of years have eroded them and worn them down.

The Appalachians contain many smaller ranges of mountains. These include the White Mountains in New Hampshire, the Green Mountains in Vermont, the Catskills in New York, the Alleghenies in Pennsylvania, and the BLUE RIDGE MOUNTAINS, which run from Pennsylvania to North Carolina. The tallest peak in the Appalachians is Mount Mitchell, in the Black Mountains of North Carolina. It is 6,684 feet (2,037 m) high.

The forests of the Appalachians are important sources of lumber and of wood pulp used in papermaking. Coal is another important resource. The soil provides much farmland for apples, grain, potatoes, and tobacco.

The Appalachian National Scenic Trail, from Maine to Georgia, is visited every year by thousands of tourists.

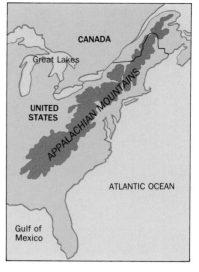

▲ It is commonly thought that the Appalachians are a very old mountain system. This is only partially true. Most of the Appalachians are less than 25 million years old, which is quite young for a mountain range. Only the highest peaks date from the Permian Period, 200 million years old.

APPLESEED, Johnny

Johnny Appleseed is the name by which John Chapman (1774–1845) has become known. As early pioneers moved west and cleared the land, Chapman followed them, planting orchards of apple trees as he went.

Legends grew up about him. Some said he was so eager to encourage the cultivation of apples in the young country that he gave the settlers many gifts of seeds and young trees for planting. Very little is really known about John Chapman, but the legend of Johnny Appleseed lives on as an inspiration to all who care about the land.

ARAPAHOS

The Arapahos are one of the INDIAN tribes that lived in the GREAT PLAINS. They moved there from what are now the North Central states. This probably happened in the early 1800s.

▲ Johnny Appleseed became one of the symbols of the pioneering spirit in America.

▲ Two Arapaho girls pose in traditional dress in Oklahoma. The Southern Arapaho people were given land in Oklahoma in 1867 by the Treaty of Medicine Lodge.

▶ A tree is planted during an Arbor Day ceremony. By planting trees young people demonstrate their interest in improving the environment.

Some Archaeological Sites in the U.S.
- **Folsom, N. Mex.** Flint spearheads have been found dating from 9000–8000 B.C.
- **Koster, Il.** This may be the oldest village in the U.S. The site spans 8,000 years (from 7500 B.C.–A.D. 1000) and covers 11 different Indian cultures.
- **Mesa Verde, Colo.** The most excavated site in the country, Mesa Verde contains remains of cave and cliff dwellings dating from A.D. 350–1300.

Two groups developed. The Northern Arapahos lived along the Platte River in Wyoming; the Southern Arapahos settled in Colorado, around the Arkansas River. Both groups hunted buffalo. Their life-style depended on the horses they got from trading with their neighbors, the KIOWAS. The Arapahos were one of the main tribes involved in the wars that took place as American settlers moved west in great numbers, taking over more and more land from the Indians. After the INDIAN WARS, the defeated Northern and Southern Arapahos were moved onto two separate reservations, in Wyoming and Oklahoma.

ARBOR DAY

Arbor Day is a day set aside for the planting of trees. It dates from 1872. Arbor Day was the idea of J. S. Morton, a member of the Nebraska State Board of Agriculture. Today it is celebrated in many states, and in a number of them is a legal holiday.

The ceremonial planting of trees on Arbor Day is often a local school activity. It is a special day on which to remember the importance of trees and forestland. Because of climate differences, Arbor Day is not the same day in every state.

ARCHAEOLOGY

Archaeology is the study of ancient peoples. In the United States, this study began in the late 1700s with the work of Thomas JEFFERSON. This scholar who became president contributed to the early methods of American archaeology. He carefully dug up and studied a large mound of earth on his lands in Virginia, uncovering a number of Indian burials.

In the 200 years since that time, thousands of mounds have been found. Some were for burials, while others were used for religious ceremonies. The MOUND BUILDERS were prehistoric Indians who lived between A.D. 600 and the time of the early Spanish explorers of North America. Some mounds were shaped like animals, such as the Great Serpent Mound in Ohio. Other famous mounds are in Cahokia, Illinois; Adena and Hopewell, Ohio; and Moundville, Alabama.

As pioneers opened up the West, other great Indian cultures were discovered. One of these was the Anasazi. These people built adobe (clay) villages like apartment buildings into the sides of cliffs. Mesa Verde, in Colorado, is the remains of one of these. The Anasazi also lived in pueblos, in which many rooms were joined together around an open space. Each pueblo formed a small village. Pueblo Bonito at Chaco Canyon, New Mexico, was built over 3,000 years ago. The HOPI, Pecos, and Zuni Indians may be descendants of the Anasazi culture.

Archaeologists have found firm evidence that people lived in America at least 12,000 years ago. They came from Asia to Alaska over a strip of land called *Beringia*. That "land bridge" is now under water. Spearheads belonging to the Clovis and FOLSOM cultures, who were wandering hunters, have been found in the West.

The VIKINGS are the first people known to have come from the Old World. The remains of their houses, found at L'Anse aux Meadows in Newfoundland, are almost a thousand years old.

**Hohokum pottery dish
A.D. 500-900**

Decoy duck 200 B.C.

Hopewell pipe A.D. 300

▲ *Archaeological excavations of Indian sites have uncovered a variety of artifacts.*

▼ *In the 1840s dozens of burial mounds were opened in the lower Mississippi Valley. This drawing was made from a painting of one of the excavations in Louisiana.*

ARCHITECTURE

Architecture is the art of designing buildings. Some buildings are very simple, designed by the people who build them; this is called *vernacular* architecture. The timber houses built by the colonists of New England in the 1600s are examples of this kind of architecture. Most buildings today, however, are designed by trained architects in a chosen style.

Many American architectural styles originally came from Europe. They were then adapted by the colonists to suit the different climate and building materials of their new homeland. For example, the simple, dignified houses called *colonial* and found in the East, are built in a style brought from England during the 1700s. Many missions in California and New Mexico show the influence of the Spanish *baroque* style of the 1600s. American public buildings often have domes and columns derived from the *classical* architecture of ancient Greece and Rome. The CAPITOL building in Washington, D.C., is an example of this *neoclassical* style; so are many of the pre–Civil War plantation houses of the southern states.

▼ Falling Water, a house in Pennsylvania, is one of Frank Lloyd Wright's most famous buildings. His houses are designed to be in harmony with the landscape.

Later other, older, European styles were revived. The *gothic* style developed in the 1100s with the building of the great medieval cathedrals. Gothic spires and pointed arches were used for many American churches and university buildings during the late 1800s. The 1800s were also the years of the INDUSTRIAL REVOLUTION, and architects designed many factories and railroad stations as well as country homes and cathedrals.

Practical inventions often influence architecture. The steel frame and the elevator made possible the first tall office buildings, which appeared in Chicago in the 1880s. Today, SKYSCRAPERS tower over most cities in the United States. Reinforced concrete, which contains steel rods or mesh, allows architects greater freedom for their designs.

From the 1930s until recently, architecture tended to be very plain and boxlike. This style is called *modernism* or *functionalism*, because its supporters insisted that a building's form must be determined by its function, or use. Today many architects are turning to more decorative, colorful styles. They use ideas from the past, such as classical columns. This trend is called *postmodernism*.

▲ *Michael Graves's Portland Building was completed in 1982 and is a good example of postmodern architecture.*

▼ *Below are some examples of different styles of American architecture over the last 350 years.*

Some American Structures

Building	Architect
White House, Washington, D.C.	James Hoban (1762–1831)
Washington Monument, Washington D.C.	Robert Mills (1781–1855)
Trinity Church, Boston	Henry Richardson (1838–1886)
Tiffany Building, New York City	Stanford White (1853–1906)
Auditorium Building, Buffalo	Louis Sullivan (1856–1924)
Harvard University Graduate Center, Boston	Walter Gropius (1883–1969)
Museum of Modern Art, New York City	Edward Durrell Stone (1902–1978)
Seagram Building, New York City	Philip Johnson (1906–) and Ludwig Mies van der Rohe (1886–1969)
Trans World Airlines Terminal, New York City	Eero Saarinen (1910–1961)
National Gallery of Art (East Building), Washington, D.C.	I.M. Pei (1917–)

AT&T Building, New York City

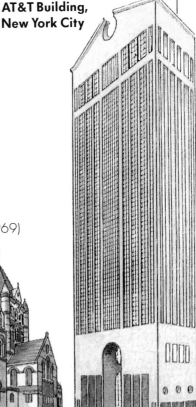

Trinity Church, Boston

Monticello, near Charlottesville, Virginia

Colonial timber house

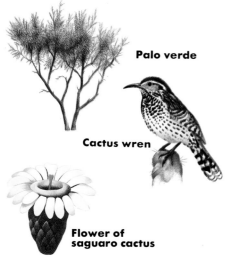

Palo verde

Cactus wren

Flower of saguaro cactus

Arizona is a state in the Southwest. Much of it is desert, and it was long thought that people would not settle there because of the burning summer heat. But irrigation has made the land productive, and air-conditioning has helped people endure the heat. Today, cotton, vegetables, and other crops are grown in Arizona. And its population has grown by a third since 1980, making it one of the fastest growing states in the nation.

In addition to agriculture, manufacturing, mining, and tourism are important industries. Most of Arizona's factories are located in and around PHOENIX, the capital and largest city, and Tucson. Molybdenum, gold, and silver are mined in Arizona. But its most important mineral is copper. Arizona supplies more than two thirds of the nation's copper. Tourism is second in importance to manufacturing. Tourists visit the state in the winter to enjoy the dry desert air. They also come to wonder at such natural attractions as the GRAND CANYON and the PAINTED DESERT.

The Spanish were the first Europeans to settle in the

▼ *The Grand Canyon's spectacular rock formations form Arizona's greatest natural wonder.*

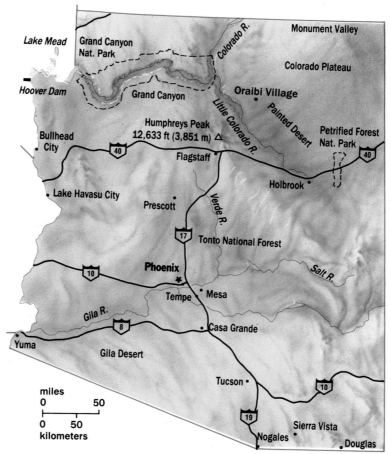

region. They ruled it from the 1500s until 1821, when it became part of newly independent Mexico. The United States took possession of Arizona in 1848. Some of the fiercest fighting between Indians and white settlers took place beginning in 1861. The APACHES, led by such men as GERONIMO and COCHISE, and the NAVAJOS were brave foes. They were not defeated until 1886.

Arizona still has one of the largest Indian populations in the country—almost 170,000. But they are far outnumbered by the state's more than 450,000 HISPANIC AMERICANS, most of whom are Mexican.

Places of Interest
- The Grand Canyon is one of the natural wonders of the world.
- The Scenic Apache Trail passes through Tonto National Forest.
- Oraibi Village in Navajo County is probably the oldest continuously inhabited settlement in the country and is just one of several Hopi villages in Arizona.
- San Xavier del Bac Mission, near Tucson, is an example of an early Arizona mission settlement.

Arizona
Capital: Phoenix
Area: 113,508 sq mi (293,986 km²). Rank: 6th
Population: 3,677,985 (1990). Rank: 24th
Statehood: February 14, 1912
Principal rivers: Colorado, Gila
Highest point: Humphreys Peak, 12,633 ft (3,851 m)
Motto: *Ditat Deus* (God Enriches)
Song: "Arizona March Song"

◄ *Graves in Boot Hill Cemetery bear witness to Tombstone's violent past. Gunfights were common in the days of the silver-mining boom in the 1800s.*

▼ *When the first Europeans arrived in Arizona, they found well-developed Indian civilizations. Tourists can still visit pueblo villages, some of which date from the 1100s.*

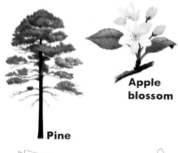

Mockingbird

Apple blossom

Pine

Arkansas is among the most beautiful southern states. It is a major agricultural state, but industry has become important in recent years. Northern and western Arkansas—the Highlands—are mountainous, with forests, lakes, and streams. Southern and eastern Arkansas—the Lowlands—are lower and more fertile. Tourists from all over the United States visit Arkansas every year to hunt in its forests, fish in its lakes, and admire its natural beauty. The Ozark and Ouachita mountain ranges in northern Arkansas are especially popular. Many visitors come to bathe in the state's natural spring waters at resorts such as Mammoth Spring and Hot Springs.

The processing of food grown on Arkansas's farms is the state's most important industry. Many factories make electric and electronic equipment. Others make paper and wood products, such as furniture. Bauxite mining—bauxite is used to make aluminum—and petroleum refining also contribute to the state's prosperity. Arkansas also has the only diamond mine in the country, at Murfreesboro. Its farms raise more broiler chick-

▼ A young visitor digs for diamonds at Crater of Diamonds State Park.

ens than those of any other state and grow one third of the total U.S. rice crop. Soybeans and cotton are also important state crops.

Arkansas belonged to France, Spain, and then France again before it became part of the United States in the LOUISIANA PURCHASE of 1803. It was a slave state before the CIVIL WAR and fought with the Confederacy in the war. Its prosperity was destroyed by the war, and Arkansas remained poor for many years.

Little Rock, located in the center of the state on the banks of the Arkansas River, is the capital and largest city of Arkansas.

▲ The State Capitol in Little Rock was modeled on the U.S. Capitol.

Places of Interest
● Crater of Diamonds State Park has the only active diamond fields in the U.S.
● Blanchard Springs Caverns, near Mountain View, attracts many visitors with its beautiful rock formations.
● Dogpatch U.S.A., near Harrison, is an amusement park with a zoo, caves, and musical entertainment.
● The steam train of Eureka Springs is one of this popular Victorian resort's many attractions.
● Hot Springs National Park is a popular spa.
● Mountain Village 1890, Bull Shoals, is a reconstruction of an early pioneer town.

▼ The Ozark Mountains lie in the Highlands of Arkansas. The region's beautiful scenery makes it popular with tourists.

Arkansas
Capital: Little Rock
Area: 52,078 sq mi (134,882 km²). Rank: 27th
Population: 2,362,239 (1990). Rank: 33rd
Statehood: June 15, 1836
Principal rivers: Arkansas, Mississippi.
Highest point: Magazine Mountain, 2,753 ft (839 m)
Motto: *Regnat Populus* (The People Rule)
Song: "Arkansas"

41

Although the armadillo has short legs, it can run quite quickly and will scurry away at the first sign of danger.

As a child Louis Armstrong would follow the brass bands through the streets of New Orleans. Later he played the trumpet on the Mississippi riverboats. He got his big break when he was asked to play second trumpet in Joe "King" Oliver's band.

▼ Neil Armstrong was the first civilian to join the astronaut training program. In 1986 he was asked to chair the commission set up to investigate the Challenger space shuttle disaster.

ARMADILLO

The armadillo is a small, burrowing mammal, covered with bony plates joined together to form a kind of armor. The armadillo hunts at night. It eats roots, small creatures such as insects, worms, and snails, and the carcasses of dead animals.

The only armadillo in the United States is the Texas armadillo. It is also known as the nine-banded armadillo because it has nine thin, movable plates between the fixed plates that cover its shoulders and haunches. The armadillo, which averages under 2 feet (60 cm) long, is edible.

ARMSTRONG, Louis

The dazzling trumpet playing of Louis Armstrong (1900–1971) was one of the glories of JAZZ. Armstrong was nicknamed "Satchmo" after someone observed that he had a mouth like a satchel. In the 1920s he became one of the first jazz players to perform improvised solos. A vocalist with an appealing, gravelly voice, Armstrong popularized a singing style called *scat*, in which nonsense syllables imitate an instrument. He also composed many jazz songs.

Satchmo was born in the birthplace of jazz, New Orleans, and grew up with the sounds of its brass bands in his ears. But his family was poor, and he was often left to fend for himself. While in a home for delinquent boys he learned to play the cornet, a trumpet-like instrument, and decided to become a musician. His talent for comedy as well as music led to parts in many films, including *High Society* and *Hello, Dolly*.

ARMSTRONG, Neil

In July 1969 astronaut Neil Armstrong (1930–) became the first person to set foot on the moon. Armstrong began his career as a Navy pilot and went on to become a civilian test pilot. He joined the SPACE PROGRAM as an astronaut in 1962, and his first space flight was just four years later. On board Gemini 8 he was involved in the first docking of vehicles in space. Three years later, during the Apollo 11 mission, he stepped onto the surface of the moon and said, "That's one small step for man, one giant leap for mankind!"

ARMY, United States

The U.S. Army is the largest and the oldest branch of the United States armed forces. Its special responsibilities are for military operations on land, but it also engages in other vital military activities such as search-and-rescue operations and civil defense. In all, the Army employs over 2 million men and women, of whom more than 750,000 are soldiers on active duty.

The Army was first formed in 1775, as the Continental Army. Its job then was to fight and defeat the British in the American REVOLUTION. Its responsibilities today are much greater. The Army's two primary roles are to defend the United States and, in the event of war, to

▲ The U.S. Army insignia, which is based on the Great Seal of the United States, was adopted in 1778.

Civil War (Union)

War of 1812

World War II

Modern colonel, U.S. Infantry

◄ Some of the uniforms soldiers have worn since Congress created the Continental Army in 1775.

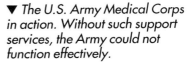

▼ The U.S. Army Medical Corps in action. Without such support services, the Army could not function effectively.

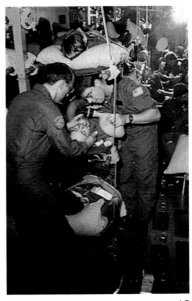

attack its enemies overseas. The Army's active-service personnel are stationed on bases in the United States and overseas, especially in Europe.

There are many different branches of the Army, but the most important are the combat units, which include the infantry, the armored forces, and the artillery. They are backed up by a wide range of other troops, such as communications and observation units, transportation units, engineers, and logistic units. All Army units must be properly trained and are supplied with the latest equipment. A large part of the Army's work and budget goes to ensuring that these basic priorities are met. The Army is run by the Department of the Army in Washington, D.C.

ART

The works of art on these pages show you some of the wonderful variety of American creative styles. Further examples of American art can be found in the articles on PAINTING, SCULPTURE, ARCHITECTURE, and FOLK ART. You might also want to look up the names of individual artists in the Index.

◀ The carved totem pole was a work of art and a sacred tribal symbol for many Indians of the Northwest.

▼ This portrait of Mr. and Mrs. Mifflin was painted by John Singleton Copley in the late 1700s.

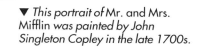

▲ Girl in Pink, by an unknown artist, is an example of American primitive art from the late 1700s or early 1800s. Primitive art is characterized by its simplicity. This is because most primitive artists were not trained artists.

▶ George Caleb Bingham recorded this scene of river life, called Fur Traders Descending the Missouri, in the mid-1800s.

▼ A statue of George Washington in Philadelphia stands as an example of American civic art for public buildings.

▲ This lamp was designed by Louis Comfort Tiffany, a major American stained glass designer of the late 1800s. Tiffany helped establish style called art nouveau.

▲ In the late 1800s, John Singer Sargent began to use soft, countryside settings for his portraits, as shown in this detail The Brook.

▼ Built in 1929, the Chrysler Building in New York City shows the influence of the art deco movement with its sleek, streamlined shape and use of geometric patterns.

► Mirror Shadow XVI is typical of the work of sculptor Louise Nevelson. Most of her sculptures are made out of wood or use objects from everyday life.

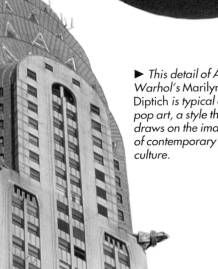

► This detail of Andy Warhol's Marilyn Diptich is typical of pop art, a style that draws on the images of contemporary culture.

45

▼ *The Brooklyn Bridge was opened in 1883, during Chester A. Arthur's term of office. It was hailed as the eighth wonder of the world.*

Chester A. Arthur was elected vice president of the United States in 1880. He became the 21st president when President James A. GARFIELD was assassinated (murdered) in 1881. As a young laywer, Arthur had been against slavery. He made a name for himself in two cases. In one, he won the freedom of two slaves. In the other, he fought for a free black's civil rights.

After joining the Republican Party, Arthur became active in New York politics. In 1871, President Ulysses S. GRANT made Arthur customs collector for the port of New York City. The customs house provided jobs to party supporters, who were known as "Stalwarts," even if they were not qualified for them. In the late 1800s many politicians were more interested in the spoils of office than in policies or issues. As customs collector, Arthur did nothing dishonest, but he did not change the system either. President Rutherford B. HAYES, who followed Grant, finally forced Arthur out of office.

Chester A. Arthur
Born: October 5, 1829, in Fairfield, Vermont
Education: Union College
Political Party: Republican
Term of office: 1881–1885
Married: 1859 to Ellen Lewis Herndon
Died: November 18, 1886, in New York City

Arthur and other Republican Stalwarts tried to have Grant renominated as the presidential candidate in 1880. But Garfield won the nomination. To win the support of the Stalwarts, the Republicans chose Arthur as the vice presidential candidate. The Republicans won the election. Many people, however, were nervous about Arthur, especially when he took over as president after Garfield's assassination. He seemed too rooted in the so-called spoils system. After Arthur became president, however, he abandoned the spoils system and reformed the civil service.

ARTICLES OF CONFEDERATION

The Articles of Confederation was a formal compact drawn up by the original 13 states in 1781. It gave the young country a body of laws that it was governed by until the CONSTITUTION was finally drawn up and approved by all the states in 1789.

Each of the states was anxious to guard its own independence and the right to govern its citizens. As a result, some powers were given only to the states and some only to CONGRESS. Matters that affected all the states (in other words, the country as a whole) were dealt with by Congress. These included the powers to declare war and establish armed forces for defense, to carry on relations with foreign countries, and to issue money. The powers to tax the people and regulate the sale of goods were given to the states.

Under the Articles of Confederation, Congress had so little power that effective government of the new nation was almost impossible. In order to prevent disorder breaking out, a committee was set up to amend the Articles. However, the committee took the bold step of drawing up a completely new constitution. This caused one delegate to remark, "We are razing the foundations of the building, when we need only repair the roof."

ASIMOV, Isaac

Isaac Asimov (1920–   ) is a biochemist and best-selling science fiction writer. He was born in the USSR and brought to the United States by his parents at the age of three. After obtaining a Ph.D. in chemistry, he was associate professor at Boston University Medical School from 1955 to 1958.

Asimov's first story was published in 1939. He has written more than 350 books and several hundred articles. He is best known for his science fiction works and has won several Hugo and Nebula awards for them. His Foundation series was given a special Hugo Award as Best All-Time Science Fiction Series. Asimov has also written detective stories, encyclopedias, textbooks, and books on many aspects of science.

▼ *Fred Astaire dances in the movie* Finian's Rainbow *(1968). Astaire received a special Academy Award in 1949 in recognition of his talent as a film entertainer.*

ASTAIRE, Fred

Fred Astaire (1899–1987), born Frederick Austerlitz, became famous as the star of a number of popular musical movies. Astaire created all his own dances. He was able to make complicated dance steps seem relaxed and easy. His style was smooth and elegant.

Astaire's first dancing partner was his sister Adele, with whom he danced on stage. His film partners included Audrey Hepburn and Cyd Charisse. But the most famous was Ginger Rogers, with whom he made ten films. Astaire was also a fine actor, who turned in excellent performances in *On the Beach* and *The Towering Inferno*.

ASTOR FAMILY

In the 1800s the Astors became one of the wealthiest and most prominent families in the United States. When John Jacob Astor arrived in New York City in 1783, he was a penniless 20-year-old German. By the time he died in 1848, he had a fortune of $20 million, made from the fur trade and from real estate. His descendants became even richer. By the 1880s they were making $5 million a year, much of it from tenements occupied by poor immigrants. The Astors themselves lived in great splendor. Mrs. William B. Astor, Jr., was the "queen" of New York society in the late 1800s. The Astor "cottage" in Rhode Island was really a mansion.

One branch of the family moved to England, where they were given titles. The Virginia-born Lady Nancy Astor became the first woman elected to Parliament.

Both the British and the American Astors have also been active in journalism. For many years Vincent Astor owned *Newsweek* magazine. He sold off the Astor real estate holdings in the 1940s and left most of his fortune to charity.

▲ *Nancy Astor dressed for a costume party in 1910. She later became Lady Astor and was elected to the British Parliament.*

ATLANTA

Atlanta, with 394,017 people, is the capital of GEORGIA and its largest city. It is one of the fastest-growing cities in the country and a major industrial and transportation center. Downtown Atlanta has many new high rises and malls, especially around Peachtree Center.

Atlanta was founded in 1837. Then it was called Terminus, because it stood at the southern end, or terminus, of the Western and Atlantic Railroad. Its name was changed to Atlanta in 1845. During the Civil War it was a Confederate supply base and was burned to the ground by General SHERMAN's Union army. The city grew rapidly after the war, when it was also made the state capital. Atlanta became famous in the 1950s and 1960s as a leading center of the CIVIL RIGHTS movement. Martin Luther KING, Jr., was born and buried in the city. Today Atlanta is the commercial and financial center of the Southeast.

▼ *Downtown Atlanta boasts one of the tallest hotels in the world, the 73-story Peachtree Center Plaza Hotel.*

ATLANTIC CHARTER

In August 1941 the United States was not yet in WORLD WAR II. It was, however, supplying arms and other materials to Britain and other Allies. U.S. President Franklin D. ROOSEVELT and British prime minister Winston Churchill met on a warship in the North Atlantic and drew up the Atlantic Charter. It declared, among other things, that the two nations were not seeking any more territory and that they supported self-government for all peoples. The Charter also stated that once the Allies had defeated the Axis powers (Germany, Italy, and Japan), they would work for a world in which nations could live in peace.

ATTUCKS, Crispus

Crispus Attucks (1723?–1770), a black man, was one of the first colonists to be killed in events that led up to the American REVOLUTION. A runaway slave, he was one of a group of extremists in Boston who protested against the presence of British troops there. On March 5, 1770, Attucks led a mob in goading some British soldiers, who finally opened fire on them. Attucks and two others were killed instantly; two other colonists died later. Attucks's statesmanlike funeral was attended by thousands. A monument to these victims of the BOSTON MASSACRE was built in Boston in 1888.

AUDUBON, John James

A love of wildlife and a talent for painting led John James Audubon (1785–1851) to undertake an enormous project: painting every known species of bird in North America. Audubon had studied art in Paris (his father was a French sea captain) and then settled in the United States. In 1820 he began traveling around the country, painting birds in their natural habitat. To support his family he also painted portraits, while his wife worked as a governess. The 435 paintings, which took him some 20 years, are remarkable for their detail and realism. To ensure accuracy, Audubon worked from freshly killed specimens, and he also observed the birds in the wild. He used watercolors, sometimes redrawing the work many times before he was satisfied. Audubon's paintings make a unique record of American bird life.

On January 1, 1942, the 26 governments then at war with Germany held a conference in Washington, D.C. They declared that they "subscribed to a common program of purposes and principles in the joint declaration ... the Atlantic Charter." This agreement was later signed by most of the free nations of the world. It formed the basis of the United Nations, which was founded in San Francisco in April–June 1945.

▼ The wild turkey was just one of the many bird species Audubon painted. His collected paintings were later published in a book called The Birds of America.

▲ *A view of the Austin skyline. Austin is one of the country's fastest-growing cities.*

▼ *The introduction of conveyor belts on automobile assembly lines in 1913 cut the cost of building cars by more than half.*

AUSTIN

Austin is the capital of TEXAS and is located in the heart of the state. It is a port on the COLORADO RIVER and is an important center for transporting crops produced in the area. Many conventions are held in Austin, which is the home of the University of Texas and many other colleges. It is named after Stephen Austin, who is sometimes called the "father of Texas." Austin became the capital of the Republic of Texas in 1836 when Texas declared its independence from Mexico. Today 465,622 people live in Austin.

AUTOMOBILE INDUSTRY

The automobile industry is one of the most important businesses in America. U.S. automobile companies produce more than 8 million cars a year, over a quarter of all the cars made in the world, as well as 3.5 million trucks and buses. Their combined value is more than $125 billion. More than 700,000 people work in this huge industry. Many other industries depend on it, too. More than half the lead and rubber used every year in the United States, and almost 20 percent of all the steel, is bought by the automobile industry.

The leading automobile companies have headquarters in or near DETROIT, Michigan. Their industry is one of the most competitive in the world. U.S. manufacturers have to work hard to keep ahead of overseas competition, especially from Japan. They invest millions of dollars every year to find ways to make their cars more economical. The three largest automobile manufacturers are General Motors, Ford, and Chrysler.

Indianapolis 500 Winners		
Year	Driver	Winning Speed (mph)
1990	Arie Luyendyk	185.984
1989	Emerson Fittipaldi	167.581
1988	Rick Mears	144.809
1987	Al Unser	162.175
1986	Bobby Rahal	170.722
1985	Danny Sullivan	152.982
1984	Rick Mears	163.612

Daytona 500 Winners			
Year	Driver	Winning Speed (mph)	Car
1990	Derrike Cope	165.761	Chevrolet
1989	Darrell Waltrip	148.466	Chevrolet
1988	Bobby Allison	137.531	Buick
1987	Bill Elliott	176.263	Ford
1986	Geoff Bodine	148.124	Chevrolet
1985	Bill Elliott	172.265	Ford
1984	Cale Yarborough	150.994	Chevrolet

AUTOMOBILE RACING

Automobile racing is one of the most popular sports in the United States. The most famous race is the Indianapolis 500, held each Memorial Day. More than 100 million television viewers worldwide watch the cars speeding at almost 200 miles per hour (320 km/hr). Between them, the two Unser brothers, Al and Bobby, have won this race seven times, and A. J. Foyt has won it four times.

Two types of automobile racing were invented in the United States. Stock car racing uses showroom models with special engines; the top race is the Daytona 500. The South has produced most of the best stock car racers, including Richard Petty and Cale Yarborough. Drag racing cars are like rockets on wheels. They developed in the 1960s from the hot rods raced in California. Modern drag racing cars, called "rails," can reach speeds of 200 miles per hour (320 km/hr).

▲ A machine lowers the body of a truck onto its chassis on a General Motors assembly line. Assembly lines have come a long way from the lines of the early 1900s. Machines now do most of the work, and many lines are even using industrial robots. The first industrial robot was used on an automobile assembly line in 1961.

▼ The 1989 24-hour endurance race held at the Daytona Speedway. Endurance racing is one of the most popular forms of sports car racing.

► *The B-2 Stealth bomber is one of the most technologically advanced aircraft in the world. It took seven years to develop and is 69 feet (21 m) long with a wingspan of 172 feet (52.4 m).*

AVIATION

The United States has always been a leader in aviation. The WRIGHT BROTHERS built the first airplane and flew it in Kitty Hawk, North Carolina, on December 17, 1903. Other Americans were pioneers of aviation. Charles LINDBERGH became the first person to fly solo across the Atlantic in 1927. Five years later Amelia EARHART broke the record for an Atlantic crossing.

Chuck Yeager became the first person to travel faster than the speed of sound in 1947. His flight was one of the first in a jet airplane. Today most airplanes are jets. The fastest planes are used by the U.S. Navy and Air Force. These can break speed records every year. A different sort of record was set in December 1986. Richard Rutan and Jeana Yeager landed their light aircraft *Voyager* in California after flying nonstop around the world without refueling. (See also AEROSPACE INDUSTRY; AIR TRANSPORTATION.)

▼ *Wilbur Wright appeared on a French magazine cover in 1908, after he demonstrated his plane in France. A year later Wilbur and his brother Orville founded the American Wright Company to manufacture planes and train pilots.*

Le Petit Journal

L'AEROPLANE DE WILBUR WRIGHT EN PLEIN VOL

Some Important Dates in American Aviation
1903 The Wright Brothers make the world's first successful airplane flight.
1918 The world's first airmail service begins.
1924 U.S. Army pilots make the first round-the-world flight.
1926 Scheduled passenger flights begin.
1927 Charles Lindbergh makes the first solo nonstop flight across the Atlantic.
1947 Air force Captain Charles Yeager makes the first supersonic flight in the X-1 rocket plane.
1949 An Air Force pilot flies a B-50 nonstop around the world.
1959 American Airlines sets up the first transcontinental jet service using Boeing 707s.
1970 Boeing 747 jumbo jets are put in service by Pan Am.
1980 The space shuttle *Columbia* makes its first successful airplane-like landing.

BADGER

A badger is a member of the WEASEL family. The American badger is found mainly on the western and central plains from southern Canada down to Mexico. Badgers spend the day underground and come out at night to hunt for food. They are 16 to 30 inches (42 to 76 cm) long and weigh about 8 to 25 pounds (3.5 to 11.5 kg). Badgers are fierce when cornered.

Badgers have very strong jaws. They eat small animals such as ground squirrels and mice, as well as insects, roots, and fruits. They have long, heavy, blunt claws on their front feet, which they use for digging. Badgers dig burrows, or dens, to live in. The burrows have tunnels that lead to sleeping and storage chambers.

BADLANDS

Badlands are areas where wind, rain, and floods have carved the land into strange shapes. Towering cliffs and ridges alternate with deep ravines and rugged masses of stone. These areas look like the uninviting terrain of some far-off planet. The soil has been eroded away so that little grows here other than a few wildflowers and sagebrush. One such region in South Dakota has been set aside as the Badlands National Park. Many visitors travel here to enjoy the wild scenery and to hunt for fossils in the cliffs. (See map, SOUTH DAKOTA.)

▼ The chambers in a badger's burrow are used for sleeping and for the young to live in. Badgers keep their burrows very clean.

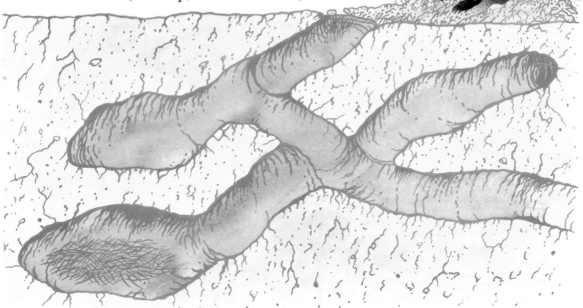

▲ *George Balanchine directs a rehearsal of the ballet* The Nutcracker.

BAEKELAND, Leo

Leo Baekeland (1863–1944) was a Belgian chemist who came to New York in 1889, where he worked for the rest of his life. He is best known for two inventions. One was a light-sensitive coating for photographic plates. This allowed photographs to be developed much faster and more easily than before and with much better results. The other, invented in 1909, was the first form of plastic. It was called Bakelite in honor of him. Bakelite is used in electric switches, pot handles, and pipe stems and as electrical insulation.

BALANCHINE, George

The most famous name in American BALLET, George Balanchine (1904–1983) was born in St. Petersburg (now Leningrad), in Russia. He studied there at the Imperial School of Ballet. Later he joined the renowned Ballets Russes, in Paris, as a dancer and choreographer (composer of dances).

  After moving to the United States in 1933, Balanchine helped to raise the standard of American ballet. The company he founded, the New York City Ballet, is known especially for the brilliant technique of its dancers. Balanchine created many ballets for the company. Although a few tell stories, most are patterns of dance movements inspired by the music. Balanchine also composed dances for stage musicals and films.

▼ *Balboa's discovery of the Pacific Ocean led to further Spanish exploration down the west coast of South America.*

BALBOA, Vasco Núñez de

Vasco Núñez de Balboa (1475?–1519) was a Spanish explorer. In 1513 he became the first European to sight the eastern shore of the Pacific Ocean.

  In 1500, Balboa set sail from Spain to make his fortune in the New World. In 1510 he fled from Hispaniola in the West Indies to escape from people to whom he owed money. The ship on which Balboa sailed arrived in Panama, where he founded a colony called Darién. Balboa became acting governor of the colony. While there, he heard of a huge sea from the local Indians. Balboa set out to discover this body of water. He eventually sighted it from a mountain on the Isthmus of Panama. He named the new ocean the Great South Sea and claimed it for Spain.

BALDWIN, James

James Baldwin (1924–1987) was a leading novelist, playwright, and essayist. He was born in Harlem in New York City, the eldest of nine children. While still in his teens, he was a part-time preacher in his stepfather's church, an experience he used as the basis of his first novel, *Go Tell It on the Mountain*. His other novels include *Giovanni's Room* and *Tell Me How Long the Train's Been Gone*, which explores the black CIVIL RIGHTS movement of the 1960s.

Baldwin's play *Blues for Mister Charlie* is a bitter attack on whites' oppression of blacks. He took an active part in the struggle for civil rights, and many of his essays deal with this issue. Collections of his essays include *Nobody Knows My Name* and *The Fire Next Time*.

▲ Many of James Baldwin's novels were a commentary on the civil rights struggle of the 1960s. His first novel, Go Tell It on the Mountain, *was written while Baldwin was living in Paris.*

BALLET

Ballet has existed in Europe for more than 300 years, but it did not become well established in North America until this century. During the 1800s, European ballet dancers occasionally visited the United States, and they were generally well received. In the early 1900s the great Russian ballerina Anna Pavlova toured to packed houses. But ballet still seemed very foreign to most Americans at that time.

The first major American company was the American Ballet—now the New York City Ballet—founded by the

During a tour in the early 1840s, Viennese ballerina Fanny Essler won the hearts of the American people with her dancing. Such was her popularity that congressmen meeting in Washington adjourned so that they would not miss her performance.

◀ *The American Ballet Theatre in a performance of the ballet* Symphonie Concertante.

American musical composers have been attracted to ballet. Aaron Copland's music for the ballet *Appalachian Spring* was an inspiration to other composers. Leonard Bernstein adapted the ballet form in his musicals *On the Town* and *West Side Story*.

wealthy patron Lincoln Kirstein and the choreographer George BALANCHINE in 1933. Balanchine's wife, Maria Tallchief, danced for the New York City Ballet. Today this is one of the world's leading ballet companies.

Many fine companies and schools now flourish in the United States. An outstanding company, the American Ballet Theatre, was founded in 1939. Its choreographers, unlike Balanchine, have generally preferred to create ballets that tell a story. Some, especially Agnes de Mille, brought a distinctively American style to ballet. They did this by combining ballet's traditional elegant steps with freer movements suitable for portraying the life of the Old West, for example, or urban themes. This trend has spread to other countries. Ballets now often include movements drawn from other kinds of dance, including modern dance and disco dancing. Another major ballet company is the Joffrey Ballet, directed by Robert Joffrey.

BALTIMORE

Baltimore is a port located on the Patapsco River, which flows into CHESAPEAKE BAY. It is the largest city in MARYLAND with 736,014 people. It is a historic city, too, founded as long ago as 1729. During the American REVOLUTION, Baltimore was the capital of the United States for a brief time. It was in Baltimore in 1814 that

▼ *Decked out with flags, the* Pride of Baltimore *sails out of Baltimore harbor, one of the world's largest natural harbors.*

Francis Scott Key wrote the "Star-Spangled Banner" after Fort McHenry held out against an attack by British warships during the WAR OF 1812. Today, the city's most important industries are shipping, iron and steel manufacturing, and tourism. Much of downtown Baltimore has been rebuilt, especially around the historic Inner Harbor area.

◄ Drive-in banks are one of the ways in which banks have developed to try to meet the customer's needs.

BANKS AND BANKING

Banks are places where people can deposit their money for safekeeping. The banks make a profit by lending this money to people and businesses and by investing it.

Most people bank at *commercial banks*. Here they can open savings accounts that earn them interest. They can open checking accounts, so that they can pay their bills with checks. And they can borrow money—to buy a car, for example. Many people use bank cards to get cash even when the banks are closed. There are more than 14,000 commercial banks in the United States. About $2 trillion is deposited in these banks.

Many people open savings accounts at *savings banks*. There are more than 3,000 of these banks in the United States. They have deposits of almost $1 trillion.

Credit unions and *savings and loan associations* are banks that lend money to their depositors, especially for home mortgages. *Investment banks* lend money to companies in return for stock in the companies. These banks can then resell the stock to make a profit.

The Federal Reserve System serves as the central bank of the United States. There are 12 banks in the system, which was set up in 1913. Its most important role is to help economic growth. It controls the supply of money in the country and keeps watch over all the other banks.

Largest U.S. Commercial Banks (by deposits)
1. Citibank NA, New York
2. Bank of America NT&SA, San Francisco
3. Chase Manhattan Bank NA, New York
4. Manufacturers Hanover Trust Co., New York
5. Morgan Guaranty Trust Co., New York
6. Security Pacific National Bank, Los Angeles
7. Wells Fargo Bank NA, San Francisco
8. Chemical Bank, New York
9. Bankers Trust Co., New York
10. First National Bank, Chicago

Washington, D.C., is one of the few cities in the world that was designed before it was built. A French engineer, Pierre Charles L'Enfant, was hired to draw up a plan for the capital. In 1789, Benjamin Banneker and Andrew Ellicott were commissioned by President George Washington to help survey and plan its construction.

▲ Sir Frederick Banting was only 30 years old when he discovered insulin.

The Six Major Baptist Denominations (by membership)
1. Southern Baptist Convention
2. National Baptist Convention, U.S.A.
3. National Baptist Convention of America
4. American Baptist Churches in the U.S.A.
5. Baptist Bible Fellowship International
6. Progressive National Baptist Convention

BANNEKER, Benjamin

Benjamin Banneker (1731–1806) was the best-known black person in the early history of the United States. A free black, Banneker taught himself mathematics and astronomy. As a young man, he built a wooden clock that kept nearly perfect time for 50 years. In 1789 he correctly predicted an eclipse of the sun. In 1791 Banneker helped survey the new DISTRICT OF COLUMBIA. At the age of 60 he began providing astronomical calculations, weather forecasts, and times of the tides for an almanac he published every year. He also sent out pamphlets against slavery and war.

BANTING, Sir Frederick

Sir Frederick Banting (1891–1941) was a Canadian doctor who in 1922 discovered how to remove a hormone called insulin from the pancreas, one of the body's vital organs. Insulin helps the body to break down sugar. People who cannot produce insulin are called diabetics and have a disease called diabetes. Banting's discovery has helped prolong the lives of millions of diabetics. In 1923, Banting and a co-worker, John Macleod, shared the Nobel Prize for medicine for the discovery of insulin.

BAPTISTS

There are well over 28 million Baptists in the United States, making them the largest Protestant group in the nation. The group consists of at least 24 separate churches. The Southern Baptist Convention is the largest of these and contains over half of all Baptists in America. Baptists become full members of their church when they are baptized. This does not usually happen in infancy but when a person is old enough to make the decision to join the church. According to Baptist practice, candidates for baptism are usually immersed in water to mark their entrance into the church.

BARDEEN, John

John Bardeen (1908–1991), an American physicist, was co-winner of the Nobel Prize for physics in 1956 and 1972. Bardeen's first Nobel Prize, shared with two Bell

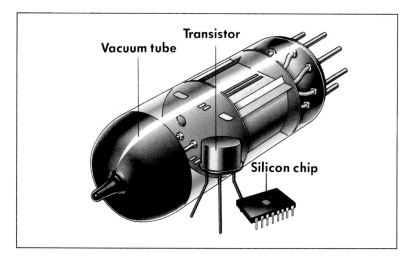

Vacuum tube

Transistor

Silicon chip

 Before the invention of the transistor, vacuum tubes were used in electronic equipment. In the 1960s and 1970s tubes were replaced by the transistor, which was smaller, used less energy, and cost less. Since then, transistors have gotten even smaller. Today over a million transistors can be put on a silicon chip just 0.25 inch (5 mm) square.

Telephone Company colleagues, W. B. SHOCKLEY and W. H. BRATTAIN, was for inventing the transistor. This device revolutionized electronics. His second Nobel Prize was shared with L. N. Cooper and J. R. Schrieffer. They further developed the theory of superconductivity. This is the ability of certain substances, called *superconductors*, to conduct electricity without resistance at very low temperatures.

BARNUM & BAILEY

Barnum & Bailey is one of the most famous CIRCUS names in the world. The circus grew largely from the work of one man, Phineas T. Barnum (1810–1891) one of the most famous showmen in the world. Barnum began his show business career by exhibiting an elderly slave he claimed was 160 years old and had been George Washington's nurse. He then exhibited Charles Stratton, a midget, as "General Tom Thumb." Later Barnum toured the United States with the famous singer Jenny Lind, the "Swedish Nightingale."

In the 1870s, Barnum set up "The Greatest Show on Earth," a touring circus and sideshow. One of his partners, James Bailey, developed this circus until the Ringling Brothers, a famous circus family, bought it in 1907. Today it is known throughout the world as the Ringling Brothers and Barnum & Bailey Circus.

BARRYMORE FAMILY

Born to actor parents, Ethel (1879–1959), John (1882–1942), and Lionel (1878–1954) Barrymore were

 An early poster for the Barnum & Bailey circus. P. T. Barnum's life was dedicated to show business, so much so that with his dying words he asked about the day's receipts at the circus.

Phineas T. Barnum could be considered a pioneer of modern advertising. He would send "advance men" out to cover a town with posters to advertise the arrival of his traveling show. Brass bands and a spectacular parade would further promote the event.

▶ From left to right, Lionel, Ethel, and John Barrymore, starring together in the movie Rasputin and the Empress.

During the 1920s, moviegoing was fast becoming America's favorite form of entertainment. In 1926 the first motion picture with a synchronized musical score was released. The movie, *Don Juan*, starring John Barrymore, marked what Warner Brothers called "the beginning of the sound era."

(1882–1942), and Lionel (1878–1954) Barrymore were among the leading figures of the American stage and screen for half a century. Ethel first made a name for herself on the London stage. In 1901 she scored a triumph on Broadway in *Captain Jinks of the Horse Marines*. She won an Oscar for her performance in the film *None but the Lonely Heart*. Her brother Lionel appeared in many films, including *Captains Courageous* and *Duel in the Sun*. He is probably best remembered for his annual portrayal, on radio, of Scrooge in *A Christmas Carol*. John, dubbed "the great profile," often played romantic leading men in such films as *Grand Hotel* and *Dinner at Eight*. However, he also gave memorable performances on stage as Shakespeare's Richard III and Hamlet. John's granddaughter, Drew (1975–   ), has carried on the family acting tradition.

▼ Clara Barton's suggestion that the Red Cross serve victims of natural disasters became part of the constitution of the Red Cross in 1884.

BARTON, Clara

Clara Barton (1821–1912) was the founder of the American RED CROSS. When the CIVIL WAR broke out in 1861, she was working in Washington, D.C., as the first woman clerk in the U.S. Patent Office. She set up an organization to take food and supplies to wounded soldiers. She even nursed the wounded herself and was soon being called "the Angel of the Battlefield." At the end of the war, President Abraham LINCOLN asked her to start an office to search for missing soldiers.

On a visit to Switzerland, Clara Barton learned of the work being done there by the International Red Cross, which had been founded in 1864. In 1881, after returning home, she founded the American branch of the Red Cross and served as its president until 1904.

BASEBALL

For many years there was a widespread belief that baseball was invented by Abner Doubleday in Cooperstown, New York, in 1839. But baseball actually developed from other bat-and-ball games that had been played long before 1839. Rules for baseball were drawn up in 1845, and it quickly became popular. The first professional league was the National League, founded in 1876. The American League followed in 1900.

Today each of the major leagues has two divisions, East and West. The National League divisions have six teams, and there are seven in American League divisions. Each fall the divisional champions have a play-off for the league championship. The winners play for the overall crown in the best-of-seven World Series in October. In early July, about halfway through the season, the best players from each league play each other in the All Star Game.

Top baseball players become national heroes. Some of their records last for decades. Babe Ruth's career record of 714 home runs was only broken in 1974, by Hank Aaron. These two players and other stars, such as Cy Young, Jackie Robinson, Lou Gehrig, Ted Williams, and Ty Cobb, are in Baseball's Hall of Fame in Cooperstown, New York.

▲ Good pitching is vital to a team's success. Orel Hershiser of the L.A. Dodgers had a record 59 consecutive scoreless innings at the end of the 1988 season.

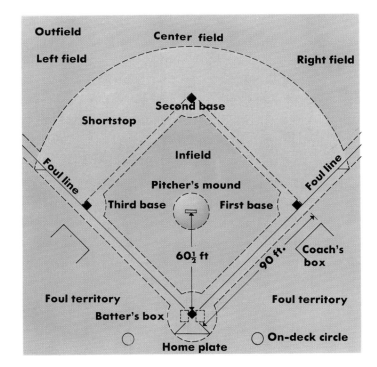

Winners of the World Series	
Year	Team
1990	Cincinnati Reds
1989	Oakland Athletics
1988	L.A. Dodgers
1987	Minnesota Twins
1986	New York Mets
1985	Kansas City Royals
1984	Detroit Tigers
1983	Baltimore Orioles
1982	St. Louis Cardinals
1981	L.A. Dodgers
1980	Philadelphia Phillies
1979	Pittsburgh Pirates
1978	New York Yankees
1977	New York Yankees
1976	Cincinnati Reds
1975	Cincinnati Reds

◄ Although the size of the outfield and foul territory may vary from ballpark to ballpark, the measurements of the infield are always the same.

▲ Count Basie formed his own band in 1935. Many famous soloists played with the band, including the saxophonist Lester Young and the drummer Jo Jones.

▶ A diagram of a regulation basketball court.

▼ James Worthy scores for the L.A. Lakers with a "dunk," one of basketball's most spectacular shots.

BASIE, Count

Count Basie (1904–1984), born William Basie, was a JAZZ composer and bandleader.

Basie became famous in the 1930s. Perhaps his greatest contribution to the field of jazz was to combine the big band "swing" sound of the 1930s with the sound of the new "modern jazz" that came into being during the early 1940s.

Basie's orchestra had a relaxed and highly colorful style of playing, with the strong use of soloists, both instrumental and vocal. Eventually, Basie concentrated less on solo playing and more on his very personal style of overall musical arrangements.

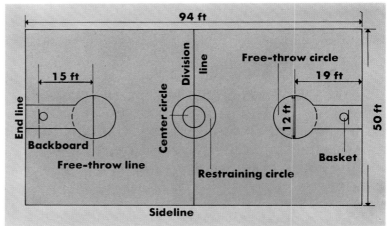

BASKETBALL

In 1891 physical-education instructor James Naismith invented basketball as a game for student athletes to play indoors between the football and baseball seasons. He stuck peach baskets on two poles, divided the players into two teams, and gave them a soccer ball to shoot at the baskets. The rules for the modern sport were soon drawn up, and basketball attracted more and more players. It is now the most popular indoor team sport in the world.

Colleges have always attracted big crowds for their games. The best college players are offered multimillion-dollar contracts to play professionally in the National Basketball Association (NBA). The NBA's Eastern Conference is divided into the Atlantic Division (six teams) and the Central Division (seven teams). The

Western Conference's Midwest Division and Pacific Division have seven teams each. Divisional and conference play-offs take place each May and June to decide the NBA Championships.

Modern players such as Michael Jordan, Magic Johnson, and Larry Bird earn top salaries for their skills. But no one seems likely to reach the scoring heights of Wilt Chamberlain, who scored 100 points in a single game in 1962. Kareem Abdul-Jabbar, another basketball great, scored 38,387 points in his 20-year career.

NBA Play-off Championships	
Year	Team
1990	Detroit Pistons
1989	Detroit Pistons
1988	L.A. Lakers
1987	L.A. Lakers
1986	Boston Celtics
1985	L.A. Lakers
1984	Boston Celtics
1983	Philadelphia 76ers
1982	L.A. Lakers
1981	Boston Celtics
1980	L.A. Lakers
1979	Seattle SuperSonics
1978	Washington Bullets
1977	Portland Trail Blazers
1976	Boston Celtics
1975	Golden State Warriors

BATS

Bats are the only mammals that can fly. Their wings are made of skin stretched between their long arms and fingers. Bats are found almost everywhere in North America, from caves and deserted log cabins in the Midwest to New York City's attics. Of the 900 species, or kinds, of bats found in the world, about 40 are found in North America.

There are no vampire bats in North America. Nor are there any of the enormous bats known as flying foxes, which are found in warmer climates. The largest North American bat is the hoary bat, which has a 16-inch (40-cm) wingspan. Many North American bats have a wingspan of about 12 inches (30 cm).

One of the most common North American species, the little brown bat, is found all over the continent except for the extreme north. Another species, the red bat, is found east of the Rocky Mountains.

Mexican freetail bat

Silver-haired bat

Big brown bat

Long-eared myotis

▲ Pictured here are four American bats. Not all bats live in big colonies. The Mexican freetail roosts in large numbers. The other three species, however, roost in small colonies or singly.

BAUM, L. Frank

L. Frank Baum (1856–1919) was an author of children's fantasy books. He created a magical land called Oz, about which he wrote over a dozen books and short stories. The first of these books was made into the

▲ *A black bear cub. The black bear is the most common bear in North America.*

▼ *Bears of North America. Although the grizzly bear is fiercer, it is not as large as the Alaskan brown bear, which grows up to 9 feet (2.7 m) long and is the largest of all.*

Grizzly bear

Black bear

Polar bear

Brown bear

famous 1939 film *The Wizard of Oz*. Judy GARLAND played Dorothy, a young girl who has a whole series of adventures in Oz. In her search for the wizard, she is threatened by a wicked witch and helped by a good witch, and she meets such wonderful characters as the Tin Man, the Scarecrow, and the Cowardly Lion.

These books were so popular that after Baum died, other people continued to write Oz stories. Baum also wrote many books under other names (*pseudonyms*).

BEARS

Bears are the largest *carnivores* (flesh-eating mammals) in North America. They eat small mammals and fish, as well as fruit, roots, and plants. Bears especially love honey. Most are good swimmers. They usually sleep through much of the winter.

The smallest North American bear is the black bear. A good climber, it lives in forests all over North America. It is often seen in national parks, where it raids trash cans and begs for food. Visitors are forbidden to feed the bears, as black bears can be dangerous, particularly when protecting their cubs.

The grizzly bear is much larger. It used to be found all over the West, but it was hunted a great deal. Today grizzlies are common only in parts of Canada and Alaska and a small area of Montana. The grizzly normally kills only for food, but it has sometimes been known to attack people.

The Kodiak bear, an Alaskan brown bear, is the largest bear in the world and the largest land carnivore. It is related to the grizzly bear. The Kodiak bear is very strong but will not usually attack people if it is left alone. It is expert at catching salmon to eat.

The polar bear lives in the Arctic region of North America, where it eats mainly seals and fish. Its white fur makes it less noticeable against the snow and ice.

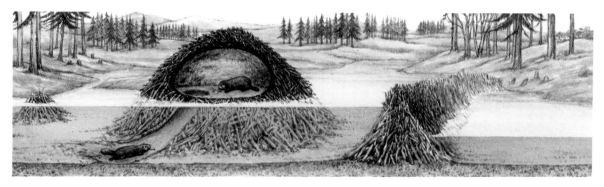

BEAVER

A beaver is a RODENT, an animal that has long front teeth for gnawing. Beavers eat bark from trees and can even fell trees by gnawing around the trunks. They cut these trees into logs with their teeth. They use the logs, along with branches, rocks, and mud, to build dams across streams and small rivers.

A pond forms behind a dam, and in it beavers build an island home known as a *lodge*. The lodge is a mound of logs and branches covered with mud, with dry earth and leaves inside. One or more families of beavers live together in the lodge. The members of this *colony* work together, constantly repairing or enlarging the dam.

Beavers are very good swimmers. Their flat, paddle-shaped tails help them swim. They also use their tails to lean on when they are gnawing trees. To warn their families of danger, they slap their tails on the water.

Beavers have been hunted so much for their thick, waterproof fur that now they are protected by the United States and Canadian governments. There are more beavers in North America than anywhere else in the world. They are about 4 feet (1.3 m) long and weigh about 60 pounds (27 kg) or more.

BEES

Bees are INSECTS that are related to ANTS and wasps. Most kinds are solitary—they live alone. Each female builds a nest. She lays one egg on some pollen in each cell in the nest. This will provide food for the larvae (young bees) after the eggs hatch. With her work done, the female seals up the nest and flies away.

The most common type of solitary bee in North America is the leaf-cutting bee. It cuts out pieces of leaves to make the cells. A relative of the leaf cutter is

▲ The entrances to a beaver lodge are underwater, but the living chamber is above water level.

▲ Beavers' teeth never stop growing. Constant gnawing on the branches and trunks of trees keeps them very sharp.

▲ The picture shows honeybees swarming. This occurs when a colony becomes overcrowded. The queen bee and many of the workers then leave to start a new colony elsewhere.

▼ The common, or American, bumblebee lives in a colony in the ground that may contain fifty to several hundred bees.

the mason bee. It makes a kind of concrete for its nest, using clay and saliva. The mining bee digs burrows in the ground for its nest. The carpenter bee builds a nest in wood or plant stems. The cuckoo bee does not build a nest at all. It lays its eggs in other bees' nests.

Bumblebees and honeybees are social rather than solitary—they live in colonies. A bumblebee colony can have several hundred bees. Most are worker bees. Some are drones, which fertilize the queen. There is one queen in each colony. Honeybee colonies contain 50,000 to 80,000 bees. Honeybees make the cells of their nests, or hives, out of beeswax. After making honey out of plant nectar, they store it in these cells. Some people raise honeybees for their honey and beeswax. Beekeeping is widely practiced in North America.

A fierce new type of honeybee, the so-called "killer bee," has spread throughout South America and as far north as the U.S.–Mexico border.

BEETLES

▼ Beetles include the most useful and the most destructive of insects. The ladybug, for example, eats garden pests such as aphids. The Japanese beetle, introduced by accident into North America, destroys cultivated plants and fruits.

A beetle is an INSECT that has hard sheaths, or wing cases, that cover and protect its wings. There are more kinds of beetles than any other creature in the world. North America has 28,000 species, almost a tenth of the total species in the world. The name beetle means "biter," for beetles have strong mouth parts. The well-

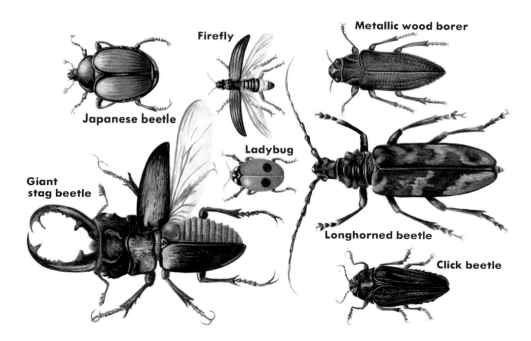

Japanese beetle

Firefly

Metallic wood borer

Giant stag beetle

Ladybug

Longhorned beetle

Click beetle

known June bug has particularly strong jaws, as does the fierce-looking stag beetle. Male stag beetles can sometimes be seen fighting, using their large jaws to grip each other. Other well-known North American beetles include the Japanese beetle, the ladybug, the Colorado potato beetle, the boll weevil, and the firefly.

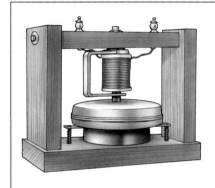

The First Bell Telephone
Alexander Bell's telephone worked by changing sound waves produced by the human voice into an electric current. This current could then be transmitted along a wire and changed back into sounds at the other end.

▲ In 1892, Alexander Graham Bell telephoned Chicago from New York City to demonstrate to businessmen the usefulness of his new invention.

BELL, Alexander Graham

Alexander Graham Bell (1847–1922) was a Scottish-born scientist, teacher, and inventor of the telephone. He came to the United States in 1871.

Bell was fascinated by the sound of the voice and how the human ear hears it. He taught the deaf, using a system invented by his father. Bell had also become fascinated with the recently invented telegraph. He believed that if electricity could carry telegraph signals, it could also carry human speech and other sounds. Others had been trying to achieve the same thing, but in 1876, Bell succeeded. The first words ever spoken over a telephone were Bell's request to his assistant: "Mr. Watson, come here. I want you." A year later, Bell established the Bell Telephone Company.

Bell later experimented in other areas, including sheep breeding and the creation of a flying machine. He also started the organization now known as the Alexander Graham Bell Association for the Deaf.

BELLOW, Saul

The novelist Saul Bellow (1915–) was born in the province of Quebec, Canada, of Russian Jewish parents but moved with them to Chicago as a child. He made use of this background in *The Adventures of Augie March*. This

When President James A. Garfield was shot by an assassin, Alexander Graham Bell developed a device that he hoped would locate the bullet inside the president's body. It was similar to a modern mine detector. Unfortunately, it could not distinguish between the bullet and the iron springs of the president's bed, and so the experiment failed. President Garfield eventually died on September 19, 1881.

novel relates the sometimes sad, sometimes comic experiences of a poor Jewish boy who refuses to settle for a safe, humdrum existence. Some of Bellow's other books, such as *Henderson the Rain King*, are about individuals who go through crises that force them to examine their lives. Another important theme in his writing is the relationship between Jews and Gentiles. This is the main theme in *The Victim*. Bellow won the 1976 Nobel Prize for literature. Three of his books—*The Adventures of Augie March*, *Herzog*, and *Mr. Sammler's Planet*—won National Book Awards.

▲ *Saul Bellow won both a Nobel Prize and a Pulitzer Prize for his works. Besides novels, Bellow has written short stories and drama.*

▼ *James Gordon Bennett, Jr., who inherited his father's keen sense of news, was the first person to introduce the idea of the "exclusive" news story.*

MR. JAMES GORDON BENNETT.

BENÉT, Stephen Vincent

The author and poet Stephen Vincent Benét (1898–1943) acquired in childhood a taste for history and literature. Perhaps his best-known work is his long narrative poem *John Brown's Body*, which vividly describes the events and personalities of the Civil War. Benét won a Pulitzer Prize for this poem. *Western Star*, published after his death, won a second Pulitzer. In addition to poetry, he wrote novels and short stories, including the story *The Devil and Daniel Webster*, which was turned into a play, a film, and an opera. *A Book of Americans*, which he wrote with his wife, Rosemary Carr, consists of portraits in verse of famous historical characters.

BENNETT, James Gordon

James Gordon Bennett (1795–1872) was a Scottish-born newspaper editor who founded the New York *Herald* in 1835. Today's NEWSPAPERS owe much to his new ideas about journalism. He broke with tradition and sent reporters out actively seeking news. During the Civil War, Bennett assigned a number of reporters to provide accurate coverage of the war as it happened. The *Herald* was the first newspaper to publish anything about stocks and finance. Bennett also helped found the Associated Press news agency.

Bennett's son, James Gordon Bennett, Jr. (1841–1918), who was born in New York City, carried on his father's work. He also established newspapers in London and Paris. It was Bennett who sent the journalist Henry M. STANLEY on his legendary expedition to find the explorer Dr. David Livingstone in Africa.

◄ *The strong colors and feeling of movement in Thomas Hart Benton's mural* Independence and the Opening of the West *are typical of the artist's work.*

BENTON, Thomas Hart

The paintings of Thomas Hart Benton (1889–1975) show life among ordinary American people, especially in the rural parts of the South and Midwest. Benton came from Missouri and was named after a great uncle who had been a U.S. senator from that state.

After studying at the Art Institute of Chicago, Benton went to study further in Paris. But he turned his back on modern European art, which was becoming more concerned with forms. He chose instead to represent simple subjects in ways that the average person could understand. Although Benton's paintings are clear, they are not truly realistic. The colors are very vivid, and the lines are swirling, suggesting movement. Benton painted a number of *murals* (large wall paintings). He also taught in art schools.

▼ *The Bering Strait is the only place where people in the United States can look across at Soviet territory.*

BERING STRAIT

The Bering Strait is a passage of water that separates ALASKA from Asia. The strait connects the Arctic Ocean and the Bering Sea. At its narrowest point, this barrier between the United States and the Soviet Union is only 36 miles (58 km) wide. In the middle of the Bering Strait are the two Diomede Islands. One belongs to the United States and the other to the Soviet Union. During the Ice Age there was a land bridge where the Bering Strait is now located. The ancestors of the American Indians reached North America by crossing that bridge.

▲ *Irving Berlin on the movie set for* This is the Army, *one of the many musicals he wrote. Others include* Annie Get Your Gun *and* Louisiana Purchase.

▼ *Leonard Bernstein rehearses the London Symphony Orchestra for a performance in Britain.*

BERLIN, Irving

Irving Berlin (1888–1989) was one of the most popular American songwriters. He was born in Russia and came to the United States in 1892.

He taught himself music and began writing songs in 1906 under his real name, Baline. By mistake, his name was printed as "Berlin," and he adopted it for the rest of his life. During his career he wrote almost 5,000 songs, some of which are all-time favorites. Among them are classics such as "God Bless America," "White Christmas," and "Alexander's Ragtime Band." He also wrote the songs for *Annie Get Your Gun* and other musicals.

Berlin insisted on publishing his own music so that he could control the money he received. To help other songwriters protect their rights he helped start the American Society of Composers, Authors, and Publishers (ASCAP).

BERNSTEIN, Leonard

Leonard Bernstein (1918–1990) was a man of many talents. He was a conductor of some of the world's great orchestras, a composer, a pianist, a writer, and a television personality. He shot to fame in 1943 when, at the last moment, he substituted for the conductor of the New York Philharmonic, who had become ill. Bernstein's conducting impressed the critics and launched him on a brilliant career as a conductor. As a composer he is best known for *West Side Story*. Among his other compositions are the ballet *Fancy Free*; *Chichester Psalms*, a setting of Hebrew psalms for choir and orchestra; and the music for the film *On the Waterfront*. Bernstein also had a gift for communicating in words, which he employed in many television programs and in several books, including *The Joy of Music*.

BERRIES

Berries are small fruits that grow on bushes, shrubs, or trailing vines. Some kinds are popular garden plants. Many types of berries are tasty and rich in vitamins. They can be eaten fresh or they can be used to make juices and wines, pastries and pies, and jellies and jams.

Berries grow wild in many parts of North America

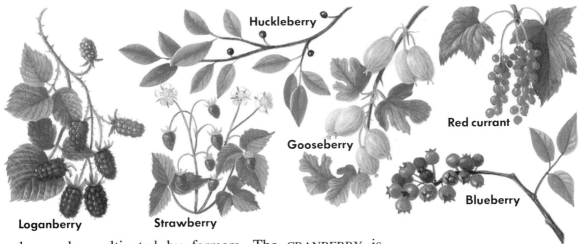

Huckleberry

Gooseberry

Red currant

Blueberry

Loganberry

Strawberry

and are also cultivated by farmers. The CRANBERRY is an important crop in Massachusetts, Wisconsin, New Jersey, and Washington. A close relative of the cranberry, the lingonberry, is sometimes called the mountain cranberry. Blueberries and huckleberries are also related to the cranberry. Maine is a leading producer of blueberries. Huckleberries grow from New England to the Rockies. Gooseberries and currants are also found across the country.

Blackberries, raspberries, and strawberries are important cultivated crops. They are members of the rose family. Blackberries, which include dewberries, boysenberries, and loganberries, grow best in the warm climate of the South. The three varieties of raspberries—red, black, and purple—are grown along the North Atlantic and Pacific coasts and in the Great Lakes region. The strawberry is the most important cultivated berry. Wisconsin, California, and Oregon are the leading strawberry-producing states.

▲ *Some of the many fruits that people call berries. Of the above, only blueberries, gooseberries, huckleberries, and red currants are considered true berries by botanists. They all have seeds inside a single fruit. Strawberries and loganberries are made up of many small fruits.*

BETHUNE, Mary McLeod

Mary McLeod Bethune (1875–1955) was an educator who spent her life working to improve education for black people, especially women.

Her Florida school for black girls later became part of the coeducational Bethune-Cookman College. In 1935 she founded the National Council of Negro Women. Bethune also worked in a number of government positions under presidents Coolidge, Hoover, Roosevelt, Truman, and Eisenhower. Under Roosevelt she was the director of the Division of Negro Affairs of the National Youth Administration.

The group of advisers who assisted Franklin D. Roosevelt during his presidency was once described by a journalist as "Roosevelt's Brain Trust." The name stuck. From 1935 to 1944, Mary McLeod Bethune served as his special adviser on the problems of minority groups in the United States.

▲ *Bighorns range in color from dark gray-brown to pale buff. However, all have creamy white patches on their rumps.*

BIGHORN SHEEP

The bighorn, or mountain sheep, is the only wild sheep found in North America. It lives on remote mountain slopes of the western United States and southwestern Canada. In California it is protected in reserves. There are three species, or kinds, of bighorn: the Rocky Mountain sheep, Dall sheep, and Stone's sheep.

Male bighorns, or rams, have long horns that sweep back in a huge curve of 39 inches (100 cm) or more. The horns of the ewes (females) are shorter and straighter.

▶ *Bighorn sheep can venture high above the treeline on steep mountainsides. Their lambs can climb up rocky slopes from the day they are born.*

BILL OF RIGHTS

The first ten amendments to the United States CONSTITUTION form what is known as the Bill of Rights, a summary of the basic rights held by all U.S. citizens. Canada has a similar summary, called the Charter of Rights and Freedoms.

When the Constitution was written, many felt it did not clearly guarantee the rights and freedoms that had been fought for in the American REVOLUTION. As a result, a number of amendments (additions) to the Constitution were proposed. The ten that became the Bill of Rights were passed by Congress in 1789 and became law in 1791, when they were approved by the required number of states.

Since 1791 sixteen other amendments have been

The first ten amendments to the U.S. Constitution became the law of the land on December 15, 1791. The amendments were known as the Bill of Rights. There were originally 12 amendments, but two that changed the method of electing members of Congress were rejected.

added, but it is the first ten that stand as a charter for the freedoms of all Americans.

Sometimes there are arguments about just what these rights actually mean. In that case the SUPREME COURT generally decides. This court has the power to interpret what the Constitution says. The court's decision becomes part of the law of the land.

United States Bill of Rights

Amendment 1
Congress shall make no law respecting an establishment of religion, or prohibiting the free exercise thereof; or abridging the freedom of speech, or of the press; or the right of the people peaceably to assemble, and to petition the government for a redress of grievances.

Amendment 2
A well-regulated militia, being necessary to the security of a free state, the right of the people to keep and bear arms shall not be infringed.

Amendment 3
No soldier shall, in time of peace, be quartered in any house without the consent of the owner, nor in time of war, but in a manner to be prescribed by law.

Amendment 4
The right of the people to be secure in their persons, houses, papers, and effects, against unreasonable searches and seizures, shall not be violated, and no warrants shall issue, but upon probable cause, supported by oath or affirmation, and particularly describing the place to be searched, and the persons or things to be seized.

Amendment 5
No persons shall be held to answer for a capital or otherwise infamous crime, unless on a presentment or indictment of a grand jury, except in cases arising in the land or naval forces, or in the militia, when in actual service in time of war or public danger; nor shall any person be subject for the same offense to be twice put in jeopardy of life or limb; nor shall be compelled in any criminal case to be a witness against himself, nor be deprived of life, liberty, or property, without due process of law; nor shall private property be taken for public use, without just compensation.

Amendment 6
In all criminal prosecutions, the accused shall enjoy the right to a speedy and public trial, by an impartial jury of the state and district wherein the crime shall have been previously ascertained by law, and to be informed of the nature and cause of the accusation; to be confronted with the witnesses against him; to have compulsory process for obtaining witnesses in his favor, and to have the assistance of counsel for his defense.

Amendment 7
In suits of common law, where the value in controversy shall exceed twenty dollars, the right of trial by jury shall be preserved, and no fact tried by a jury, shall be otherwise reexamined in any court of the United States, than according to the rules of the common law.

Amendment 8
Excessive bail shall not be required, nor excessive fines imposed, nor cruel and unusual punishment inflicted.

Amendment 9
The enumeration in the Constitution, of certain rights, shall not be construed to deny or disparage others retained by the people.

Amendment 10
The powers not delegated to the United States by the Constitution, nor prohibited by it to the states, are reserved to the states respectively, or to the people.

Robin
10 in (25 cm)

Mockingbird
10½ in (27 cm)

Eastern goldfinch
5 in (13 cm)

Black-capped chickadee
5¼ in (13 cm)

Cardinal
8½ in (22 cm)

BIRDS OF NORTH AMERICA

Birds are animals with feathers. They are warmblooded, like mammals, and they lay eggs, like reptiles. Nearly all birds can fly. There are about 8,700 kinds, or *species*, of birds in the world.

North America is home to many bird species. At times there may be as many as 20 billion birds on the continent. Some are only summer visitors. They raise their young and then *migrate*, or travel, to warmer climates for the winter. But many other birds spend their entire lives in North America.

The land and climate of North America are varied, so there are many different *habitats* for birds. Birds live in the habitat that suits them best. Snow geese, for example, breed along the icy coast of Alaska. Far to the south, in the hot deserts of Arizona, cactus wrens make their nests in cacti.

Sparrows, robins, and jays are among the most commonly seen U.S. birds. But North American birds vary enormously, in size and in other ways. The calliope hummingbird of southern California is only about 2.75 inches (7 cm) long. The California condor measures up to 9 feet (2.6 m) from wing tip to wing tip. It is the largest flying bird in the world.

The California condor is one of several North American birds that are in danger of dying out, or becoming *extinct*. Only about 40 of these birds remain, all in captivity. *Endangered species* such as the condor are protected by law in the United States. The bald eagle, the national bird of the United States, is another of these protected species.

See also BIRDS OF PREY; CARDINAL; CONDOR; DUCKS AND GEESE; EAGLE; ENDANGERED ANIMALS AND PLANTS; GULLS AND TERNS; HAWK; HERON; HUMMINGBIRD; KINGFISHER; MOCKINGBIRD; OWLS; PELICAN; PIGEON; QUAIL; ROBIN; TURKEY; VULTURE; WATER BIRDS; WOODPECKER.

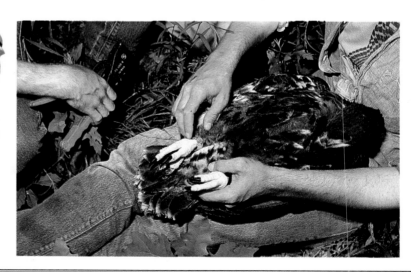

▶ A young eagle is banded. Bird banding provides us with useful information about the behavior of different species.

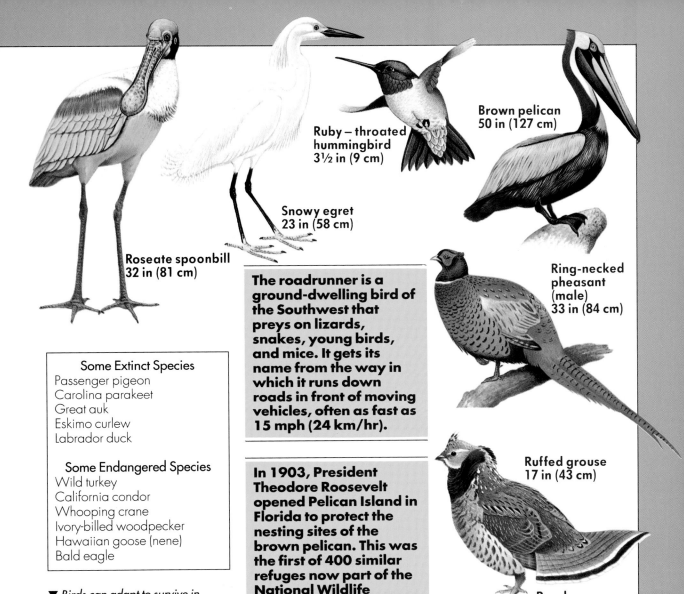

Roseate spoonbill
32 in (81 cm)

Ruby – throated
hummingbird
3½ in (9 cm)

Snowy egret
23 in (58 cm)

Brown pelican
50 in (127 cm)

Ring-necked
pheasant
(male)
33 in (84 cm)

Some Extinct Species
Passenger pigeon
Carolina parakeet
Great auk
Eskimo curlew
Labrador duck

Some Endangered Species
Wild turkey
California condor
Whooping crane
Ivory-billed woodpecker
Hawaiian goose (nene)
Bald eagle

▼ *Birds can adapt to survive in different habitats. The cactus wren, for example, lives in the desert, nesting among cactus spines.*

The roadrunner is a ground-dwelling bird of the Southwest that preys on lizards, snakes, young birds, and mice. It gets its name from the way in which it runs down roads in front of moving vehicles, often as fast as 15 mph (24 km/hr).

In 1903, President Theodore Roosevelt opened Pelican Island in Florida to protect the nesting sites of the brown pelican. This was the first of 400 similar refuges now part of the National Wildlife Refuge System.

Ruffed grouse
17 in (43 cm)

Roadrunner
22 in (56 cm)

Great horned owl
22 in (56 cm)

Bald eagle

Turkey vulture

Prairie falcon

▲ Although the hooked beaks of the birds of prey pictured above look extremely vicious, the birds depend on their talons as their main weapon. Their beaks are only used when feeding.

▲ The bison originally came from Eurasia and migrated to North America in prehistoric times over a land bridge across the Bering Strait.

BIRDS OF PREY

Birds that hunt other animals for food are called birds of prey. They all have sharp claws, or talons, for catching and killing their prey and curved beaks for eating.

North America's largest birds of prey are the California CONDOR and the EAGLE. Buzzards, or turkey VULTURES, are birds of prey found all over North America. Most hunt in the daytime, but OWLS are birds of prey that hunt at night. The great horned owl and the screech owl are the most widespread owls in North America.

North America has many species of HAWKS. The sharp-shinned hawk and Cooper's hawk are typical of the group known as "true hawks." They live in woodlands over much of North America. Another group of hawks is the *buteos*. The most common of these is the red-tailed hawk, which lives in woods and open country.

Falcons are a type of hawk, too. One falcon, the American kestrel, or sparrowhawk, is a familiar sight in the western mountains and prairies. The peregrine falcon, which also lives in the West, is the fastest diver of all. It swoops down on its prey at a speed of up to 180 miles per hour (290 km/hr). A relative of the falcon is the osprey, a fish-eating hawk. It is found on the East Coast in particular and is an endangered species, protected by law.

North America has four species of kites. The swallow-tailed kite is the most graceful and elegant of all birds of prey. It lives in the southern swamps, along with the agile Mississippi kite.

BISON

The bison is a large mammal. It is commonly called the buffalo, although it is not a true buffalo. The bison is similar to the ox, but it is much larger and is covered with long, shaggy fur. It eats grass and leaves, the bark and twigs of trees, and shrubs.

There are two kinds of American bison, the plains bison and the wood bison. The wood bison is slightly larger. Millions of bison once filled the plains and prairies. By the beginning of this century, however, hunters had killed some 50 million bison, and they were almost extinct. Herds are now protected within national parks so that the bison can increase in numbers.

BLACK AMERICANS

Most Black Americans are descended from African slaves brought to North America in the 17th and 18th centuries. Their original homelands were in West Africa, where we find such countries as Ghana and Sierra Leone. Until recently, they were called Negroes, which is the Spanish word for "black." Today many blacks prefer to be called African-Americans. There are more than 29 million blacks in the United States, making up about 13 percent of the population.

The story of Black Americans is mainly that of a long struggle to win equality in a society dominated by whites. Even after slavery was abolished, blacks who lived in the South were not free in the full sense of the word. They worked for low wages and were generally

▲ Africans were brought to North America to work as slaves on the plantations of the South. By the early 1800s, about 700,000 slaves lived in the southern states.

▲ New York City's first black mayor, David Dinkins (left), was elected in 1989. Award-winning author Maya Angelou (right) has written several books based on her own life.

prevented from getting an education. A few pioneering black educators, such as Booker T. WASHINGTON, established schools and colleges, but educated blacks were treated with more hostility than those who "kept their place." Fear of violence from the KU KLUX KLAN prevented southern blacks from exercising their right to vote. Even in the North, prejudice kept most blacks in low-paying jobs and poor neighborhoods.

Despite the prejudice, blacks have distinguished themselves in government, business, the arts, and the professions. Blacks have also excelled in many sports. JAZZ—possibly the most important musical develop-

Notable Black Americans
(with biographies in this encyclopedia)

20th-Century Leaders

Ralph Abernathy
Ralph Bunche
Shirley Chisholm
W.E.B. DuBois
Marcus Garvey
Jesse Jackson
Martin Luther King, Jr.
Malcolm X
Adam Clayton Powell
Colin L. Powell
A. Philip Randolph
Roy Wilkins
Andrew Young
Whitney M. Young

The Arts

Marian Anderson
Louis Armstrong
James Baldwin
Gwendolyn Brooks
Countee Cullen
Langston Hughes
Paul Robeson

ment of the 20th century—has its roots in Black American culture.

Thanks to the CIVIL RIGHTS movement, more blacks now get a good education and good jobs than formerly, although there is still a long way to go. At the same time, black leaders, writers, and artists are urging their people to develop a sense of pride in their own culture. The phrase "Black is beautiful" is a reminder to blacks (and whites) that they have much to be proud of.

BLACKFOOT

The Blackfoot are an important group of three tribes which lived in the area where Montana and the Canadian provinces of Saskatchewan and Alberta lie today. They were the Siksika (Blackfoot proper), the Piegan, and the Blood. They spoke an Algonquian language.

Like other PLAINS tribes, the Blackfoot depended on hunting the buffalo. It provided the food they ate. Buffalo hide was made into tents, or tepees. At first the Blackfoot hunted and traveled on foot. They were at the mercy of the SHOSHONI, who moved into the Great Plains with horses. Then the Blackfoot began to take horses from other tribes. With horses and weapons they obtained in trade with the settlers, they became very strong. Today they live as farmers and ranchers.

BLACK HAWK

Black Hawk (1767–1838) was a Sauk Indian leader who fought to prevent white settlers from taking his people's lands. His Sauk name was *Ma-ka-tai-me-she-kia-kiak*—Black Sparrow Hawk.

In 1804, other chiefs signed away the Sauk lands in Illinois. Most of the Sauk moved by 1830, but Black Hawk and his tribe refused. Armed volunteers forced the Indians to leave their homes. A period of fighting, known as the Black Hawk War, ended in a massacre. Soldiers ignored a flag of truce and killed almost every Indian. Black Hawk himself was taken prisoner for a time and then settled on a reservation.

▼ *A Blackfoot Indian wearing the traditional skin shirt and leggings. In the winter a bison robe was wrapped around the shoulders.*

BLACKWELL, Elizabeth

Elizabeth Blackwell (1821–1910) was the first woman to obtain a Doctor of Medicine (M.D.) degree from an

American medical school. Born in England, she came to the United States with her family when she was a young girl. She received a good education, but many medical schools rejected her before the Geneva (N.Y.) Medical School agreed to admit her. She graduated first in her class. After training in Paris and London, she opened the New York Infirmary for Women and Children, which provided free health care for the poor and training for women who wanted to become doctors. In 1869, Dr. Blackwell returned to England, where she helped found the London School of Medicine for Women.

BLUE RIDGE MOUNTAINS

Part of the APPALACHIAN MOUNTAINS, the Blue Ridge Mountains are famous for their scenery. The range extends 615 miles (990 km) from southeastern Pennsylvania through Maryland, Virginia, and North and South Carolina to northern Georgia. The highest peaks are in North Carolina. Many rivers and streams run through the mountains. Though famous for their isolation and beauty, the mountains are threatened by POLLUTION and by industrial and housing development.

▲ The Blue Ridge Mountains get their name from the blue haze that, from a distance, seems to surround the mountains.

BOBCAT

The bobcat, or lynx, is a wild CAT found almost all over the United States, in southwestern Canada, and in northern Mexico. It is at home in most habitats, especially open scrubland and forests with rocky areas. The bobcat generally comes out to hunt at night, feeding on rodents, rabbits, other small mammals, and birds. When it is really hungry, it will even attack deer and sheep.

▼ Bobcats thrive in the mountain forests and stony terrain of the southwestern states.

The bobcat is about 24 to 30 inches (60 to 100 cm) long and weighs about 29 pounds (13 kg). It makes a home, or lair, in the hollow of a fallen tree or among the roots of a large bush.

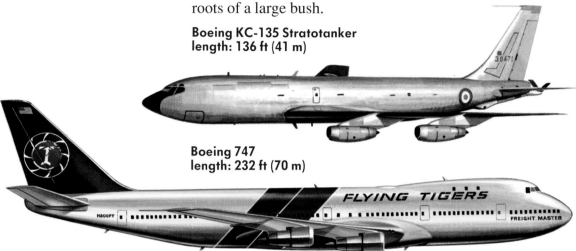

**Boeing KC-135 Stratotanker
length: 136 ft (41 m)**

**Boeing 747
length: 232 ft (70 m)**

▲ *The Boeing 747 was the first jumbo jet. It can fly 6,000 miles (9,650 km) nonstop. The KC-135 Stratotanker is used to refuel military planes in flight.*

BOEING, William Edward

William Edward Boeing (1881–1956) is one of the most famous names in aviation. In 1916, in Seattle, Washington, he helped set up the Pacific Aero Products Company. This later became the Boeing Company, with Boeing himself as its president. Today it is the largest AEROSPACE company in the United States, employing more than 100,000 people. Everybody knows Boeing's most famous plane, the 747, or jumbo jet, the most successful commercial airliner ever built. But Boeing has built many other successful jets, including the 707, the 727, and the 737. The company also makes military airplanes and parts for spacecraft.

▼ *Humphrey Bogart won an Academy Award for Best Actor for his performance in* The African Queen.

BOGART, Humphrey

Humphrey Bogart (1899–1957) was one of America's best-loved film stars. He was best known for his hard-boiled, no-nonsense characters, especially the detectives Philip Marlowe, whom he played in *The Big Sleep*, and Sam Spade, whom he played in *The Maltese Falcon*. These films helped establish a new kind of thriller, one that was glamorous and seedy at the same time. Even today, people love to imitate the rasping voice and world-weary attitude Bogart brought to these parts. His other famous films include *The Treasure of the Sierra Madre* and *The African Queen*.

BOONE, Daniel

Daniel Boone (1734–1820) was a famous American pioneer. Just before the American Revolution, he helped blaze the WILDERNESS ROAD through the Cumberland Gap in the Allegheny Mountains. It was along this trail that thousands of settlers made their way westward to Kentucky and beyond, expanding the frontier of the young American nation.

From Boone's earliest childhood, first in Pennsylvania and later in North Carolina, he was at home in the wilderness. He learned how to hunt and trap and to live in the forests like an Indian. In 1775 he led his family and others along the Wilderness Road into Kentucky, where he had already built the settlement of Boonesborough. Three years later Boone was captured by the Shawnee Indians. After learning that the Indians were going to attack Boonesborough, he escaped and led the successful defense against the attack. More and more people were now coming to Kentucky. Boone, who liked the wilderness, moved west to Missouri.

BOOTH, Edwin

Edwin Booth (1833–1893) was a famous actor of the late 1800s. He was especially admired for his portrayal of Shakespeare's Hamlet. The son of an English actor, Junius Brutus Booth, Edwin was only 15 when he first appeared on stage. By his late twenties he was a star in New York. When Booth's brother, John Wilkes BOOTH, assassinated President Abraham LINCOLN, Edwin retired briefly from the stage.

▲ While held captive by the Indians, Daniel Boone was forced to "run the gauntlet." This was a test of courage in which Boone had to run unarmed between two rows of fierce warriors.

▼ Edwin Booth's roles in Shakespeare's plays made him a star on both sides of the Atlantic. He is pictured here dressed as Hamlet.

▲ *John Wilkes Booth crept into the president's box and shot Lincoln at point-blank range. Brandishing a dagger, he leapt to the stage, breaking his leg, and fled.*

▼ *The John Hancock towers, old and new, rise up over Boston's Back Bay district.*

BOOTH, John Wilkes

John Wilkes Booth (1838–1865) was the person who assassinated President Abraham LINCOLN. Like his brother, Edwin BOOTH, he was an actor. Known for his support of slavery and pro-Southern views, he soon found additional work as a secret Confederate agent. Booth's hatred of Lincoln led him to organize a plot to kill the president. On April 14, 1865, just after the end of the CIVIL WAR, he entered Ford's Theater in Washington, where Lincoln was attending a play, and shot the president in the head. Booth escaped to a farm in Virginia, but Federal troops found him. He was either killed by the soldiers or took his own life.

BOSTON

Boston is the capital of MASSACHUSETTS and its largest city, with a population of about 574,200. It is one of the oldest and most historic American cities, founded by PURITAN settlers in 1630. Boston still has many fine old buildings, especially from the colonial period. It was in Boston that many of the events leading up to the American REVOLUTION took place. In the 1800s, Boston grew into a great port and industrial center, where many immigrants, especially from Ireland and Italy, settled. Boston is still an important port, and it has also become a leading financial, business, and transportation center. The many colleges and universities in the Boston area, including Harvard University and the Massachusetts Institute of Technology, have also made the city a major educational center. Boston is on the Atlantic coast, 200 miles (320 km) northeast of New York City.

BOSTON MASSACRE

The Boston Massacre was one of the events that led to the American REVOLUTION. On March 5, 1770, a mob of colonists, protesting the presence of British troops in Boston, started hurling snowballs and stones at a soldier who was standing guard at the Boston Customs House. About twenty soldiers joined him and confronted the mob with fixed bayonets. Finally one soldier, who had been hit with a club, opened fire, and others followed. Five colonists were killed. Radical colonists quickly named the incident the "Boston massacre" to whip up resentment against the presence of British troops.

Between 1615 and 1617 an epidemic of measles, scarlet fever, and other diseases was responsible for wiping out almost the whole Indian population of the Shawmut peninsula. The diseases had been carried to the region by European explorers. Shawmut was renamed Boston on September 7, 1630, by John Winthrop, governor of Massachusetts.

▼ The event now known as the Boston Massacre occurred when British soldiers were confronted with an unruly mob and lost control. The crowd had been pelting them with snowballs and calling them "lobster-backs," a reference to their red coats.

BOSTON TEA PARTY

The Boston Tea Party was one of the events that led to the American REVOLUTION. In 1773, the British Parliament gave the East India Company the right to sell tea to the American colonies at a low price. This meant that the company had a *monopoly*—no one else could match its low price. The colonists feared that the British would try to set up other monopolies, hurting local businesses. They also resented a tax imposed on tea. Some ports refused to admit the British tea ships. In Boston, when two ships arrived, colonists demanded

The Boston Tea Party inspired a number of copycat "tea parties." In April 1774, a band of New Yorkers, dressed as Indians, dumped British tea in the East River. In October of the same year, the patriots of Annapolis, Maryland, burned the *Peggy Stewart*, a British vessel, and its cargo of tea.

▲ *Samuel Adams led his fellow patriots in the Boston Tea Party. They were disguised as Indians.*

▶ *The Brooklyn Botanic Garden, seen here in June, is an oasis of quiet in New York City.*

Some Botanical Gardens in the U.S.
Arnold Arboretum, Jamaica Plain and Weston, Massachusetts
Brooklyn Botanic Garden and Arboretum, Brooklyn, New York
Fairchild Tropical Garden, Miami, Florida
Longwood Gardens, Kennett Square, Pennsylvania
Los Angeles City and County Arboretum, Arcadia, California
Missouri Botanical Garden, St. Louis
New York Botanical Garden, Bronx, New York
Rancho Santa Ana Botanic Garden, Claremont, California
United States National Arboretum, Washington, D.C.

that the governor order them to leave. When he refused, a group of SONS OF LIBERTY dressed up as Indians and boarded the ships during the night of December 16, 1773. They dumped 342 chests of tea into Boston Harbor. The British then passed more severe laws against the colonists, increasing their anger.

BOTANICAL GARDENS

A botanical garden is a large park where plants are grown for scientific research or public display. The plants are clearly labeled, and people can examine them and learn more about the way they grow. The plants are also studied by scientists doing research.

One of the largest botanical gardens in the United States is the New York Botanical Garden in New York City. The Brooklyn Botanic Garden, also in New York City, has a special Fragrance Garden for the blind, as

well as a children's garden. One of North America's few tropical botanical gardens is the Fairchild Tropical Garden in Miami, Florida. The Missouri Botanical Garden in St. Louis has one of North America's finest collections of orchids, as well as a Japanese Garden.

BOURKE-WHITE, Margaret

The news photographer Margaret Bourke-White (1906–1971) covered many important events of the 20th century. She began her career in 1927, specializing in pictures of buildings and industry. As a photographer for *Life* magazine, she covered some of the battles of WORLD WAR II. She also photographed the horrors of

◄ Margaret Bourke-White's photographs revealed the beauty that people often ignore around them. This photograph of the George Washington Bridge, which links New York and New Jersey, was taken around the time of the bridge's opening in 1931.

Margaret Bourke-White's photograph of Fort Peck Dam in Montana was chosen for *Life*'s first cover as a news magazine. The dam, completed four years later in 1940, was a typical subject for Bourke-White's camera. It represented the national will to fight the Depression with large-scale public works projects.

▼ Nathaniel Bowditch's combined skills in mathematics and astronomy made nautical research easy for him.

the Nazi concentration camps. Later she photographed the struggle for independence in India. Books of her photographs include *Shooting the Russian War* and *Halfway to Freedom*.

BOWDITCH, Nathaniel

Nathaniel Bowditch (1773–1838) was a mathematician and astronomer. He was raised in the seaport of Salem, Massachusetts. Bowditch had little formal education, but he had a great thirst for knowledge. He taught himself mathematics, French, and Latin. When only in his teens, he wrote a complete almanac. His most important book, *The New American Practical Navigator*, is still a standard reference book for sailors.

▲ *The Bowie knife has a large blade with a curved edge. It was designed as a single all-purpose implement, useful for hunting as well as for defense.*

BOWIE, James

James Bowie (1796–1836) was a frontiersman, adventurer, Indian fighter, and a hero of the Mexican War. Born in Georgia, Bowie spent much of his life in Texas, which was then part of Mexico. He became a Mexican citizen, but he took part in the Texas Revolution and died at the siege of the Alamo, sharing command of the defense of the fort against the Mexicans. Bowie is often credited with designing the Bowie knife, a weapon favored by American frontiersmen. But some experts believe that his brother, Rezin, actually designed it.

BOWLING

There are more than 11,000 bowling alleys in the United States. Millions of people bowl each year.

Bowling was introduced to America by the Dutch in the 1600s. They used nine pins, and men would bet on the outcome of the games. The American colonies banned bowling as a result. Bowlers got around the law by using ten pins rather than the nine used before. Today there are many kinds of bowling games, such as duckpins, fivepins, lawn bowling, candlepins, and boccie. But tenpin bowling is the most popular game. Dozens of tournaments organized by such groups as the Professional Bowlers Association and the Ladies Professional Bowlers Tour are televised. Today's champion bowlers include Marshall Holman, Mike Aulby, Earl Anthony, and Robin Romeo.

▼ *Joe Louis became world heavyweight champion in 1937. He defended the title 25 times before his retirement in 1949.*

BOXING

The sport of boxing has many critics, but it is still extremely popular. More than 750 million people around the world watched heavyweight champion Mike Tyson's defeat in January 1990, when James Douglas defied predictions and knocked him out.

Fears of illegal gambling, as well as the bloody results of bare-knuckle fights, meant that boxing was against the law in most states until early this century. New York became the first state to legalize boxing under the Walker Law, passed in 1920. This called for strict regulations and the use of padded boxing gloves. The Golden Age of boxing over the next two decades brought world fame to fighters such as Jack DEMPSEY,

◀ *Mike Tyson's 30-month reign as undisputed world heavyweight champion began with his victory over Tony Tucker (right) on August 1, 1987.*

Some Famous American Boxers	
Heavyweight Champions	
John L. Sullivan	1882–1892
James J. Corbett	1892–1897
Jack Johnson	1908–1915
Jack Dempsey	1919–1926
Joe Louis	1937–1949
Rocky Marciano	1952–1956
Muhammad Ali	1964–1967 1974–1978
Mike Tyson	1987–1990
Middleweight Champions	
Sugar Ray Robinson	1951–1952 1955–1957 1958–1959
Welterweight Champions	
Sugar Ray Robinson	1946–1951
Sugar Ray Leonard	1980–1982

Gene Tunney, and Joe Louis. After World War II, television made "the Saturday night fight" as popular as "Monday night football" is today. Later, such boxers as Muhammad Ali, George Foreman, and Sugar Ray Leonard further increased the sport's popularity.

BOY SCOUTS *See* Scouts

BRADFORD, William

William Bradford (1590–1657) was a leader of the Pilgrims and governor of Plymouth Colony for more than 30 years between 1621 and 1656. He helped draw up the Mayflower Compact. This agreement laid the foundations for the colony's self-government. He encouraged the development of democratic institutions, such as the town meeting, and established a generally peaceful relationship with the local Indians. Plymouth Colony prospered under his leadership.

BRADLEY, Omar Nelson

Omar Bradley (1893–1981) served in the U.S. Army for more than 35 years. He attained the rank of General of the Army. During World War II he proved himself a brilliant commander in North Africa and in the invasion of Sicily in 1943. The next year he was put in charge of the American forces that landed on the beaches at Normandy, France, on D Day. Bradley was made chief of staff of the Army in 1948, and a year later he became the first chairman of the Joint Chiefs of Staff.

Governor William Bradford did not approve of celebrations. Despite this, he established the first feast of Thanksgiving to celebrate the successful harvest in the autumn of 1621.

▲ *Marlon Brando played Johnny, the tough leader of a motorcycle gang, in* The Wild Ones.

BRADY, Mathew

The photographer Mathew Brady (1823–1896) is best known for his pictures of the CIVIL WAR. He began his career as a fashionable portrait photographer, photographing many famous people.

To photograph the Civil War, Brady hired a team of 20 photographers. Brady himself was present at several battles. Action photographs were not yet possible, but Brady's pictures of weary, wounded, and dead soldiers form a moving record of the war. Taking these pictures cost Brady $100,000. But he earned very little from them and died a poor man.

BRANDO, Marlon

Marlon Brando (1924–) is one of the most famous actors of this century. He first became known as a powerful stage actor, but he soon went to HOLLYWOOD. Some of his classic film performances include Marc Antony in *Julius Caesar* and Stanley Kowalski in *A Streetcar Named Desire*. He won an ACADEMY AWARD in 1954 for his role in *On the Waterfront*. His rare later roles include Don Corleone in *The Godfather*, which won him another Oscar (1972).

BRANT, Joseph

Joseph Brant (1742–1807) was a MOHAWK chief. His Indian name was Thayendaneegea. Brant was a good friend to the British and fought for them in the FRENCH AND INDIAN WAR. His sister married Sir William Johnson, who became superintendent of the Iroquois tribes in what is now upstate New York. Brant even visited Britain, but he returned to America to fight for the British in the American REVOLUTION. After the war, Britain gave him a grant of land in Canada.

▼ *Walter Brattain's work on semiconductors and transistors opened the world of electronics for modern use.*

BRATTAIN, Walter

Walter Brattain (1902–1987) was a physicist who invented the transistor in 1947 with fellow scientists William B. SHOCKLEY and John BARDEEN. In 1956 all three, who worked at Bell Telephone Laboratories, were awarded the Nobel Prize for physics for their invention. The transistor revolutionized electronics. It helped make possible many of the electronic products we take for granted today, such as personal computers and communications satellites.

BRIDGES

▲ *The Chesapeake Bay Bridge-Tunnel in Virginia is 17.5 miles (28.2 km) long. It includes two stretches of tunnel beneath busy shipping lanes.*

Bridge building has always been one of the greatest challenges facing engineers and builders in the United States. Most famous bridges are suspension bridges. Suspension bridges are suspended from cables hung between two tall towers. The U.S. bridge with the longest suspended span is the Verrazano-Narrows Bridge, linking Staten Island and Brooklyn in New York City. The span between its towers is 4,260 feet (1,298 m).

The Golden Gate Bridge in San Francisco has a

Some Notable American Bridges			
Kind of Bridge	Total Length	Year Opened	Bridge
Suspension	26,372 ft (8,017 m)	1957	Mackinac Straits, Michigan
Suspension	13,700 ft (4,176 m)	1964	Verrazano-Narrows, New York
Suspension	8,981 ft (2,737 m)	1937	Golden Gate, California
Cantilever	13,915 ft (4,241 m)	1974	Commodore John Barry, Pennsylvania – New Jersey
Steel arch	8,460 ft (2,579 m)	1931	Bayonne, New Jersey – Staten Island, New York
Combination	154,387 ft (47,057 m)	1956 and 1969	Lake Pontchartrain Causeway, Louisiana

shorter span, but its two bridge towers are the highest in the world—746 feet (227 m) above the water level. In the 18th and 19th centuries, many covered wooden bridges were built. The roof protected passengers as well as the structure of the bridge itself. Most of these bridges fell victim to fires, but the remaining covered bridges (mainly in New England) are popular with tourists.

Engineers still build drawbridges to raise when tall ships have to pass through. Drawbridges that open on a hinge (like medieval castle drawbridges) are called bascule bridges. Chicago has five bascule bridges with a span of more than 240 feet (74 m).

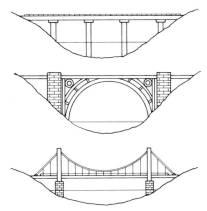

▲ Standard bridge designs include beam (top), arch (center), and suspension.

▶ The 5-mile (8-km)-long Mackinac Bridge links Michigan's Upper and Lower peninsulas.

▼ Nevada's bristlecone pines survive for thousands of years in poor soil and arid conditions. Most other trees would die within a month.

BRISTLECONE PINE

Bristlecone pine trees are the oldest living trees in the world. The oldest one of all, named Methuselah, is almost 4,700 years old. These trees grow mainly in mountainous areas in the southwestern states.

The trees grow very slowly and are only about 10 to 30 feet (3 to 8 m) tall. Bristlecone pines that grow in the eastern states are dwarf trees and may grow to only 3 feet (1 m). Gnarled and twisted by the wind, they do not grow at elevations below about 8,000 feet (2,600 m). The few bunches of needles growing on each tree stay on the tree for up to 30 years. This helps the trees endure long droughts.

BRITISH COLUMBIA

British Columbia is Canada's westernmost province and the only province on the Pacific coast. It is also the country's third largest province in size and in population.

Much of British Columbia is wild and rugged, with spectacular forests, rivers, and lakes. The Rocky Mountains lie along British Columbia's border with the province of Alberta. Numerous rivers, such as the Fraser, reach inland from the rocky coast. Away from the ocean, the winter climate can be as harsh as the terrain. Settlement in these regions has been difficult. But the province's vast natural resources, especially timber, coal, copper, and lead, have drawn many eastern Canadians to British Columbia since it was opened up in the 1800s. Most people live in the southwestern part of the province, in and around the cities of Vancouver, the largest city and port, and Victoria, the capital. Victoria is located on the 285-mile (460-km)-long Vancouver Island. The weather in the southwest is warm, with frequent rain. Parts of the coast here are fertile and low-lying, with many farms. There are also numerous fishing villages and towns.

▲ Snowcapped mountains loom over the excellent natural harbor of Horseshoe Bay, in west Vancouver.

Flowering dogwood

British Columbia
Capital: Victoria
Area: 365,900 sq mi (947,800 km²). Rank: 3rd
Population: 3,044,200 (1989). Rank: 3rd
Entry into Confederation: July 20, 1871 (6th province)
Highest point: Mt. Fairweather, 15,300 ft (4,663 m)

On April 17, 1982, the British North America Act was replaced with the Constitution Act, the new governing document of Canada.

Each year since 1947, Broadway has honored its best productions with the Tony Awards. These are given for the best play and musical, best actor and actress, and other achievements.

▼ The neon lights are always bright on Broadway. Illuminated movie and theater marquees compete with dazzling billboard ads and headlights from passing traffic.

BRITISH NORTH AMERICA ACT

Passed by the British Parliament in 1867, the British North America Act created the Canadian Confederation. It also served as CANADA's constitution. The new nation consisted of the provinces of Nova Scotia, New Brunswick, Ontario, and Quebec. By 1873 all of the other provinces except Newfoundland had joined. The act provided for a government similar to that of Britain, with a parliament and a prime minister. The British North America Act served as Canada's written constitution until 1982, when the British Parliament passed the Canada Act. This, in effect, transferred Canada's constitution to Canada from Britain.

BROADWAY

Broadway is the best-known street in NEW YORK CITY. From its start at the southern tip of Manhattan it runs 15.5 miles (25 km) north, eventually crossing into the Bronx and ending at the city's northern border. Broadway passes Wall Street and the famous financial district, but its most noted stretch is just north of Times Square, where Broadway becomes the center of the theater district. Most of New York's famous plays and shows have been staged in Broadway theaters. High rents nowadays have closed many theaters.

BROOKS, Gwendolyn

Gwendolyn Brooks (1917–) won the PULITZER PRIZE for poetry in 1950 for her collection of poems entitled *Annie Allen*. Brooks has spent most of her life in Chicago. Her observations of racial hatred and discrimination in the Chicago neighborhood where she lived inspired her early work, such as *Bronzeville Boys and Girls*. Using short, sharp phrases and simple rhymes, she wrote of everyday things and experiences as they affected the lives of black people. She became the poet laureate of Illinois in 1968.

BROWN, John

John Brown (1800–1859) was an ABOLITIONIST who believed that force was necessary to free the slaves. He was considered a radical by some in the abolitionist movement. In 1856, Brown, four of his sons, and other abolitionists were involved in some bloody fighting between pro- and anti-slavery settlers in Kansas. On the night of October 16, 1859, he and 21 armed co-conspirators captured the federal arsenal at Harpers Ferry, Virginia. Several people were killed on both sides. Two days later, Federal troops commanded by Col. Robert E. LEE forced the band to surrender. Brown was tried and convicted of treason against Vir-

▲ Gwendolyn Brooks was born in Kansas, but her poems deal with ghetto life in Chicago.

▼ John Brown lost two sons in the Harpers Ferry raid. His own execution made him a martyr for the anti-slavery movement.

At the 1896 Democratic National Convention, Bryan made one of the most famous political speeches in the history of the United States. He was calling for the free coinage of silver at a fixed rate with gold. He believed that if the government issued silver coins as well as gold, it would help the country's farmers and therefore improve the whole economy. Bryan ended his rousing speech with the much quoted words: "You shall not crucify mankind upon a cross of gold."

▼ *Not long before his death in 1925, William Jennings Bryan was the attorney for the prosecution in the famous Scopes trial in Tennessee. John Scopes, a teacher, had been charged with teaching the theory of evolution in violation of state law. Bryan used his great oratory skill to present a religious view of creation. Scopes was convicted but not before defense attorney Clarence Darrow had put Bryan through some fierce cross-examination.*

ginia, promoting a slave revolt, and murder. He was hanged in December. Many Northerners considered him a martyr, and during the CIVIL WAR "John Brown's Body" was a popular Union song.

BRUCE, Blanche Kelso

Blanche Kelso Bruce (1841–1898) was the first black American to serve a full term in the U.S. Senate. Bruce was born a slave in Virginia, but was tutored by his master's son and attended Oberlin College in Ohio. He set up two schools for blacks in Kansas and Missouri. After the CIVIL WAR, Bruce became a planter in Mississippi. He later became involved in Republican politics, and in 1874 was elected to the U.S. Senate. As senator he actively promoted the rights of minorities, including Indians and immigrants from Asia.

BRYAN, William Jennings

William Jennings Bryan (1806–1925) was a great orator and political leader. A lawyer, Bryan entered politics in the 1880s as a Democratic congressman from Nebraska. He ran for president in 1896 as an opponent of the gold standard, a major issue of the day. Although he lost the election, he remained an important Democratic leader. He later served as President Woodrow WILSON's secretary of state. He resigned because he thought Wilson's policies would bring the country into WORLD WAR I. Bryan returned to lecturing and the law until his death in 1925.

James Buchanan was the 15th president of the United States. He served during the years just before the CIVIL WAR. Before his election, Buchanan, who was a lawyer, served in the Pennsylvania legislature and the U.S. House of Representatives. He also served as minister to Russia, U.S. senator, secretary of state under President James K. POLK, and minister to Great Britain. A Democrat, he was elected president in 1856.

When Buchanan came to office, the United States was heading toward civil war. In Kansas, pro-slavery and anti-slavery groups were fighting. Buchanan felt that slavery was wrong, but he wanted to preserve the Union. Because pro-slavery people controlled the government of Kansas, Buchanan was ready to allow Kansas to join the Union as a slave state. This angered many Northerners.

In 1857, Buchanan became involved in the Dred Scott case. The Supreme Court had ruled that the slave Dred Scott could not take legal action in a federal (national) court to obtain his freedom, because slaves

▼ On January 9, 1861, South Carolina troops fired on the federal ship Star of the West. President Buchanan had sent the ship to supply troops stationed around Charleston Harbor.

were not U.S. citizens. Buchanan supported this position, which further annoyed Northerners.

In 1859, John BROWN made his famous raid on the arsenal at Harpers Ferry. The United States was on the brink of civil war. The DEMOCRATIC PARTY was split, and Republican Abraham LINCOLN won the election. As a result, seven southern states seceded (withdrew) from the Union during Buchanan's last months in office. He stated that they had no right to secede, but also that he had no power to stop them. In March 1861 he handed over the reins of government to Lincoln.

James Buchanan
Born: April 23, 1791, near Mercersburg, Pennsylvania
Education: Dickinson College, Carlisle, Pennsylvania
Political Party: Democratic
Term of office: 1857–1861
Died: June 1, 1868, in Lancaster, Pennsylvania

▲ Many of Pearl Buck's 65 books and hundreds of stories tried to foster understanding between Asia and the West.

BUCK, Pearl S.

Pearl Buck (1892–1973) was a novelist who wrote about life in China. She spent most of her childhood in that country, where her parents were missionaries. Her best-known book, *The Good Earth*, tells of a Chinese peasant and his wife whose struggles and patience are eventually rewarded with prosperity. This novel won the 1932 PULITZER PRIZE; later writings won her the Nobel Prize for literature in 1938. After World War II, Pearl Buck did charitable work, helping Asian orphans and retarded children. She told the story of her own life in *My Several Worlds*.

BUFFALO *See* Bison

BUFFALO BILL *See* Cody, William F.

BUGS

The fearsome assassin bug is known for its painful stab and resulting swelling. Despite this, it is very useful as a pest control. Because the assassin bug feeds on the insects that destroy crops, it has proved to be a farmer's friend.

People often use the word "bug" to refer to any INSECT. But to scientists, bugs are only those insects that have long, pointed, beaklike mouthparts. Bugs use their mouthparts for sucking the juices of plants or the blood of humans or other animals.

Bugs can be found nearly everywhere. Some, such as water boatmen, backswimmers, and water scorpions, live in the water. But most bugs live on land.

Many bugs are helpful because they destroy weeds or insect pests. But often bugs are harmful because they attack crops. Plant bugs, lace bugs, and stinkbugs, for example, are all serious pests. A number of bugs, such

► Bugs come in all different shapes and sizes. The giant water bug can grow to 2.5 inches (6 cm), while the lace bug grows to a mere 0.25 inch (0.6 cm). Bugs vary in color too. Often the colors are designed to act as camouflage or to warn off predators. All bugs belong to the insect order Hemiptera.

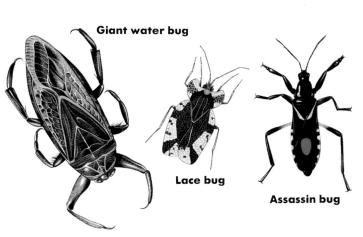

Giant water bug

Lace bug

Assassin bug

as the bedbug, bite humans or animals. Some even pass on germs.

To hide from their prey and their enemies, some bugs, such as the ambush bug, are colored to blend in with their background. Others, like the stinkbug, smell nasty or have an unpleasant taste. Many advertise this fact by being brightly colored.

A young bug, after hatching from an egg, is called a *nymph*. It looks very much like an adult bug but does not have wings.

Despite their names, ladybugs, mealy bugs, doodlebugs, and sowbugs are not true bugs.

BULL RUN, Battles of

Two CIVIL WAR battles were fought near the stream called Bull Run, near Manassas, in northern Virginia. They are known in the North as the Battles of Bull Run, and in the South as the Battles of Manassas. The first battle, on July 21, 1861, was the opening engagement of an intended Union attack on Richmond. Both sides were inexperienced. The Union forces seemed at first to have the advantage, but the arrival of Confederate reinforcements stopped them and they retreated to Washington. The battle demonstrated to Northerners that they would not be able to win the war quickly.

The following year, on August 29–30, General LEE's Confederate army met another Union army in the same place and defeated them, with heavy casualties on both sides. More than 27,000 Union and Confederate soldiers were killed, captured, or wounded during the two Battles of Bull Run.

▲ *Many Northerners thought that the first Battle of Bull Run would end the Civil War quickly. Some Washington residents even took picnics and watched. The fierce battle that followed, with its many casualties, came as a terrible shock.*

Casualties at the second Battle of Bull Run were heavy. Following this major Confederate victory, Union troops were cleared out of Virginia for the first time during the Civil War.

The famous Battle of Bunker Hill actually took place on Breed's Hill, a short distance away. The American troops set up bulwarks on Breed's Hill but lacked the supplies they needed to defeat the British outright. However, the British army was forced to charge the hill three times before the Americans finally withdrew.

BUNCHE, Ralph

Ralph Bunche (1904–1971) was a distinguished diplomat. During the 1940s he played an important role in setting up the UNITED NATIONS. His special area of knowledge was in dealing with colonies or former colonies. His skill as a negotiator was also highly prized. After the establishment of the state of Israel in 1948, war broke out in the Middle East between Israel and its Arab neighbors. Bunche conducted talks that led to an armistice. This great achievement won him the Nobel Peace Prize in 1950. He later held several important positions in the United Nations.

BUNKER HILL, Battle of

The Battle of Bunker Hill, at Boston, was the first major battle of the American REVOLUTION. It was actually fought on nearby Breed's Hill. British troops controlled Boston, and they planned to occupy the hills across the Charles River from the city. The colonists learned of this plan and sent their forces to Breed's Hill before the British could do so. On June 17, 1775, British troops attacked. The British captured both hills, but 1,000 out of 2,300 British soldiers were killed. Of the 3,200 Americans in the battle, 450 were killed or wounded.

▼ The American troops at Bunker Hill had very little ammunition. As the British marched toward them in rows, American Colonel William Prescott told his men to wait. He gave his now-famous order: "Don't fire until you see the whites of their eyes."

BUNYAN, Paul

In American FOLKLORE, Paul Bunyan is a legendary figure, a lumberjack of superhuman size and strength. He is the hero of many "tall tales," in which frontiersmen would try to outdo each other in telling ever more incredible stories. In one story, for example, it is claimed that Bunyan created the Grand Canyon by dragging his pickax along the ground. In another, his giant blue ox, Babe, hauled the logs from an entire forest. The character may have been based on a real person, a French Canadian named Paul Bunyon who ran a logging camp in the mid-1800s. The feats of the fictional Paul Bunyan first appeared in print in a lumber company's advertisement in 1914. Since then, they have been celebrated in several books, in poems by Robert Frost and others, and in an operetta by the British composer Benjamin Britten.

BURBANK, Luther

Luther Burbank (1849–1926) was a plant breeder who developed hundreds of new kinds of vegetables, fruits, and flowers. Burbank was fascinated by the possibility of creating new kinds of plants from already existing ones. The reason for doing this was so that the new plants would combine the strengths of the older ones—for instance, a vegetable with an interesting flavor and texture that would also withstand harsh weather. Among his most well-known creations are the Burbank (or Idaho) potato and the Shasta daisy.

▲ Most Paul Bunyan stories also include tall tales about his blue ox, Babe. Babe was supposed to have measured 42 ax handles long and could drink a river dry.

▲ *Aaron Burr's political career ended when he killed Alexander Hamilton in a duel. By the mid-1800s dueling was banned in most of the United States.*

BURR, Aaron

Aaron Burr (1756–1836) was an American political leader who became vice president under Thomas JEFFERSON.

A lawyer, Burr entered New York state politics in the 1780s. He was elected to the U.S. Senate in 1791. In the meantime, however, he had acquired a political enemy, Alexander HAMILTON. When Burr and Thomas Jefferson tied in the presidential election of 1800, Hamilton worked to secure Burr's defeat. Burr then served as vice president under Jefferson. But in 1804, before his term was finished, he fought a duel with Hamilton in which Hamilton was killed. Under threat of arrest for murder, Burr joined a friend, General James Wilkinson, in a plot to invade Mexico and found a new country that would have included part of the Louisiana Territory. Wilkinson betrayed Burr, who was tried for treason. He was acquitted, but his political career was finished.

▶ *Johnny Weissmuller, the first actor to play Tarzan in the movies, wrestles with a young elephant. The Tarzan movies introduced millions of people to Edgar Rice Burroughs's books. They have been translated into 50 languages.*

Edgar Rice Burroughs had no experience of either English high society or the African jungle before he wrote his Tarzan novels. Instead he had been a storekeeper, gold miner, cowboy, and even light-bulb salesman.

BURROUGHS, Edgar Rice

The writer Edgar Rice Burroughs (1875–1950) created Tarzan, one of the most popular characters in fiction. Tarzan, the son of an English nobleman, is abandoned in Africa as a baby when his parents are killed. He is brought up by apes and learns their language. Burroughs wrote the first Tarzan book, *Tarzan of the Apes*, in 1914. It was an immediate success, and he went on to write another 25 Tarzan books.

BUSH, George

George Bush is the 41st president of the United States. Born in Massachusetts, he served as a U.S. Navy pilot during World War II. Later, after moving to Texas, he helped found an oil company and then entered politics. Between 1967 and 1977, Bush was a U.S. congressman, ambassador to the United Nations, envoy to China, and director of the Central Intelligence Agency (CIA). He served as vice president under Ronald REAGAN from 1981 to 1989.

Bush was elected president in 1988. In foreign affairs, his first two years in office were marked by friendlier relations with the Soviet Union. But twice he sent U.S. troops overseas. In December 1989 he ordered U.S. troops to invade Panama and overthrow that country's dictator, General Manuel Antonio Noriega. Bush sent U.S. troops overseas again in August 1990, after Iraq had invaded and occupied the oil-rich country of Kuwait. By the end of the year hundreds of thousands of troops were stationed in Saudi Arabia, a neighbor of Kuwait in the Middle East. Troops from some European and Arab countries joined them to protect Saudi Arabia's oil fields and to force Iraq out of Kuwait.

In domestic affairs, Bush had inherited a huge budget deficit. The government was spending much more than it was taking in from taxes and other sources. When Bush was running for president, he promised "no new taxes." But in 1990 he backed a bill to reduce the deficit by raising taxes. The higher taxes and the declining economy of the United States lost Bush's Republican Party votes in the 1990 elections.

George Bush
Born: June 12, 1924, in Milton, Massachusetts
Education: Yale University
Political party: Republican
Term of office: 1989–
Married: 1945 to Barbara Price

▼ *George Bush (center) commanded an X-2 Naval Air fighter plane in World War II.*

◄ *President Bush, seen here with former British Prime Minister Margaret Thatcher. Even before he became president, Bush had met many world leaders during his years as vice president.*

BUTTERFLIES AND MOTHS

Butterflies and moths are flying INSECTS whose wings are covered in tiny, colored scales. Most feed by sucking sweet juices, known as nectar, from flowers. There are about 12,000 different kinds, or *species*, of butterflies in the world and about 120,000 species of moths. Of these, there are about 700 species of butterflies and 9,000 species of moths in North America.

The colors and patterns on the wings of butterflies and moths help to protect them from being eaten by other ani-

The Life Cycle of a Butterfly

Butterfly lays eggs

Eggs

Newly-hatched larva

Fully-grown caterpillar

Three pupal stages

Adult butterfly

Butterfly or Moth?

It isn't always easy to tell a butterfly from a moth. There are some differences, but there are many exceptions to the rules. Butterflies usually have thin bodies, while those of moths are shorter and fatter. Most butterflies fly during the day; moths fly at night. A moth usually rests with its wings flat. Many butterflies rest with their wings held together above their bodies.

Tiger moth

Wood nymph (butterfly)

▼ Butterflies and moths can be identified easily by wing shape and coloring.

▲ The life cycle of the butterfly. From the eggs hatches the caterpiller, or larva. This becomes a pupa from which the adult butterfly will emerge.

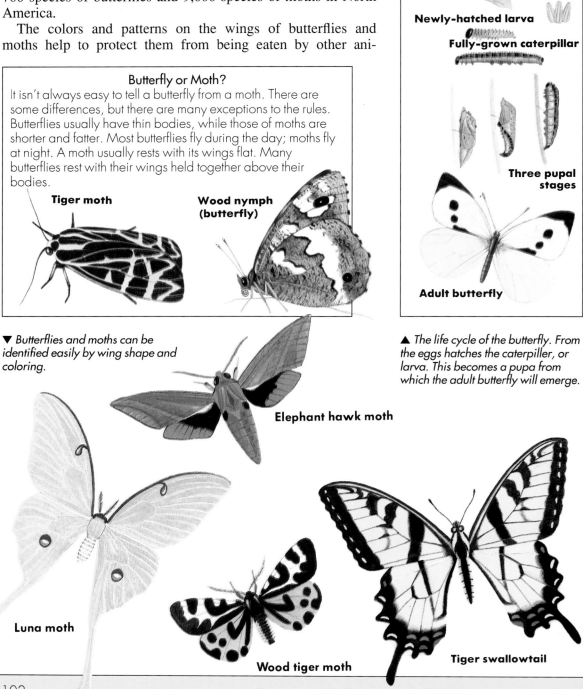

Elephant hawk moth

Luna moth

Wood tiger moth

Tiger swallowtail

mals. Some, such as hawk moths, look so much like their surroundings that they are practically invisible. Others, such as monarch butterflies, have an unpleasant taste or are poisonous. They are usually brightly colored, so that their enemies will easily remember to avoid them. There are some butterflies and moths that look like (or *mimic*) a poisonous type of butterfly. Their enemies avoid them even though they do not actually taste bad themselves. Viceroy butterflies, for example, mimic monarchs.

Butterflies known as hairstreaks have spots that look like eyes at the tip of each back wing. These false eyes cause their enemies to snap at the wrong part, so that the butterfly escapes.

Because many species are similar in a number of ways, they are grouped into large categories. Skippers are insects that share characteristics of butterflies and moths. They are usually classed as a separate group.

▲ *A cluster of monarch butterflies swarms in a tree during the annual migration from their winter quarters in Mexico to their breeding grounds in the United States and Canada.*

Monarch

Red admiral

Mourning cloak

Blue

Cabbage white

Butterfly Families

Fritillaries: Regal fritillary
Blues, Coppers, and Hairstreaks: American copper, Spring azure
Brush-footed butterflies: Mourning cloak
Sulphurs and Whites: Common sulphur
Satyrs and Wood nymphs: Pearly eye
Swallowtails: Black swallowtail
Metalmarks: Northern metalmark
Milkweed butterflies: Monarch
Snout butterflies: Southern snout butterfly

▲ *Charles Lindbergh congratulates Richard Byrd for his flight over the South Pole. Just two years before, in 1927, Lindbergh had made his historic transatlantic flight.*

Despite freezing fingers and an aircraft with an oil leak, Byrd and Bennett circled the North Pole several times. The journey lasted 15 hours and 51 minutes. In 1909, Robert E. Peary and Matthew Henson had taken eight months to reach the North Pole by dogsled.

▶ *On November 28, 1929, Byrd became the first person to fly over the South Pole. He set off from his base camp, called "Little America," on the Ross Ice Shelf at the Bay of Whales, and the round trip took him 19 hours.*

BUZZARD *See* Vulture

BYRD, Richard E.

Richard Byrd (1888–1957) was America's greatest Antarctic explorer. He learned to fly in the Navy, after graduating from the U.S. Naval Academy in 1912. In 1926, during an expedition to the Arctic, he and his co-pilot, Floyd Bennett, became the first persons to fly over the North Pole. Byrd later passed on some advice on navigation to Charles LINDBERGH, who was preparing for his own transatlantic flight. Byrd soon turned his attention to Antarctica. He led an expedition to that frozen continent in 1928, and in the following year he became the first person to fly over the South Pole. Soon after, he was promoted to rear admiral. Byrd led four other expeditions to Antarctica, the last in 1956, to explore and map the continent and to conduct scientific studies. During his 1933–1935 expedition, Byrd stayed alone in a weather station built under the snow and ice for five months. His small hut was located farther south than any human occupation up to that time. He wrote about this adventure in the book *Alone*.

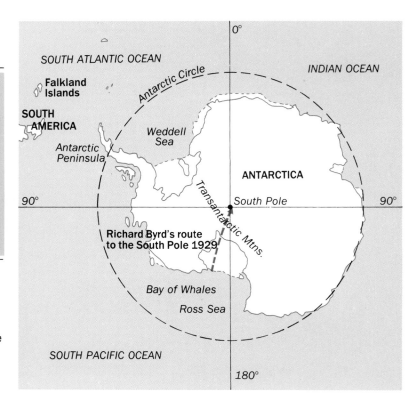

CABINET

The Cabinet is a group of presidential advisers. It includes the heads, or secretaries, of the major government departments, plus the attorney general. The Cabinet is not the only group that helps shape the government's policies. Some presidents have used their own advisers even more than they have used the Cabinet for decision making.

Though the CONSTITUTION does not call for a Cabinet, over the years it has become a central part of the United States government. The president nominates the members of the Cabinet, and they must then be approved by the Senate. He often chooses them not just because he thinks they will be able to perform their jobs efficiently, but because they share his political goals. As a result, when a new president is elected, the members of the old Cabinet resign, and the new president appoints a new Cabinet.

◄ The 1989 Cabinet, with President George Bush and Vice President Dan Quayle, poses at one of its first weekly meetings in the Cabinet Room of the White House.

CABLE CAR

A cable car is a passenger vehicle pulled by a cable that is constantly moving. The cable cars of a ski lift hang from the cable that extends up the slope. SAN FRANCISCO has a system of cable cars for public transportation. The cars run on rails, with the cable submerged in a channel below the rails. The American inventor Andrew S. Hallidie developed the first cable car. His cable car system was first used in San Francisco, in 1873. Cable cars remain a popular and effective way of traveling along San Francisco's hilly streets.

Members of the Cabinet
Secretary of State
Secretary of the Treasury
Secretary of Defense
Secretary of the Interior
Secretary of Agriculture
Secretary of Commerce
Secretary of Labor
Secretary of Health and Human Services
Secretary of Housing and Urban Development
Secretary of Transportation
Secretary of Energy
Secretary of Education
Secretary of Veterans Affairs
Attorney General

One of the most important outcomes of John Cabot's voyages was his discovery of the dense schools of cod off the southeastern coast of Newfoundland. News of the rich fishing grounds on the Grand Banks spread, and fishing crews have been attracted there ever since.

▶ John Cabot's exploration of the Canadian coast and the St. Lawrence River opened up present-day Canada for England.

CABOT, John and Sebastian

John Cabot (1450?–1498?) and his son Sebastian (1476?–1557) were of Italian origin, but they explored the New World for England. In an attempt to compete with Spain's colonizing activities, Henry VII of England commissioned John Cabot to search for new lands. In 1497, Cabot arrived on the coast of Canada (possibly Newfoundland), which he claimed for the English king. Cabot's explorations of this territory prepared the way for England's colonization of Canada. On a second voyage, in 1498, Cabot was lost at sea. His son Sebastian, who had accompanied him on his first voyage, later worked for Spain as well as for England. At one time he was cartographer, or mapmaker, to Henry VIII, and in 1544 he produced a famous map of the world.

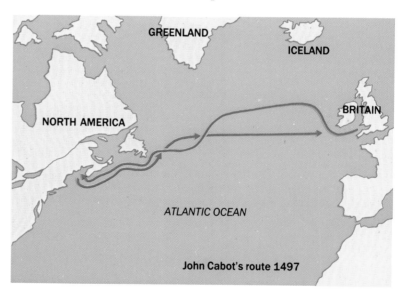

John Cabot's route 1497

▲ Juan Rodriguez Cabrillo explored the California coast as far north as what is now the border with Oregon.

CABRILLO, Juan Rodriguez

Very little is known about the life of the explorer Juan Rodriguez Cabrillo (died 1543?), except that he was the first European to discover California. He may have been born in Portugal, but he fought and explored for Spain. It is believed that he founded the town of Oaxaca, in Mexico, and that he was one of the conquerors of the part of Central America now including Guatemala, Nicaragua, and El Salvador. In 1542 he sailed up the west coast of North America with an exploration party. He explored much of the coast of California, including the areas around San Diego and Monterey.

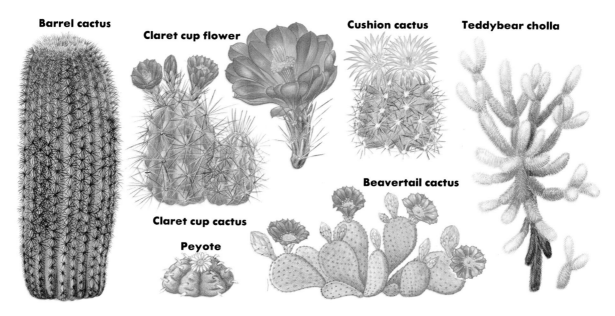

Barrel cactus

Claret cup flower

Cushion cactus

Teddybear cholla

Claret cup cactus

Peyote

Beavertail cactus

CACTUSES

A cactus is a plant that can store a large amount of water in its stem. Cactuses are native to North and South America, where they are the most common desert vegetation.

Cactuses have developed differently than other plants. The stems and branches do the work that in other plants is done by the leaves. Instead of leaves, a cactus usually has hairs, needles, or spines. These protect it from animals. The thick, waxy skin of the cactus keeps the water in instead of allowing it to evaporate, as in other plants. The roots grow near the surface of the ground and can quickly take in water when it does rain.

The best-known cactuses are the prickly pears. Their fruits look like pears and can be eaten. The largest cactuses are the saguaro cactuses. These can be up to 40 feet (12 m) tall. Pincushion cactuses grow from Mexico to Canada and are often grown as houseplants. Barrel cactuses can be up to 12 feet (3.5 m) tall and several feet thick. One type of barrel cactus, the bisnaga, may live more than 1,000 years.

CADDOS

The Caddos are an INDIAN people who came from the southeastern plains. They lived largely in what is now Arkansas, Oklahoma, Louisiana, and Texas. Their language, Caddoan, was spoken by a number of other

▲ The 2,000 species of cactuses have developed some unusual shapes to adapt to special conditions of rainfall and elevation.

▼ The saguaro cactus blossoms for only a few days each spring.

tribes, including the PAWNEE. In the 1500s the Spanish found the Caddos to be fierce warriors. Most Caddos were hunters and farmers, who came into conflict with the nomadic tribes that followed the game as it moved over the plains. When war broke out between Indians and the white settlers, the Caddos offered themselves as scouts to the army as a way of fighting their enemies, the hunting tribes. Today, some 1,200 Caddos live on a reservation in Oklahoma.

▼ *Caddo women were skilled makers of highly decorated pottery, which was traded widely with other tribes.*

CADILLAC, Antoine de la Mothe

Mt. Cadillac in Maine, the highest point on the Atlantic coast of the United States, is named for the soldier-explorer, as are Cadillac, Michigan, and the Cadillac automobile.

Antoine de la Mothe, sieur de Cadillac (1658–1730) was a French soldier and colonist who founded the city of Detroit. He fought in battles against the IROQUOIS Indians in Canada and for three years served as commandant of the French trading post of Mackinac (in Michigan). In 1701 he founded a new post called Fort Pontchartrain du Detroit, now called simply Detroit. Later, Cadillac was governor of Louisiana. But he made a number of enemies and was recalled to France.

CAGE, John

A performance of John Cage's highly original *Imaginary Landscape No. 4* requires 24 musicians, a conductor, and 12 radios. To make sure that no two performances are ever the same, each radio is tuned to a different station and the volume of the radios is changed during the piece.

John Cage (1912–) is a composer who has spent much of his career exploring new musical sounds. He has placed spoons, pieces of wood, rubber bands, and other objects on piano strings to create new sounds. He calls this his "prepared piano." Cage is also known for his chance, or random, music. In this he uses musicians and radios. As the musicians play, the radios are tuned in to different stations. Some Cage compositions even include the sound of slamming doors or electrical generators. Many people think that Cage's music is strange. But others regard him as a musical genius.

CAGNEY, James

James Cagney (1899–1986) was a great movie actor who is best known for his roles in gangster films of the 1930s. But his early training was as a song and dance man in Vaudeville, skills he also brought to Hollywood. It was for his role as the Broadway musical star George M. Cohan in *Yankee Doodle Dandy* that Cagney won an ACADEMY AWARD as best actor in 1942. The toughness that made him ideal as a gangster also made him believable in military and spy roles, such as the World War II film *13 Rue Madeleine*.

CAJUNS

The Cajuns are a group of people who live in the bayou region of southern Louisiana. Their French ancestors had lived in Nova Scotia, Canada. This land had been discovered by the English and later settled by the French, who called it Acadia. The two countries fought over who owned it. Finally, the Treaty of Utrecht (1713) gave the land to the English. But the settlers fought English rule. In 1755 the English forced the Acadians to move from their homes; 4,000 were taken to Louisiana. This group came to be called Cajuns.

▲ James Cagney was a small, wiry man, but his expression and voice could be wonderfully menacing for the role of "tough guy" that he so often played.

The French-speaking, Roman Catholic Cajuns number about 250,000. They maintain their old traditions and speak an old form of French into which are mixed words taken from English, German, Spanish, and various Indian languages.

◄ Cajun music is ideal for open-air dances where the whole community takes part. The words of Cajun songs are often in old-fashioned French.

▲ *Calamity Jane's fame spread when she showed off her skills in a Wild West touring company.*

▼ *Alexander Calder created many mobile sculptures. But even his static (nonmoving) art, such as this sculpture in San Diego, California, always has a sense of movement.*

CALAMITY JANE

Calamity Jane (1852?–1903), who was born Martha Jane Canary, was a frontierswoman and adventuress. Although not the glamorous and high-principled heroine portrayed in the popular novels of the late 1800s, the real Calamity Jane was a skilled horsewoman and a crack shot. Most of her adult life was spent in the mining town of Deadwood, South Dakota, where her wearing of men's clothing was cheerfully tolerated. For a while she rode with the 7th U.S. Cavalry, and she may have served as a scout for General Custer. It is believed that her nickname resulted from her warning men that if they offended her they were inviting calamity.

CALDER, Alexander

Alexander Calder (1898–1976) was one of the most important sculptors of this century and the first American sculptor to be known across the world. He obtained a degree in engineering before enrolling at the Art Students League in New York City in 1923. Calder is most famous for his *mobiles*—sculptures that are made of colored sheets of metal and are wired together so that they gently move in the air. They seem familiar today, but in 1932, when Calder made his first mobiles, people considered them daringly new. Later, Calder created *stabiles*, sculptures that look like mobiles but do not move.

CALGARY

Calgary is the largest city in the province of ALBERTA and the center of the Canadian oil industry. Founded in 1875, it is located just east of the Canadian Rocky Mountains. Calgary has long been an important cattle center. The Calgary Stampede, an annual rodeo festival, is world famous. Today, Calgary is also a major industrial, financial, and transportation center. Downtown Calgary, with its malls and high rises, reflects the city's prosperity. In 1988, Calgary hosted the Winter Olympics. Winter sports enthusiasts now take advantage of the city's many fine winter sports facilities.

Many Americans live in Calgary, largely because there are about 400 oil companies based in the city.

CALHOUN, John C.

John C. Calhoun (1782–1850) was an important Southern political leader in the years before the CIVIL WAR. He strongly defended states' rights and believed that an individual state could declare an act of Congress unconstitutional and refuse to obey it. This was known as the theory of *nullification*. Calhoun was from South Carolina. He was a planter and a politician who served for many years in Congress and as vice president under John Quincy ADAMS and Andrew JACKSON. He was also secretary of war under President James MONROE and secretary of state under President John TYLER. Calhoun was an outspoken defender of slavery, and during his 15 years as a senator from South Carolina, he fought to keep slavery alive and to have new slave states admitted to the Union.

▼ John C. Calhoun's fiery speeches supported the Southern cause in the decades before the Civil War.

CALIFORNIA

California is the third largest state. Only Alaska and Texas are larger. It is situated on the Pacific coast and stretches 780 miles (1,260 km) from the Mexican border in the south to the Oregon border in the north. The SIERRA NEVADA and the MOJAVE DESERT cover much of eastern California. California has the largest population of any state. Many people are attracted by the state's sunny climate, great natural beauty, strong economy, and relaxed life-style. In the 1800s, California was a promised land to both Americans and immigrants. Hundreds of thousands made the difficult journey west in covered wagons.

The largest city in California is LOS ANGELES. It is a major manufacturing and financial center and the hub of the motion picture and television industries. SAN DIEGO and SAN FRANCISCO are also thriving cities. The capital is Sacramento. The first Europeans to settle in California were Spaniards, in the 1500s. In 1822, California became part of Mexico, after that country won its independence from Spain. Then, in 1848, after

California valley quail

Golden poppy

California redwood

PACIFIC OCEAN

miles
0   100

0   100
kilometers

Places of Interest
● Disneyland, near Anaheim, was designed by Walt Disney. Most of the exhibits and rides are based on characters from his films.
● Yosemite National Park is just one of six national parks in California. Its magnificent scenery includes Yosemite Falls, one of the world's highest waterfalls.
● The Redwood Highway takes you from San Francisco to Oregon through impressive groves of redwood trees. These trees are the tallest in the world.
● The mission at Santa Barbara was founded in 1786 by Franciscan friars. It is one of several similar missions set up to convert the Indians to Christianity.
● Death Valley National Monument is a desert wilderness and includes the lowest point, 282 feet (86 m) below sea level, in the Western Hemisphere.

the MEXICAN WAR, it became an American territory. Two years later, it became the 31st state.

Today, much of California depends on farming, especially along the fertile Central Valley that runs up the middle of the state. Oil is one of the many important industries. Many "high-tech" industries are situated in "Silicon Valley" in northern California. Tourism is important, too. Natural attractions such as parks, forests, and mountains, and man-made attractions such as Disneyland, draw millions of visitors.

◄ *Upper Yosemite Falls in Yosemite National Park is 1,430 feet (436 m) high, the highest waterfall in the country.*

▼ *Malibu, located just west of Los Angeles, is the home of many wealthy celebrities.*

► *Laguna Beach is one of California's finest harbors. Its fine sands and safe waters also make it popular with swimmers.*

California
Capital: Sacramento
Area: 156,299 sq mi (404,814 km²). Rank: 3rd
Population: 29,839,250 (1990). Rank: 1st
Statehood: September 9, 1850
Principal rivers: Sacramento, Colorado
Highest point: Mt. Whitney, 14,495 ft (4,418 m)
Motto: *Eureka* (I Have Found It)
Song: "I Love You, California"

113

Canada
Capital: Ottawa
Official languages: English and French
Area: 3,849,662 sq mi (9,970,610 km²)
Population: 26,527,000 (1990 est.)
Government: Parliamentary democracy
Highest point: Mt. Logan, 19,524 ft (5,951 m)
Principal rivers: St. Lawrence, 1,900 mi (3,058 km); Mackenzie, 1,071 mi (1,724 km)
National anthem: "O Canada"

CANADA

Canada is the second largest country in the world. Its land area covers more than 3,558,000 square miles (9,215,000 km²). It extends east to west from the Atlantic to the Pacific. The United States forms Canada's southern border. To the north, it extends almost as far as the North Pole. Despite its size, Canada's population is small—only one tenth that of the United States. Most Canadians live in a narrow belt only 125 miles (200 km) from the U.S. border. This is where the largest cities and most important industries are. TORONTO, in the province of ONTARIO, and MONTREAL, in the province of QUEBEC, are the two biggest cities. OTTAWA, the capital, is small by comparison.

The vast forests of Canada's interior have made it the world's biggest producer of pulpwood. There are important mineral reserves, too, especially of oil, iron, nickel, uranium, and gold. These have helped Canada become one of the most important industrial countries in the world. Canada also has huge farms and cattle ranches, especially in the Prairie Provinces of MANITOBA, SASKATCHEWAN, and ALBERTA.

▲ *Peggy's Cove in Nova Scotia is typical of the small fishing villages in Canada's Maritime Provinces.*

The first settlers in Canada caught fish in its rivers and lakes and trapped animals in its forests. Many were French, and about 20 percent of all Canadians still speak French. In the province of Quebec, 80 percent of the people speak French. But the largest group of immigrants were British, and Canada still has close links with Britain. Canada is a member of the British Commonwealth.

▲ *The Canadian Parliament meets in the federal capital of Ottawa. The building is patterned on the British Houses of Parliament.*

Canada has the longest coastline of any country in the world — about 152,000 miles (244,000 km). It is bordered by the Pacific Ocean on the west, the Arctic Ocean on the north, and the Atlantic Ocean on the east.

◀ *The Canadian Rockies are even wilder and more unspoiled than those in the United States.*

▶ *Many of Canada's first settlers spent whole winters without seeing another family.*

CANADIAN HISTORY

The first Europeans to arrive on Canadian soil were the Vikings. They settled briefly in NEWFOUNDLAND sometime around A.D. 1000. Much later, in 1497, the explorer John CABOT claimed this region for England. But it was the French who first put down roots in the land we know as Canada. French fishermen, fur trappers, and missionaries settled along the St. Lawrence River and in the Great Lakes region. They traded with the Indians and converted many of them to Christianity.

The colony of NEW FRANCE prospered from the beginning of the 1600s until the mid-1700s. In the meantime, however, Britain was also colonizing the region. Several wars broke out between these rival powers, and in 1763 the treaty ending the FRENCH AND INDIAN WAR (Seven Years' War) gave Britain control of Canada.

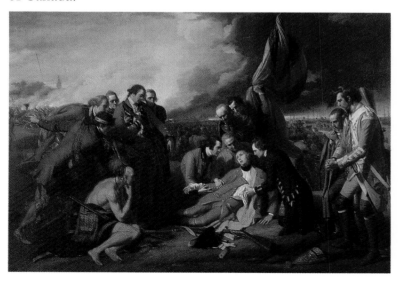

▶ *The Death of Wolfe, a painting by Benjamin West, depicts the dying British General James Wolfe at the Battle of Quebec, fought against the French during the French and Indian War. Wolfe and the French commander, the Marquis de Montcalm, were killed in the battle, but the British won the day.*

Over the next hundred years, Canada consisted of several provinces, ruled mainly from Britain, though with their own elected assemblies. The population increased rapidly and began to move westward. The growing need for unity led, in 1867, to the BRITISH NORTH AMERICA ACT, which established the Canadian Confederation. Full independence from Britain was achieved in 1931, though Canada remains a member of the British Commonwealth of Nations.

The period after World War II saw a rapid development of Canadian industry and a new level of prosperity. Another wave of immigration, mainly from Europe, added to the nation's cultural diversity.

In recent years the unity of the country has been threatened. Some French Canadians, fearing that their culture is in danger of being submerged by the English-speaking majority, have agitated for independence for the province of QUEBEC. The Canadian government has responded with several measures to preserve the French language and play down the ties with Britain, but Anglo-French tensions remain.

▲ In 1982, Prime Minister Pierre Trudeau announced the Constitution Act, a milestone for Canadian self-government.

◀ The Canadian Pacific Railway, finished in 1885, linked Canada from coast to coast. At the ceremony held to complete the link, the final spike, made of gold, was driven in.

CANADIAN SHIELD

The Shield is a geological term used to describe the huge land mass surrounding Hudson Bay in the center of Canada. The Shield is extremely hard land, with a thin layer of topsoil covering bedrock composed mainly of granite. This bedrock was formed as mountains more than 600 million years ago. Natural erosion and several Ice Ages since then have worn it down. A typical Shield landscape is one of low, rolling hills with many small lakes and rivers. Parts of the Shield extend south into the states of Minnesota, Wisconsin, and New York.

▲ The rocky Canadian Shield covers more than half of Canada's land area.

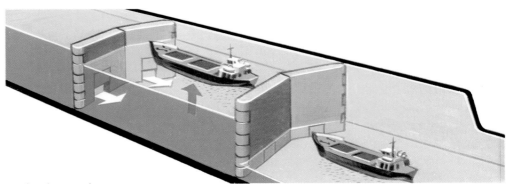

▲ Ships are raised or lowered through canal locks in a series of steps. Water fills the lock to raise the ship up a level, and the gates are opened to allow the ship through. The gates must then be shut and the water level lowered again through sluice gates before the next ship at the lower level can enter the lock.

CANALS

Canals are waterways dug across land. Some are used for supplying water to crops or for drainage. Large canals are used by barges or ships. These inland waterways connect rivers, lakes, seas, or cities.

The first major canal in the United States was the ERIE CANAL, finished in 1825. It joined Lake Erie with the HUDSON RIVER, thus linking the GREAT LAKES with the Atlantic Ocean. This allowed the products of the Great Lakes region to be shipped to Europe by way of the port of New York City. As a result, Rochester, Buffalo, and other cities along the canal grew rapidly, and New York City became North America's greatest port. In 1918 the Erie Canal was made part of the New York State Barge Canal System.

After the Erie Canal, many more canals were built, especially in Ohio and Indiana. They were used by barges pulled along by mules or horses that walked on a

▲ St. Lambert Lock in Quebec is part of the man-made section of the St. Lawrence Seaway. Ships can carry cargo along the seaway from the Great Lakes to the Atlantic.

▶ The St. Lawrence River is a natural canal as it passes Quebec City. It is deep enough even for huge, seagoing tankers.

path alongside the canal. Beginning in the late 1800s, however, the railroad proved a faster and less expensive means of transportation. Most of the old canals are no longer used.

Important North American canals in use today include the Sacramento Canal in California and the Houston Ship Canal in Texas. The ST. LAWRENCE SEAWAY is a whole series of canals. It allows large seagoing vessels to travel between the Great Lakes and the Atlantic. The PANAMA CANAL in Central America provides a shortcut for ships between the Atlantic and Pacific oceans.

The Largest Canyons in the U.S.
Glen Canyon, Utah, Arizona
Grand Canyon, Arizona
King's Canyon, California
Bighorn Canyon, Wyoming
Canyon de Chelly, Arizona
Black Canyon, Colorado
Walnut Canyon, Arizona

CANYONS

A canyon is a long, narrow valley between high cliffs. It usually has a river or stream flowing through it. The desert region known as the Colorado Plateau, covering parts of Arizona, Utah, Colorado, and New Mexico, is a vast maze of deep canyons. The most spectacular is the GRAND CANYON, which in some places is more than one mile (1.6 km) deep. Canyons are carved out by rivers over millions of years. The layers of exposed rock at the top are the youngest. On the canyon floor, the rock may be hundreds of millions of years old.

CAPE CANAVERAL

Cape Canaveral, on the east coast of Florida, is the site of the John F. Kennedy Space Center. The National Aeronautics and Space Administration (NASA) Launch

◄ The Peekaboo Loop Trail winds through the spectacular rock formations of Bryce Canyon in Utah. Water, wind, and weather have eroded away the softer rock, leaving the harder rock behind.

▼ The Cape Canaveral launchpad is over 20 stories high. Hundreds of local people are NASA employees.

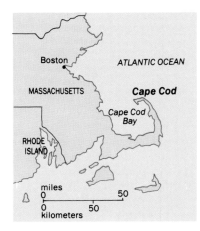

▼ *Cape Cod has some of the best beaches along America's Atlantic coast. Surfers prefer the wild waves of the ocean side, facing east. The shallower—and calmer—waters of Cape Cod Bay are ideal for vacationers.*

Operations Center is at this space center. Cape Canaveral has been the launching site for most American space vehicles. The first satellite was sent into orbit in 1958. Every manned U.S. rocket, from the tiny Mercury probes in the early 1960s to today's space shuttles, has been launched from Cape Canaveral. The Cape is also the site of the Air Force Missile Test Center.

In 1963, Cape Canaveral was renamed Cape Kennedy, in honor of President John F. Kennedy. In 1973 the name was changed back to Cape Canaveral.

CAPE COD

Cape Cod is a sandy, hook-shaped peninsula that extends eastward about 65 miles (105 km) from the MASSACHUSETTS mainland. The coastline is irregular, with many bays and harbors. The islands of Martha's Vineyard and Nantucket lie to the south of Cape Cod.

The Pilgrims landed briefly at the tip of Cape Cod in 1620, before continuing across Cape Cod Bay to Plymouth. The site of their first landfall is now called First Encounter Beach. Tourism has replaced fishing as Cape Cod's leading industry. The winter population of about 180,000 rises to more than 1.5 million each summer.

▼ *The Capitol is built according to the architectural rules of ancient Rome. Many state capitols also use the domes and columns that were features of classical Roman buildings.*

CAPITOL, U.S.

The Capitol is the building in the center of WASHINGTON, D.C., where Congress meets to make the laws of the United States. Its white exterior and huge dome are familiar as a symbol of American democracy. The Capitol takes its name from the Capitoleum, the temple of Jupiter built on the Capitoline Hill in ancient Rome. Rome's senate sometimes met on the Capitoline Hill. The building borrowed more than just its name from Rome. The architecture follows Rome's classical style. Inside the Capitol there are three main areas. In the center, under the dome, is the Great Rotunda, where important ceremonies are held. To the north is the Senate Chamber, where the Senate meets, and to the south is the House Chamber, where the House of Representatives meets.

Work on the Capitol began in 1793, when George WASHINGTON laid the cornerstone. The building was completed in 1800 but was burned down by the British during the WAR OF 1812. It was rebuilt by 1829.

CARDINAL

The cardinal is one of North America's most colorful songbirds. It is found in hedgerows and at the edges of woodlands. Cardinals can also be spotted in parks, gardens, orchards, and farmland.

The cardinal is about 8 inches (20 cm) long. The male has the well-known bright red coloring. The female is brown with some red on its crest, wings, and tail. The cardinal eats seeds, berries, green shoots, insects, and larvae (young insects). Its song is a clear, whistling sound, either high or low pitched.

Cardinals build their nests in trees or tall bushes. After the nesting season, they merge into small groups and roam through the countryside.

Sometimes called the redbird, the cardinal is one of the most colorful crested birds of North America. It migrates northward in spring, but rarely goes farther north than the state of Massachusetts.

▼ Many Caribbean islands, such as this one in the country of St. Vincent and the Grenadines, are popular vacation spots. Tourism often provides the chief source of income for the islands.

CARIBBEAN SEA

The Caribbean Sea is an arm of the Atlantic Ocean. It is bounded by Central and South America and the islands of the West Indies. The sea was named after the Carib Indians, who lived on some of these islands. The Caribbean is one of the world's busiest waterways, because ships using the PANAMA CANAL must pass through it. The climate is tropical, and it is a major winter vacation area, particularly for North Americans. The four largest West Indian islands—Cuba, Hispaniola (Dominican Republic and Haiti), PUERTO RICO, and Jamaica—are known as the Greater Antilles. The Lesser Antilles is made up of hundreds of small islands, including the U.S. VIRGIN ISLANDS. The people of Puerto Rico and the U.S. Virgin Islands are U.S. citizens.

▼ The Caribbean Sea is a passageway for ships carrying many goods to and from the United States.

▶ Two caribou bulls show off their large, branched antlers. Both sexes have antlers, but the female's are smaller and less elaborate. Caribou gather in large herds in the late fall and migrate south to escape the Arctic winter, sometimes traveling over 800 miles (1,300 km). When spring comes, they return north. Their migration routes were taken into account when oil and gas pipelines were laid in Alaska and Canada.

As a caribou moves, a tendon in its foot rubs against a bone and makes a clicking noise. This click becomes very noticeable when caribou gather in herds to migrate; the sound of the continuous clicking of more than 100,000 caribou is unforgettable.

▼ Stokely Carmichael coined the term "Black Power" during a civil rights march in 1966. He was encouraging blacks to make their voices heard in America by exercising their right to vote.

CARIBOU

The caribou is the North American reindeer. It lives in Alaska and northern Canada. At one time it was also found much farther south, but its numbers have been much reduced. Some Inuit (ESKIMOS) and INDIANS eat caribou meat and use its hide to make clothing.

The caribou, like other reindeer, is the only kind of DEER in which both male and female have antlers. They eat grass, sedges, the shoots of trees, mosses, and lichens. Caribou live in herds, migrating long distances south for the winter. The caribou living in the northern tundra are known as barren-ground caribou. Caribou found in the woodlands farther south are called woodland caribou.

CARMICHAEL, Stokely

Stokely Carmichael (1941–) was a leader of the black CIVIL RIGHTS movement in the 1960s. Born on the island of Trinidad, Carmichael grew up in Harlem, in New York City. In 1960, as a student at Howard University, he helped to form the Student Nonviolent Coordinating Committee (SNCC). This racially mixed group led peaceful protests against segregation. After Carmichael was elected chairman of the SNCC in 1966, the group adopted the idea of Black Power. Black Power meant the gaining of political power and economic control. Carmichael later led the militant Black Panther Party.

CARNEGIE, Andrew

Andrew Carnegie (1835–1919) was a famous industrialist and philanthropist. Born in Scotland, he came to the United States with his family when he was 12. He was very successful in the steel industry and became one of the richest men of his time. Carnegie believed that riches should be used for the good of society, so he gave much of his fortune away. He created almost 2,000 public libraries in the United States so that books and knowledge could be within everyone's reach. He also sponsored the building of Carnegie Hall in New York City for concerts. Today, his work continues through such institutions as the Carnegie Corporation and the Carnegie Foundation for the Advancement of Teaching.

▲ During his lifetime, Andrew Carnegie gave more than $350 million to charitable causes.

◄ Carnegie Hall is in the heart of New York City. Musicians consider it an honor to play there.

CARSON, Kit

▼ Legends about Kit Carson sprang up in a series of novels written in the 1860s and 1870s.

Christopher ("Kit") Carson (1809–1868) was a legendary hero of the American western frontier. At the age of 15 he ran away from his home in Missouri and joined a group of traders headed for Santa Fe. In the West he made his living by trading and fur trapping. He was later asked to serve as a guide for John C. FRÉMONT's expeditions across the Rocky Mountains. As a soldier, he fought bravely in the MEXICAN WAR. During the CIVIL WAR, he was a Union brigadier general and fought Confederate forces in New Mexico. In 1868 the government appointed him superintendent of Indian affairs for the Colorado Territory. Many people admired Carson. Several towns are named after him, including Carson City, the capital of Nevada.

James Earl (Jimmy) Carter, Jr., was the 39th president of the United States. Before he ran for the presidency, Carter, a Democrat, was governor of Georgia (1971–1975).

Soon after taking office as president in 1977, Carter fulfilled an election promise and pardoned those who had avoided the draft during the VIETNAM WAR. Carter's honesty and easygoing manner at first made him a popular figure in the White House. His commitment to human rights, at home and abroad, added to his popularity. Carter's biggest problem within the United States was inflation (rising prices). An energy crisis and the high price of oil were the main causes. Carter created a new Department of Energy.

One of Carter's major achievements was the 1979

▶ President Carter's informal approach at the Camp David Agreement lessened tension between Egypt and Israel.

Jimmy Carter
Born: October 1, 1924, in Plains, Georgia
Education: U.S. Naval Academy
Political party: Democratic
Term of office: 1977–1981
Married: 1946 to Rosalynn Smith

Camp David Agreement, when Prime Minister Begin of Israel and President Sadat of Egypt signed a historic peace treaty. Also in 1979, Carter and the Soviet Union signed a treaty known as SALT 2, limiting nuclear weapons. But when the Soviets invaded Afghanistan six months later, Carter withdrew the treaty. The United States also stopped selling grain to the Soviet Union and boycotted the 1980 Moscow Olympic Games.

The worst crisis of Carter's presidency came when 63 Americans were taken hostage in Iran. Carter sent a military force to rescue them, but the effort failed. Carter's popularity declined as a result of the crisis, and he was beaten by Ronald REAGAN in the 1980 election. The hostages were finally released on Carter's last day of office.

▼ Jimmy Carter's hometown of Plains, Georgia, was a quiet rural community when he was a boy in the 1920s.

CARTIER, Jacques

The French navigator Jacques Cartier (1491–1557) made three voyages to Canada. He was the first European to sail the whole navigable length of the ST. LAWRENCE RIVER. Cartier claimed the region for France.

Cartier first sailed to Canada in 1534. On his second voyage, in 1535, he was told by the Indians of a land farther west that was rich in gold and precious stones. In 1541, King Francis I of France sent Cartier back to Canada, along with a nobleman named de Roberval, to establish a colony there. The venture was unsuccessful. And the supposed gold and diamonds that he took back to France proved worthless. But Cartier's voyages paved the way for the French empire in North America.

CARTOON *See* Comic Art; Motion Pictures

CARVER, George Washington

The son of slave parents, George Washington Carver (1864?–1943) became a leading agricultural chemist. As an orphaned boy, living on a Missouri plantation, Carver developed an interest in plants and animals. He recieved a masters degree in science from Iowa State Agricultural College in 1896. Carver then went to Tuskegee Institute, in Alabama, where he taught and experimented with different crops. He discovered that peanuts and soybeans could enrich soil that had been exhausted by many years of growing cotton. He also discovered many uses for these crops, and so helped southern farmers to become more prosperous. Carver's work earned him honors in the United States and abroad and the respect of world leaders.

CASSATT, Mary

Mary Cassatt (1844–1926) was an important painter. Born in Pennsylvania, she moved to France when she was 22. There she met a group of painters called the Impressionists, who strongly influenced her work. They painted scenes from everyday life and tried to give their *impression* of them. Their aim was to create a sense of scenes glimpsed rather than studied.

▲ George Washington Carver's studies into soils and crops led to many breakthroughs in farming. He developed more than 300 by-products from different crops.

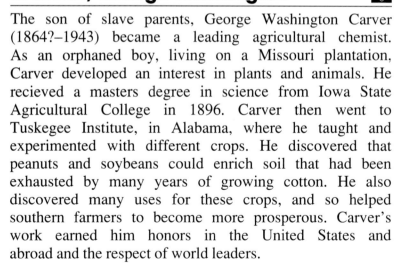

▼ Mother and Child, *a painting by Mary Cassatt. Many of her finest works were tender studies of motherhood.*

Jaguar

Lynx

Bobcat

Cougar

Ocelot

Cougar cub

▲ Most North American wild cats live in undeveloped areas west of the Mississippi River. People are their worst enemy. The jaguar was found in the Southwest up until the early 1900s, though now it is restricted to Central and South America.

▼ Carrie Catt's tireless work over three decades helped secure the vote for women.

CATS

Wild cats and domestic cats are all part of the same family. Domestic cats are extremely popular in the United States as pets. There are more than 58 million cats in U.S. households. Popular breeds of domestic cats include the American short-hair, the Siamese, the Maine Coon, and the Persian.

Of the several wild cats found in North America, the COUGAR (also known as the mountain lion or puma) is the most common. It lives in wilderness areas from British Columbia to South America. The smaller BOBCAT, or lynx, lives in forested areas and scrubland all over the United States. The jaguar was once the largest wild cat to be found in North America. Today, however, it is an endangered species and is found only in Mexico and Central and South America.

CATHER, Willa Sibert

Willa Cather (1873–1947) was a great American writer of short stories and novels. She was raised in Nebraska, and many of her stories painted a realistic picture of the harsh life of immigrants living on the prairies in the late 1800s. Among her best-known stories are *My Antonia* and *O Pioneers!*. *One of Ours*, the story of a young Nebraska farmer who is killed in World War I, won a Pulitzer Prize.

CATT, Carrie Chapman

Carrie Chapman Catt (1859–1947) was a leader in the fight for WOMEN'S RIGHTS. A teacher by profession, and one of the first woman school superintendents in the country, she began to work for the Iowa Woman Suffrage Association in 1887. Her husband, George Catt, encouraged her in this work. From 1900 to 1904 and from 1915 to 1920 she was president of the National American Woman Suffrage Association. When women finally won the vote in 1920, she reorganized this group into the League of Women Voters.

CAVES

Caves are usually found in rocks such as limestone and gypsum, which are easily dissolved by water. The most extensive caves, usually called caverns, extend for miles underground. About 130 caves in the United States are open to the public. Some of the most dramatic are located in the Appalachian Mountains. Mammoth Cave, in central Kentucky, was discovered in 1799. Its 194 miles (312 km) of explored passages form a national park. Carlsbad Caverns in New Mexico make up another national park. The caverns extend for 68 square miles (177 km^2) and are said to be the largest in the world. They include a stalagmite that is 62 feet (19 m) tall.

▲ Carlsbad Caverns in New Mexico are a national park. Visitors can go 829 feet (253 m) below ground.

CENSUS

The Constitution called for a population census "within three years after the first meeting of the Congress of the United States and within every subsequent term of ten years." The first census, held in 1790, counted 3,929,214 Americans. The 1990 census found the U.S. population to be 249,632,692.

The Bureau of the Census, founded in 1902, conducts this research. The population figures are used to determine how many members each state will have in the U.S. House of Representatives. Some government aid to states is also determined by these population figures. The Census Bureau also conducts censuses of manufacturing, businesses, transportation, agriculture, and fishing. These censuses are conducted more frequently than the population census.

CENTRAL INTELLIGENCE AGENCY

The Central Intelligence Agency (CIA) collects intelligence (information) about other countries that is impor-

Caves to Visit in the U.S.
Carlsbad Caverns, New Mexico, are spread over three different levels.
Luray Cavern, Virginia, contains many stalactites and stalagmites of different colors.
Mammoth Cave, Kentucky, has 194 miles (312 km) of underground passageways.
Wind Cave, South Dakota, is a series of limestone caverns with interesting "boxwork" crystal formations.
Wyandotte Cave, Indiana, contains the highest known underground mountain, Monumental Mountain.

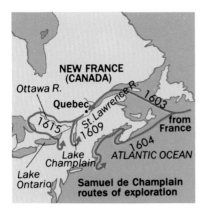

NEW FRANCE
(CANADA)
Ottawa R.
Quebec
St. Lawrence R.
1603
from
France
1615
1609
1604
Lake
Champlain
ATLANTIC OCEAN
Lake
Ontario
Samuel de Champlain
routes of exploration

▲ Samuel de Champlain's expeditions opened up valuable fur-trading routes into the heart of North America.

▶ Samuel de Champlain charted the course of the St. Lawrence River in 1603. A century later, when this map was made, more than 95 percent of all French settlers lived along the river.

tant to the security of the United States. It also conducts covert (secret) operations against the enemies of the United States. Many countries have similar agencies. Although Congress has to be informed about the work of the CIA, little information is made public.

The CIA was set up in 1947. Its headquarters are in Washington, D.C., but many CIA agents work overseas. The CIA also employs many foreign agents. While the CIA is important to U.S. security, not all its operations are successful. The failure of some has caused embarrassment to the government.

CHANDLER, Samuel de

CHAMPLAIN, Samuel de

Samuel de Champlain (1567?–1635) was a French navigator and explorer who founded the city of QUEBEC in Canada. He first visited North America in 1603, when he explored the ST. LAWRENCE SEAWAY. Later he explored the northeastern coast from Nova Scotia south to Cape Cod. In 1608 he set up a trading post at Quebec. Champlain managed to establish friendly relations with the local Algonquin and Huron Indians, which helped the settlement to prosper. In 1609, he discovered Lake Champlain. Three years later, he was appointed governor of French Canada. By the time Champlain died, the colony extended the length of the St. Lawrence River.

As Samuel de Champlain explored the St. Lawrence River, he had more than fur trading in mind. He was convinced that a Northwest Passage to Asia branched off the river.

One of Raymond Chandler's most famous thrillers, *The Big Sleep*, was made into a film in 1946 starring Humphrey Bogart. The script for the film, however, was written by another novelist, William Faulkner.

CHANDLER, Raymond

Raymond Chandler (1888–1959) was a leading writer of crime stories. The hero of his books was Philip Marlowe, a tough private eye. The stories are set in the seedy world of Los Angeles crime. Some of his best-known books include *The Big Sleep*, *The Long Goodbye*, and *Farewell, My Lovely*. Chandler also wrote a number of movie scripts, mostly based on his own books. Humphrey BOGART played Philip Marlowe in the movie *The Big Sleep*.

CHAPLIN, Charlie

Charlie Chaplin (1889–1977) was the most successful comedian in the age of silent movies. At the height of his fame in the 1920s, he was known and loved throughout the world for his portrayal of the Little Tramp in films such as *The Kid* and *The Gold Rush*. Later, Chaplin wrote, directed, and starred in a number of serious films. Charlie Chaplin was born in England. He came to the United States in 1910 where he lived until 1952. Chaplin died in Switzerland.

▲ A scene from The Gold Rush, one of Charlie Chaplin's best-known films.

CHEROKEES

The Cherokees are an INDIAN people who originally lived as farmers and hunters in what is now North Carolina and northern Georgia. Because colonists tried to take their land, the Cherokees sided with the British during the American REVOLUTION. Later, the Army

▼ The U.S. government offered the Cherokee nation $5.7 million to resettle in Oklahoma. More than 90 percent of the Cherokees refused, so troops were used to force them to move.

▲ *Chesapeake Bay's many harbors are ideal for pleasure boats. The bay is also an important source of seafood, particularly oysters and crabs.*

The Chesapeake Bay Retriever is the only retriever developed in the United States. According to legend, an English ship with dogs aboard was shipwrecked on the Maryland shore of the bay in 1807. The dogs were given by the ship's crew to their rescuers, and the new breed was developed from them.

forcibly removed some 15,000 Cherokees from their land and resettled them in Oklahoma. Four thousand died from disease, starvation, and the cold as they were made to march across the country during the brutal winter of 1838–1839. This terrible journey has become known as the "Trail of Tears." In Oklahoma the Cherokees, CHICKASAWS, CHOCTAWS, CREEKS, and SEMINOLES were known as the Five Civilized Tribes. There are more than 100,000 Cherokees today. Nearly half of them live in Oklahoma.

CHESAPEAKE BAY

Chesapeake Bay is an inlet of the Atlantic Ocean. It is 200 miles (320 km) long and is bounded by Virginia and Maryland. "Chesapeake" is an Algonquian word meaning "country on a big river." When John SMITH, who helped found JAMESTOWN SETTLEMENT, explored the bay in 1608, he said, "Heaven and earth never agreed better to frame a place for man's habitation." Several rivers, including the Potomac and Susquehanna, run into it. BALTIMORE, Maryland, and Norfolk, Virginia, are the two most important ports on the bay. The city of ANNAPOLIS, on the bay's western shore, is the site of the U.S. Naval Academy.

CHEVROLET, Louis

Louis Chevrolet (1879–1941) was an automobile racer and manufacturer. Born in Switzerland, he emigrated to the United States in 1900. Fascinated by cars, he became a racing driver. In his first race, in 1905, he defeated a famous American driver named Barney Oldfield, and he went on to set many speed records. He designed the first Chevrolet car in 1911.

▶ *Louis Chevrolet (with black hat and mustache) stands beside the* Frontenac, *the car he designed for the 1921 Indianapolis 500 automobile race. Tommy Milton (left) drove the* Frontenac *to victory that year. Another Chevrolet automobile had won the previous year's race.*

CHEYENNES

The Cheyennes are an important PLAINS INDIAN tribe. In 1851 they divided into two groups, the Northern and Southern Cheyennes. The Northern lived in South Dakota, the Southern along the Arkansas River. The Northern Cheyennes fiercely resisted white settlement. In 1876 they were at the Battle of the Little Bighorn, where General George CUSTER was killed. They were finally defeated. In 1884 the government granted them a reservation on the Tongue River in Montana. Today, several thousand still live there. The Southern Cheyennes have a reservation in Oklahoma.

▲ This Cheyenne man belongs to the Northern Cheyennes, who live on a reservation in Montana set up by the U.S. government in 1884.

◄ Chicago is the birthplace of the skyscraper. The John Hancock Center (top left) and the Standard Oil Building (top right) are two of the city's tallest buildings. The Sears Tower, also in Chicago but not shown in this picture, is the world's tallest building at 110 stories.

CHICAGO

Chicago, ILLINOIS, is the third largest city in the United States, with a population of almost 3 million. Situated on the southwestern shore of Lake Michigan, it is one of the most important transportation centers in the country. Vast quantities of industrial goods and raw materials flow through Chicago's huge railroad yards. Its O'Hare Airport is the busiest airport in the country. The city is also a major financial center. Chicago began as a trading settlement outside Fort Dearborn, which was built in 1803. It grew rich as a cattle town. A fire destroyed downtown Chicago in 1871, but the city was rebuilt and it became a major industrial center.

In 1871, Chicago was swept by a devastating fire that started in a barn and left almost 100,000 people homeless. In two days it caused tens of millions of dollars in damage. When the city was rebuilt, wooden buildings were replaced with stone ones.

▲ *The Chinooks were skillful fishermen. In this old photograph a Chinook is spearing salmon in the rapids of the Columbia River.*

▶ *Chipmunks are related to squirrels and woodchucks. They have large pouches in their cheeks to carry food. Their burrows are used for protection and food storage.*

The name Manitoba is thought to have come from the Chippewa Indian word *manitou*, meaning "Great Spirit." Wisconsin's name comes from a Chippewa word meaning "gathering of the waters."

CHINOOKS

The Chinooks were a tribe of INDIANS of the Pacific Northwest. They lived along the shores of the Columbia River in Washington and Oregon. In the past, the Chinooks lived simply, fishing mostly for salmon and gathering food from the forest. When European explorers seeking goods first came to the Northwest, the Chinooks traded with them. There are very few Indians of pure Chinook stock left; their descendants live mainly in the state of Washington.

CHIPMUNK

The chipmunk is a type of GROUND SQUIRREL. The eastern chipmunk is larger than the various types of western chipmunks. Chipmunks make a shrill chirping noise, and most types live in burrows they dig in the ground. Chipmunks are good climbers; they often climb trees and bushes looking for nuts, seeds, berries, and insects to eat. The food is carried in the large pouches in their cheeks, then stored in their burrows until they need it.

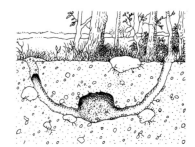

CHIPPEWAS

The Chippewas are one of the Great Lakes Algonquian INDIAN tribes. They originally lived around Lake Superior, in both the United States and Canada. (In Canada they are called the Ojibway or Ojibwa.) The Chippewas lived in small groups of houses. For their food they hunted, fished, and gathered wild rice. They have a history of conflict with the SIOUX. There is a record from 1678–79 of a Frenchman named Duluth negotiating a treaty between the two tribes. During the FRENCH AND INDIAN WARS the Chippewas supported the

French. Today they are active in many professions. Some Chippewas live on reservations in North Dakota and Minnesota.

 The Chippewas bent branches to make the frames for their wigwams. The outer layer was made from either birchbark or animal hides.

CHISHOLM, Shirley

Shirley Chisholm (1924–) was the first black woman to be elected to the U.S. House of Representatives. Born in Brooklyn, New York, she graduated from Brooklyn College and went on to get a master's degree from Columbia University. She served as an educational consultant to New York's Bureau of Child Welfare in the early 1960s. Her political career began in 1964, when she was elected, as a Democrat, to the New York State Assembly. Then in 1968 she was elected to the House of Representatives, where she served until 1983. She has promoted the rights of women and minorities.

CHOCTAWS

The Choctaws are an INDIAN tribe that originally lived in the region that is now Mississippi and Alabama. They were farmers and hunters. The Choctaws were among the tribes that were forced to move to Indian Territory (Oklahoma) in the 1830s. Almost a quarter of the Choctaws died before they reached the Indian Territory, and many more died after they arrived. During the CIVIL WAR, Choctaws fought on both sides of the conflict. The Choctaws have a long tradition of defending themselves and other tribes, and they were publicly

 Shirley Chisholm campaigned for the Democratic presidential nomination in 1972. Although she lost, she showed that a black woman could aim for the top job in the nation.

▲ George Catlin painted this scene of Choctaw Indians performing a ceremonial dance. Dances and ceremony played an important part in the cultural life of the Choctaws, whose original name was okla homa, meaning "red people."

Christian Churches in the U.S.	
Church	Membership
Roman Catholic	53,500,000
Baptist	26,101,500
Methodist	12,656,593
Lutheran	8,404,028
Orthodox	4,241,478
Latter-day Saints	4,194,286
Pentecostal	3,645,525
Episcopal	2,462,300
Holiness	1,212,757
Christian Churches and Churches of Christ	1,071,995
Jehovah's Witnesses	773,219
Church of Christ, Scientist	700,000
Adventist	696,194
Reformed	585,121
Salvation Army	434,002
Roman Rite	347,022
Mennonite	233,958
Unitarian Universalist Association	173,167
Friends (Quaker)	111,311
Brethren	100,162

active in the struggle for Indian rights that took place earlier this century. Today there are some 10,000 Choctaws. Most live on reservations in Oklahoma.

CHRISTIANITY

Christianity, the religion based on the teachings of Jesus Christ, is the major religion in the United States. Of the 250 million people in the United States, just under 60 percent belong to some religious group. Of these, more than 90 percent are members of a religious group that holds Christian beliefs.

The ROMAN CATHOLIC CHURCH is the largest single group (about 53.5 million). Its head is the Pope in Rome. In the United States there are 34 archdioceses (a district that comes under the control of an archbishop).

The second largest group is the BAPTISTS (over 26 million). METHODISTS number almost 13 million. Their beliefs are based on the teachings of John Wesley, a preacher in England in the 1700s. They baptize both infants and adults.

There are almost 8.5 million LUTHERANS in America. They follow the teachings set down by Martin Luther in Germany in the early 1500s. Episcopalians number about 2.5 million, but they are part of the larger Anglican Communion, which has many member churches throughout the world.

In addition, there are other significant Christian groups, including the Orthodox churches, the Pentecostals, the Presbyterians, the Church of Christ Disciples, and the United Church of Christ. Smaller groups include the Reformed churches, the MENNONITES (and Amish), the Society of Friends, and the Adventists. (See also PROTESTANTISM.)

▼ A church service in Tucson, Arizona, unites three generations of one family.

▼ Church weddings are solemn but happy occasions.

CHRISTIAN SCIENCE

Christian Science is a religious movement that was founded by Mary Baker EDDY (1821–1910). In 1879, in Boston, she founded what is called the Mother Church —The First Church of Christ, Scientist. This church is still the headquarters of the movement, which has now spread throughout the world.

Christian Science emphasizes healing by purely spiritual means. It holds that God is goodness. Sickness and evil mean that this goodness has temporarily been lost. People can regain the goodness by prayer. Christian Scientists believe that through reading God's word in the Bible, people can come closer to God and eventually destroy physical and spiritual illness. Christian Science beliefs are contained in Mrs. Eddy's book, *Science and Health with Key to the Scriptures*.

▼ The Mother Church in Boston's Christian Science Center is the headquarters of the Christian Science movement.

CIRCUS

A circus is a touring show with trained animals, clowns, acrobats, and other performers. Some circuses still perform under a large tent called the "Big Top." The various acts are performed in a round area, or ring.

▲ *Circus posters have always attracted audiences who are drawn to the spectacle of such daring acts as walking the tightwire.*

The first real circus in North America performed in 1793 in Philadelphia. President George Washington was one of the spectators. The most famous circuses were the Ringling Brothers Circus and the BARNUM & BAILEY Circus. At one time the Ringling Brothers Circus toured for six months of the year, covering 15,000 miles (24,000 km). The two circuses are now one; it performs in permanent indoor arenas.

Trained animals, clowns, and trapeze and tightwire artists are the most popular performers in a circus. In North America, many circuses begin with a big parade, or "spec" (for spectacle). All of the performers wear dazzling costumes and march around the arena as the band plays and the clowns entertain.

Large circuses that are still performed outside may have many smaller tents housing wild animals in cages. But the main show always takes place in the Big Top.

▶ *Modern circus animals are as highly trained as the human performers.*

City planning in English-speaking North America began in 1692 when William Penn worked out a plan for the city of Philadelphia. In 1807, town planners divided Upper Manhattan into 2,000 rectangular blocks, 200 feet (61 m) wide. This monotonous but convenient design became the pattern for many other U.S. cities.

CITIES

A city is a community in which large numbers of people live. The U.S. government defines a city as a community of more than 2,500 people having an agreed form of local government. In the United States, there are more than 2,300 cities with 10,000 or more people. About half of all Americans live in these communities.

People live in cities for many reasons. There are many kinds of businesses in cities, so many people work there. Cities are also cultural and recreational centers. City life, however, has many problems. Many cities have high pollution levels

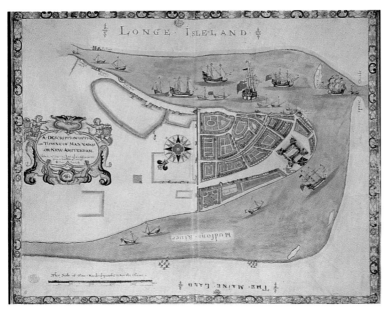

◄ *This map of the southern tip of Manhattan was drawn in 1664. In that same year it ceased to be Dutch New Amsterdam and became British New York.*

The 25 Largest Cities in the U.S.	
City	Population
New York, N.Y.	7,322,564
Los Angeles, Calif.	3,485,398
Chicago, Ill.	2,783,726
Houston, Tex.	1,630,553
Philadelphia, Pa.	1,585,577
San Diego, Calif.	1,110,549
Detroit, Mich.	1,027,974
Dallas, Tex.	1,006,877
Phoenix, Ariz.	983,403
San Antonio, Tex.	935,933
San Jose, Calif.	782,248
Indianapolis, Ind.	741,952
Baltimore, Md.	736,014
San Francisco, Calif.	723,959
Jacksonville, Fla.	672,971
Columbus, Ohio	632,910
Milwaukee, Wis.	628,088
Memphis, Tenn.	610,337
Washington, D.C.	606,900
Boston, Mass.	574,283
Seattle, Wash.	516,259
El Paso, Tex.	515,342
Nashville-Davidson, Tenn.	510,784
Cleveland, Ohio	505,616
New Orleans, La.	496,938

caused by traffic and factories. Noise, crime, and racial conflicts also detract from the quality of life. The lack of decent housing is another problem.

Because of these problems, many people have moved away from cities to the surrounding suburbs. Others have moved from the older cities of the North to developing cities in the South and the Southwest, in the area called the Sunbelt.

ST. AUGUSTINE, Florida, is the oldest city in North America. It was founded by the Spanish in 1565. The next cities to be established were BOSTON, New Amsterdam (which became NEW YORK), PHILADELPHIA, and BALTIMORE. Today, New York is the country's largest city. It has 7.4 million people. LOS ANGELES has 3.4 million, and CHICAGO has almost 3 million.

The national population census of 1920 was a turning point in U.S. history. It marked the first time that city dwellers outnumbered rural residents.

◄ *Cincinnati's location along the Ohio River made it a bustling port during the 1800s. Today it is a major industrial center.*

▼ Many pickers are needed to harvest the oranges grown around Bakersfield in California. Much is still done by hand.

▼ The United States produces many types of citrus fruit. They are all rich in Vitamin C.

CITIZENSHIP

A citizen is a full member of a country. By holding citizenship, a person is entitled to certain rights and privileges. A citizen also has certain duties and obligations. U.S. citizens, for example, have the right to vote beginning at the age of 18 and the right to protection while living abroad. In return, they owe allegiance to the U.S. government. In the event of war, they may have to serve in the armed forces.

The Fourteenth Amendment to the U.S. Constitution states that all persons born in the United States are citizens. (Children whose parents are foreign diplomats are exceptions.) People not born in the United States can become naturalized citizens. This is a legal process in which the person swears allegiance to the United States and gives up loyalty to his or her country of birth. Naturalized citizens have the same rights and duties as other citizens. They may not, however, become president or vice president.

CITRUS FRUIT

Citrus fruits have thick rinds with juicy pulp inside. They grow on trees in warm regions. Citrus fruits include oranges, grapefruits, and lemons. Less well known citrus fruits include the mandarin, kumquat, and tangelo.

The United States is the world's leading grower of citrus fruits. Florida produces about two thirds of the sweet oranges and grapefruits grown in the United States. The Dancy tangerine is the most important type of mandarin grown in Florida. California and Arizona are also important grapefruit producers, and California produces more fresh lemons than anywhere else in the United States.

Orange

Lemon

Grapefruit

Lime

Kumquat

Tangerine

CIVIL RIGHTS

Civil rights are those rights guaranteed to an individual by law and custom. The American BILL OF RIGHTS, for example, guarantees freedom of speech and religion. It also guarantees a free press, the right to own property, and the right to a speedy trial by jury.

BLACK AMERICANS were long denied many civil rights. The Thirteenth Amendment to the U.S. Constitution abolished slavery. The Fourteenth Amendment made blacks citizens, and the Fifteenth Amendment gave black men the right to vote. Still, many states kept blacks from voting. And in the late 1800s, many states passed laws that required the segregation (separation) of races in everything from transportation to schools. In 1896 the Supreme Court ruled that "separate but equal" facilities were constitutional.

In 1954, however, the Supreme Court ruled that separate facilities were, by their very nature, unequal and therefore unconstitutional. This ruling launched the civil rights movement of the 1950s and 1960s. In 1957 the government set up a Commission on Civil Rights. And the Civil Rights Act of 1964 banned discrimination in public places and in employment. Other minorities, such as the elderly and the handicapped, have also relied on these laws to preserve their rights.

Women in the United States also have suffered from discrimination. They fought for many years before the Nineteenth Amendment to the Constitution gave them the right to vote in 1920. The Civil Rights Act of 1964 protects them, as well as blacks, from job discrimination. The women's movement continues to fight for WOMEN'S RIGHTS.

CIVIL SERVICE

People who work for the government and are not in the military and not elected to office are in the civil service. These people are called civil servants. Civil servants work for the federal, state, and local governments. They carry out the everyday work of the government. More than 3 million people work for the federal government, and almost 14 million people work for state and local governments. Almost three fourths of the people the federal government employs work for the Department of Defense and the Postal Service.

▲ Neighborhood rallies and marches help keep civil rights issues in the public eye.

Some Important Dates in Civil Rights Legislation

1791 The first ten amendments to the Constitution, now known as the Bill of Rights, become law.
1865 The Thirteenth Amendment abolishes slavery in the U.S.
1868 The Fourteenth Amendment grants citizenship to all former slaves.
1870 The Fifteenth Amendment prohibits all states from denying a person the vote because of his race.
1920 The Nineteenth Amendment gives women the right to vote.
1955 The U.S. Supreme Court orders all schools to desegregate with "all deliberate speed."
1957 The Commission on Civil Rights is set up to investigate charges of denial of civil rights.
1964 The Civil Rights Act prohibits discrimination on the basis of race, color, religion, natural origin, or sex. The Equal Employment Opportunity Commission is set up.
1969 The Supreme Court orders schools to desegregate.

CIVIL WAR

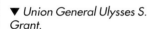

◄ *This recruiting poster offers a $100 bounty (award), payable at the end of the war.*

▲ *The attack on Fort Sumter in South Carolina triggered the Civil War.*

▼ *Union General Ulysses S. Grant.*

The Civil War (1861–1865) was fought between the northern states (the Union) and those southern states (the Confederacy) that had seceded, or withdrawn, from the Union. The war was fought over the issues of states' rights and slavery. The southern states believed that they had the right to make their own laws without interference by the federal government—especially laws that had to do with slavery. They needed slaves to work on their large farms, or plantations, and felt that the southern economy would be ruined if slaves were freed. Many Northerners wanted to abolish, or end, slavery.

When Abraham Lincoln was elected president in 1860, the South feared that he would abolish slavery. Beginning in December 1860, 11 southern states seceded. They formed the Confederate States of America.

Major Battles of the Civil War				
Battle	Date	Location	Total Casualties	Victory
Bull Run				
First	1861	Virginia	4,600	Confederate
Second	1862	Virginia	25,300	Confederate
Shiloh	1862	Tennessee	23,700	Union
Antietam (Sharpsburg)	1862	Maryland	26,100	Union
Fredericksburg	1862	Virginia	17,900	Confederate
Chancellorsville	1863	Virginia	30,000	Confederate
Vicksburg, Siege of	1863	Mississippi	17,400	Union
Gettysburg	1863	Pennsylvania	43,400	Union
Chickamauga	1863	Georgia	34,000	Confederate
Wilderness	1864	Virginia	25,400	Union
Petersburg, Siege of	1864	Virginia	70,000	Union

During the Civil War, more than twice as many soldiers died of diseases such as typhoid, malaria, and dysentery than were killed in battle. The North lost 364,000 soldiers (about one in five); the South lost 258,000 soldiers (about one in four).

▶ The Battle of Chickamauga, fought in Georgia in 1863, was the Confederacy's last important victory in the war.

The war started on April 12, 1861, when Confederate troops fired on Fort Sumter, South Carolina. The Confederates won a number of victories early in the war. In July 1863, however, the tide turned at the Battle of Gettysburg in Pennsylvania. This Confederate defeat was followed by others, and in the fall of 1864 Union General William T. Sherman captured Atlanta, Georgia. He followed this victory with a "march to the sea," during which he destroyed much of the countryside. On April 9, 1865, Confederate General Robert E. Lee surrendered to Grant.

The cost of the Civil War was staggering. More than 600,000 Americans died—almost as many as in all other American wars combined. But the Union was preserved. See also BOOTH, John Wilkes; BULL RUN; CONFEDERATE STATES OF AMERICA; EMANCIPATION PROCLAMATION; GETTYSBURG, Battle of; GRANT, Ulysses S.; LEE, Robert E.; LINCOLN, Abraham; SHERMAN, William Tecumseh.

The photographs of wounded soldiers (left) and Confederate General Robert E. Lee (right) were taken by Mathew Brady. He was a pioneer of photography and took more than 3,500 pictures of Civil War battles and camp life. Some were posed portraits of officers, but most showed ordinary soldiers in terrible conditions.

▲ *These butter clams have been gathered from mudflats along the Pacific Northwest coast. Clams suck in water and filter it for food.*

▼ *In 1779, George Rogers Clark forced the British to surrender Fort Sackville, which controlled the town of Vincennes.*

CLAM

A clam is a saltwater shellfish. There are more than 12,000 species of clams worldwide. Clams are called bivalves. They have two shells, called valves, held together by a type of hinge called a ligament. Several types of clams are collected for eating in the United States. The most popular Pacific variety is the long and narrow razor clam. Atlantic soft-shell clams are fried, steamed, or used in thick soup called chowder. They are found mainly along muddy New England beaches. The shells of hard-shell clams, called quahogs, were made into wampum, a type of money used by ALGONQUIN Indians.

CLARK, George Rogers

George Rogers Clark (1752–1818) was a soldier and frontier leader during the American REVOLUTION. Clark was born in Virginia and settled in what is now Kentucky.

When war broke out, Clark obtained permission from Virginia's governor, Patrick HENRY, to organize troops for the defense of the frontier. In 1778 his forces, numbering about 175, marched through the wilderness and captured the British posts of Kaskaskia and Cahokia, on the Mississippi River. The following year, they took Vincennes, in Indiana. Because promised reinforcements failed to arrive, Clark had to abandon his conquests. But these victories ensured that this area, then called the Northwest Territory, was given to the United States by Britain after the Revolution.

CLAY, Henry

Henry Clay (1777–1852) was one of the ablest political leaders during the years before the CIVIL WAR. He ran for president three times but was never elected. However, he made his mark in other ways. 'Clay represented Kentucky in the House of Representatives and the Senate for many years, first as a Jeffersonian Republican and then as a Whig. He also served as secretary of state under John Quincy ADAMS.

Clay is best remembered for steering through Congress a series of compromises that held the Union together in the stormy years before the Civil War.

Because of his work, Clay became known as the Great Compromiser. In the Missouri Compromise (1820), Missouri was admitted to the Union as a slave state with Maine as a free state. This preserved the existing balance between slave and free states. Clay's compromise tariff of 1833 managed to prevent South Carolina from leaving the Union. Two years before he died, Clay authored the Compromise of 1850. This series of laws admitted California as a free state but made concessions to the South that helped to postpone the Civil War for another 11 years.

CLEMENS, Samuel L. *See* Twain, Mark

CLEVELAND

Cleveland is the second largest city in OHIO, with a population of more than 505,000. It is located on the southern shore of Lake Erie and is a major Great Lakes port and transportation center. Founded in 1796, Cleveland prospered in the 1900s because of its steelworks and became one of the largest cities in the Midwest. Today, it is an important center for the manufacture of automobile parts, machine tools, plastics, and paints. Downtown Cleveland today is modern and busy, with fine buildings and parks. In 1967, with the election of Carl Stokes, Cleveland became the first major U.S. city to have a black mayor.

▲ Henry Clay was known in the Senate as the Great Compromiser because he understood both the North and the South. The Civil War might have been prevented if he had lived longer.

Cleveland's role as an industrial leader was confirmed during the Civil War. The city's iron ore and coal were mined for steel production. This was to meet the Union's growing demands for railroad equipment, heavy machinery, and ships.

◀ Cleveland is an important Great Lakes port. It is also the home of one football team, the Cleveland Browns (NFL), one baseball team, the Cleveland Indians (AL), and the Cleveland Symphony, one of the nation's leading orchestras.

Grover Cleveland
Born: March 18, 1837, in Caldwell, New Jersey
Education: Left school at 14; legal training
Political party: Democratic
Terms of office: 1885–1889 and 1893–1897
Married: 1886 to Frances Folsom
Died: June 24, 1908, in Princeton, New Jersey

▶ *France's gift of the Statue of Liberty in 1886 was a highlight of the Cleveland presidency.*

▼ *Frances Folsom was 21 years old when she married Grover Cleveland. He was 49. The wedding was held in the White House.*

Grover Cleveland was president of the United States twice. These two separate terms of office meant that he was both the 22nd and 24th president. Cleveland, a lawyer, had been mayor of Buffalo, New York, and then governor of New York. He was the first Democrat to be elected president in 28 years.

After his election in 1884, Cleveland maintained his record of honesty and integrity. He proved that he was not afraid to do what he considered right even if it made him unpopular. One of his aims was to reduce the very high tariff (tax on imported goods) that was creating economic problems. However, the Republican-controlled Senate resisted this. In 1888, Cleveland lost the election to the Republican candidate, Benjamin HARRISON, but in 1892 he won by a large margin.

Early in his second term there was a severe economic

depression. Cleveland wanted to end the issuing of silver (rather than gold) money, which he believed would cause inflation (rising prices). But the measures he took upset the supporters of silver. Cleveland had other problems as well. In 1894 police broke up a march of the unemployed on Washington. During a railroad strike in Chicago, Cleveland sent in federal troops.

During this term, British Guiana and Venezuela were involved in a boundary dispute. Cleveland warned the British that their claims went against the MONROE DOCTRINE. Finally, they backed down.

Because of Cleveland's support for the gold standard and for a lower tariff, the Democrats did not renominate him in 1896.

 The builders of the Mesa Verde cliff dwellings used the rocky overhang and the caves to keep the apartments shady and cool.

CLIFF DWELLERS

The cliff dwellers were INDIAN tribes in the Southwest who lived in caves or homes built in cliff overhangs. Eventually these homes were built in layers on top of each other, so that the cliff wall looked like a strange apartment complex. The only way to reach the homes was by a ladder that was taken away when not in use to protect the Indians from attack. There were watchtowers from which possible invaders could be seen. The cliff complexes also had large, decorated underground rooms called *kivas* that were used as community meeting places and for special ceremonies.

The best known of the cliff dwellers were the Anasazi Indians. They were the ancestors of the PUEBLO Indians. The Anasazi abandoned their cliff dwellings about A.D. 1300. The Cliff Palace at Mesa Verde in Colorado has over 200 rooms and 23 kivas. It is a United States National Park.

CLIMATE

The climate is an average of weather conditions occurring over several decades. The United States, with its vast area, contains examples of the main types of world climates. At one extreme is the wet, semi-tropical climate, seen mainly in the Hawaiian Islands and southern Florida. Annual rainfall in that climate often exceeds 100 inches (250 cm). At the other extreme are the polar climates of northern Alaska. Here winter temperatures

▼ Information collected by weather stations and satellites provides an accurate picture of temperature patterns across the country.

Average January temperatures

	Degrees Fahrenheit	Degrees Celsius
	Over 60	Over 16
	45 to 60	7 to 16
	30 to 45	−1 to 7
	15 to 30	−9 to −1
	0 to 15	−18 to −9
	−15 to 0	−26 to −18
	Below −15	Below −26

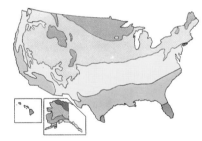

Average July temperatures

	Degrees Fahrenheit	Degrees Celsius
	Over 90	Over 32
	75 to 90	24 to 32
	60 to 75	16 to 24
	45 to 60	7 to 16
	Below 45	Below 7

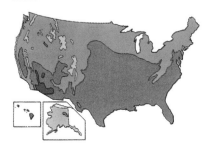

dip below −50°F (−45°C). Arizona, New Mexico, and eastern California are arid. Rainfall can be less than 10 inches (25 cm) a year, and summer temperatures soar to 120°F (50°C). The MOJAVE and other DESERTS are in this region. By contrast, the coasts of Washington and Oregon, in the northwest, are among the rainiest places in the United States. Most of the United States, however, has a temperate climate. There is regular rainfall and temperatures are not extreme during most of the year.

COAL See Mining Industry

COAST GUARD, U.S.

The U.S. Coast Guard is a branch of the armed services. It does exactly what its name suggests: it guards the coasts of the United States. This involves it in many different duties, but the purpose of them all is the same: to ensure that U.S. maritime laws are enforced and that all kinds of ships can go about their business safely. In many ways, members of the Coast Guard are the police of the sea.

Among the Coast Guard's most important jobs are

▲ The U.S. Coast Guard dates from 1790, when it was called the Revenue Marine. Its job at that time was to fight pirates and smugglers.

▼ The prompt arrival of a Coast Guard vessel can prevent a boating accident from becoming a tragedy.

helping in emergencies and arresting smugglers. But its many day-to-day tasks include maintaining navigational aids such as buoys and lighthouses, reporting weather for the National Weather Service, and overseeing safety regulations for every kind of seagoing vessel. Almost 40,000 people work for the Coast Guard, and it has hundreds of different ships, from small motorboats to large cutters. The Coast Guard was founded in 1790. It is part of the Department of Transportation. During a war, however, the Coast Guard operates under the Department of the Navy.

COCHISE

Cochise (1812?–1874) was a great chief of the Chiricahua APACHES, an Indian tribe that lived in what are now New Mexico and Arizona. In 1861 he and his people were mistakenly accused of stealing and of kidnapping a white child. Cochise denied the charges, but he was imprisoned. He escaped, taking some hostages because the Army was holding some of his relatives. Eventually both sides killed their hostages. A war broke out that involved other tribes and led to great loss of life over a number of years.

At first, attempts at settlement failed because of mutual distrust and massacres by the whites. In 1872, General Oliver Howard, with the help of Thomas Jeffords, a frontiersman, finally negotiated peace with Cochise. Chief Cochise died before his tribe was moved to the Chiricahua reservation in Arizona. Jeffords became the Indian agent.

COCHRAN, Jacqueline

Jacqueline Cochran (1910?–1980) was a famous aviator. During her career she held more flying records than anyone else. In 1938 she set two speed records and became the first woman to win the Bendix Transcontinental Air Race. During World War II, Cochran organized the Women Airforce Service Pilots (WASPS). In 1953, she broke the men's and women's world speed records. She later became the first woman to fly faster than the speed of sound and to fly at *twice* the speed of sound. In 1961 Cochrane broke her 1953 world speed record. In 1964 she flew an airplane faster than any woman ever had, at 1,429 miles (2,300 km) per hour.

A remarkable friendship grew between the Apache Indian chief Cochise and a mail contractor, Thomas Jeffords. In an attempt to stop some of the violence between his couriers and the Apaches, Jeffords met with Cochise alone and the two men declared peace, although the war with the settlers went on. When Cochise signed the treaty that ended his raids in exchange for a reservation, he insisted that Thomas Jeffords be appointed the Indian agent.

▼ The pilot Jacqueline Cochran was the first civilian woman to be awarded the Distinguished Service Medal.

CODY, William F.

William F. Cody (1846–1917), better known as "Buffalo Bill," was a frontier scout and showman. Cody led an adventurous life. He carried mail for the PONY EXPRESS and was a scout for the Union during the CIVIL WAR. He became a buffalo hunter and was credited with having killed 4,000, a feat that led to his nickname. After a brief time as an Army scout and Indian fighter, he began a career as an entertainer. He eventually formed a company called "Buffalo Bill's Wild West Show." The show toured the United States and Canada and even performed in Europe. During the show, Buffalo Bill reenacted some of his legendary exploits against the Indians and demonstrated his skill as a marksman. The city of Cody, Wyoming, is named after him.

Buffalo Bill Cody's Wild West Shows were more popular with easterners and Europeans than with natives of the American West itself. His first show, at Omaha, Nebraska, in 1883, was only a partial success. Many customers complained about paying for action they could normally see for free.

▶ Buffalo Bill's Wild West Show included other legendary figures, such as Calamity Jane and the Apache chief Geronimo.

COHAN, George M.

George M. Cohan (1878–1942) wrote many famous songs and plays. He was born in Providence, Rhode Island. As a child he performed in a vaudeville act with his family and began writing when he was a teenager. He also acted in plays and produced them. He was a well-known figure on BROADWAY. The 1942 movie *Yankee Doodle Dandy* and the 1968 musical *George M!* were about his life. Some of Cohan's most famous songs are "You're a Grand Old Flag," "Give My Regards to Broadway," and "I'm a Yankee Doodle Dandy." He was given a special medal by Congress for his World War I song "Over There." His best-known performances were in *Ah, Wilderness!* and *I'd Rather Be Right*.

Written on April 6, 1917, the day the United States declared war against Germany and entered World War I, the song "Over There" by George M. Cohan was an immediate hit. Its stirring words, "The Yanks are coming," probably made it one of the most inspiring calls-to-arms ever written.

COINS

The United States issues more than 15 billion coins each year. The coins are produced in the federal mints in Philadelphia, Denver, and San Francisco. Individual states cannot issue their own coins. Six types of coins are in current use: the cent (penny), 5-cents (nickel), 10-cents (dime), 25-cents (quarter), 50-cents (half-dollar), and dollar. Nearly 173 billion coins are in circulation, including 129 billion pennies, 11.5 billion nickels, 16.4 billion dimes, and 15.6 billion quarters. Many other U.S. coins, such as the half-cent and the $20 gold piece, are no longer produced.

▼ Coins commemorate famous people and places, such as presidents Washington, Lincoln, and Roosevelt, and Jefferson's home, Monticello.

COLD WAR

The term Cold War describes the tension between democratic and Communist countries that began after

◄ The friendly relations between President Ronald Reagan and Soviet leader Mikhail Gorbachev helped reduce Cold War tensions in the late 1980s.

▲ *This commencement ceremony at State University of New York at Stony Brook is one of thousands that take place each spring in the United States.*

The 10 Oldest Universities and Colleges in the U.S.	
University	Founded
Harvard University, Cambridge, Mass.	1636
College of William and Mary, Williamsburg, Va.	1693
Yale University, New Haven, Conn.	1701
University of Pennsylvania, Philadelphia, Pa.	1740
Princeton University, Princeton, N.J.	1746
Washington and Lee University, Lexington, Va.	1749
Columbia University, New York, N.Y.	1754
Brown University, Providence, R.I.	1764
Rutgers, The State University of New Jersey, New Brunswick, N.J.	1766
Dartmouth College, Hanover, N.H.	1769

▶ *College courses in science and engineering make use of fully equipped laboratories.*

WORLD WAR II. The United States and its allies in the West felt threatened by the Soviet Union's efforts to promote Communism and extend its control and influence around the world. Both sides built up large military arsenals. Actual fighting, or "hot war," nearly broke out over a number of incidents, including the CUBAN MISSILE CRISIS of 1962. In addition, conflicts such as the KOREAN WAR and the VIETNAM WAR were seen as part of the effort to contain Communism. The Cold War seemed to end in 1990. Soviet leader Mikhail Gorbachev allowed the Communist countries of Eastern Europe to elect democratic governments. And U.S.–Soviet relations improved dramatically.

COLLEGES AND UNIVERSITIES

Colleges and universities are schools where students go to continue their education after they graduate from high school. Students may go to a four-year college or to a two-year junior, or community, college.

The oldest university in the United States is Harvard University. It was founded in 1636. Today there are more than 3,400 colleges and universities in the country. About 12.5 million students are enrolled in these schools, including 350,000 foreign students. More than three quarters of all students go to public schools, those sponsored by local and state governments and the federal government. The average cost of tuition and

◄ Some college classes are conducted in an informal manner, even outdoors if the weather permits.

room and board at a four-year public school is about $4,600 per year for state residents and $7,400 per year for nonresidents. About one quarter of all students attend private colleges and universities. The average cost per year at these institutions is $11,000, but some can cost as much as $20,000.

More than 1.3 million degrees are awarded each year; 75 percent of these are bachelor's degrees, and 22 percent are master's degrees. More than 33,000 doctoral degrees are earned each year. For many students, a higher education is a means to getting a good job, which is why more people earn business degrees than any other kind.

Students who want to go to college take national tests called SATs (Scholastic Aptitude Tests) and ACTs (American College Tests). The results show how good a student's basic skills are. Some colleges also give an entrance examination of their own.

10 Most Popular Majors
Business administration
Accounting
Elementary education
Management
Psychology
Political science
Communications
Electrical engineering
Marketing
Premedicine, predental,
preveterinary

COLLINS, Michael

Michael Collins (1930–) was the astronaut who piloted the command module during the Apollo 11 mission to the moon in July 1969. Collins remained in the command module, circling the moon, while Neil ARMSTRONG and Edwin ALDRIN landed on the moon's surface in the lunar module.

Before the Apollo 11 mission, Collins was the co-pilot of the Gemini 10 flight, with John Young, in July 1966. During this flight he walked in space. In 1971, Collins became the director of the National Air and Space Museum in Washington, D.C.

▼ During the Apollo 11 mission, Michael Collins manned the command module Columbia while Neil Armstrong and Buzz Aldrin made their historic landing on the moon.

151

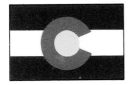

Lark bunting

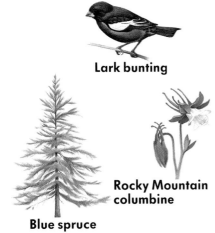

Rocky Mountain columbine

Blue spruce

Colorado is known as the Centennial State. This is because it became a state in 1876, 100 years after the signing of the Declaration of Independence. Colorado is one of the ROCKY MOUNTAIN states. Over half the state is ruggedly mountainous. The eastern part of the state, which is flatter, forms the western edge of the Great Plains. These plains are where most of Colorado's people live, especially in and around the city of DENVER, the capital and largest city.

Towering mountains make Colorado one of the most dramatically beautiful states in the country. In winter, visitors come to ski at famous resorts such as Aspen and Vail. In summer, they come to walk, camp, hunt and fish, and to admire the scenery. Tourism is one of the most important businesses in Colorado.

The eastern part of Colorado became part of the United States in 1803, as part of the LOUISIANA PURCHASE. After the western half was taken from Mexico in 1848, settlers began to flock to the area.

▶ *Pikes Peak, in Colorado's eastern Rockies, was one of the most famous landmarks for the wagon trains of the pioneers. It is named for Zebulon Pike, the explorer who first traveled through there in the early 1800s.*

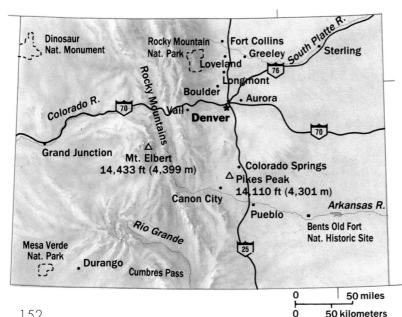

Colorado
Capital: Denver
Area: 103,595 sq mi (268,290 km²). Rank: 8th
Population: 3,307,912 (1990). Rank: 26th
Statehood: August 1, 1876
Principal rivers: Colorado, South Platte, Arkansas
Highest point: Mt. Elbert, 14,433 ft (4,399 m)
Motto: *Nil Sine Numine* (Nothing Without Providence)
Song: "Where the Columbines Grow"

0   50 miles
0   50 kilometers

Many were drawn by tales of gold in its mountains. Through the 1850s, the population swelled rapidly and many mining communities were founded.

Gold and silver are still mined in Colorado, and Denver is the site of a U.S. Mint, where COINS are produced, or minted. But today petroleum is the state's most important mineral. Many oil companies are based in Denver. Other industries include finance and manufacturing, especially in Denver. Colorado is an important agricultural state, too. Cattle and sheep are raised all over the state, and wheat is grown on the plains.

Places of Interest
● Mesa Verde National Park, near Cortez, has Indian cliff dwellings that are almost a thousand years old.
● The U.S. Mint, in Denver, produces millions of coins every year.
● Bent's Old Fort, near La Junta, is a reconstruction of a trading post originally completed in 1833. The fort was Colorado's first permanent settlement.

▶ *The Garden of the Gods is a colorful rock formation created by volcanoes more than 50 million years ago.*

▼ *A covered bridge leads to the famous ski resort of Vail. Thousands of skiers, including former president Gerald Ford, prefer Colorado snow because it is dry and powdery.*

▲ Dams in four states harness the waters of the Colorado River. The dams provide irrigation for farming and reduce erosion caused by the river.

▶ The Powell Expedition of 1869 (right) explored the Colorado River through the Grand Canyon. Over millions of years, the waters of the river have eaten through the layers of surrounding rock to create deep canyons with vertical walls (far right).

▼ The famous Lewis and Clark Expedition followed the Columbia River to reach the Pacific Ocean in 1805. For nearly three weeks they braved dangerous rapids and hostile Indians along the Columbia River.

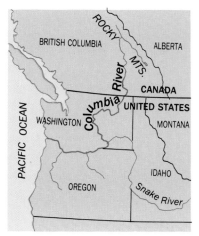

COLORADO RIVER

The Colorado River is one of the longest rivers in the United States. It is along the Colorado River, in Arizona, that the GRAND CANYON, America's most famous natural wonder, is located. The Colorado River is 1,450 miles (2,333 km) long. It flows southwest from the Rocky Mountains through Colorado, Utah, and Arizona to the Gulf of California in Mexico. Seven other rivers flow into it, including the Little Colorado River and the Gila River. A number of DAMS have been built across the Colorado River to regulate its flow and to provide power for electricity. The most famous is the Hoover Dam, built by the federal government in 1936.

COLUMBIA RIVER

The Columbia River is one of the longest and most important rivers in North America. It flows north through British Columbia in Canada and then south to Washington state before heading west to the Pacific Ocean. This westernmost section of the river forms most of the border between Washington and Oregon. Portland, Oregon's most important port, is on the Williamette River, a tributary of the Columbia. In all, the river is 1,243 miles (2,000 km) long. The Columbia River is the single largest source of electricity in the northwestern United States. Thirteen huge DAMS have been built on the river. The largest is the Grand Coulee Dam, in Washington. It provides more electricity than any other power plant in the country.

COLUMBUS

Columbus, the capital of OHIO, is located on the Scioto River near the center of the state. This central location was the main reason the site was chosen as the state capital. Construction began in 1812 and Columbus became the capital in 1816. About 632,900 people live in the city today. The state government employs many people in Columbus, but even more work in the manufacturing industries there. Heavy machinery such as coal-mining equipment is produced, as well as paints, shoes, refrigerators, and many other household items. Columbus was one of the first U.S. cities to recognize environmental problems. Since 1952 the city's downtown area has been redeveloped, new housing has been built, and tough anti-pollution laws have been enacted.

▲ The Columbus Civic Center has a riverside location. It contains city and state government buildings and the 555-foot (168-m) Lincoln–Leveque Tower.

COLUMBUS, Christopher

Christopher Columbus (1451–1506) was a great explorer and seaman. Born in Genoa, in Italy, he sailed for the Spanish King Ferdinand and Queen Isabella. In 1492 Columbus made the historic voyage in which he reached the New World.

Columbus had become convinced that it would be possible to reach Asia by sailing west from Europe in-

▼ Columbus sought honors and riches so that his descendants would be spared the poverty he faced as a child in Genoa.

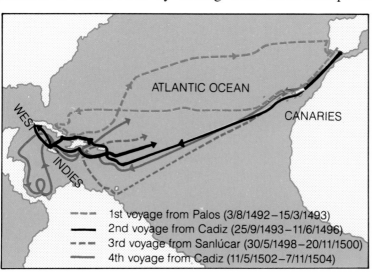

ATLANTIC OCEAN

WEST INDIES

CANARIES

- - - 1st voyage from Palos (3/8/1492–15/3/1493)
—— 2nd voyage from Cadiz (25/9/1493–11/6/1496)
- - - 3rd voyage from Sanlúcar (30/5/1498–20/11/1500)
—— 4th voyage from Cadiz (11/5/1502–7/11/1504)

◄ Christopher Columbus made four voyages to the Americas between 1492 and 1504. He explored the islands of the Caribbean as well as the coast of Central and South America.

155

stead of east. He set out in 1492 with three small ships, the *Santa Maria*, the *Niña*, and the *Pinta*, and a crew of 90. The first land he reached was an island in the Bahamas, southeast of Florida. But Columbus was sure he had reached Asia. On later voyages he discovered other Caribbean islands and parts of Central and South America, while searching for gold. He founded several Spanish colonies in these lands. But his inability to get along with people involved him in several conflicts, and the Spanish monarchs took away his command. He died less than two years after he returned to Spain from his fourth voyage. But his voyages opened up the settlement of the Western Hemisphere.

COMANCHES

The Comanches are an INDIAN tribe that originally lived on the southern Great Plains. Their skill with horses made them successful hunters of buffalo. The Comanches often raided other tribes to obtain horses and slaves. Beginning in the 1700s, the Comanches fought to keep white settlers out of their lands. When the Americans tried to restrict the Comanches to land in southwestern Oklahoma, war broke out. The Texas Rangers were formed to control the Comanches, but they did not have much success at first. In 1858 the Rangers started a major campaign against the tribe. The Comanches finally surrendered in 1875. Chief QUANAH PARKER led his people to the reservation. Today thousands of Comanches live on a reservation in Oklahoma.

▼ *In this painting by George Catlin a Comanche ropes a wild stallion. The Comanches were skilled riders and depended on horses for hunting buffalo.*

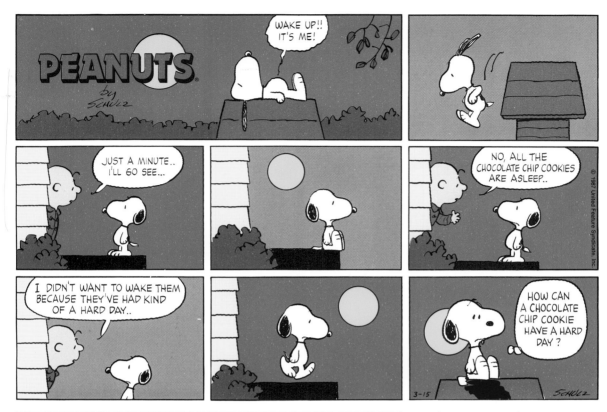

Speech bubbles within the comic:
WAKE UP!! IT'S ME!
JUST A MINUTE.. I'LL GO SEE...
NO, ALL THE CHOCOLATE CHIP COOKIES ARE ASLEEP..
I DIDN'T WANT TO WAKE THEM BECAUSE THEY'VE HAD KIND OF A HARD DAY..
HOW CAN A CHOCOLATE CHIP COOKIE HAVE A HARD DAY ?

COMICS

Comic strips have been a popular feature of newspapers for nearly a century. A strip is a series of several cartoons. Comic books developed as collections of comic strips. The first comic strips, nicknamed the "funnies," appeared in newspapers in the 1890s. William Randolph HEARST's *New York Journal* introduced the first color comic pages in 1896. The Golden Age of comic art lasted from then until World War II, with millions of readers following their favorite cartoons each day. Superheroes such as Superman, Spiderman, and Batman were created in the 1930s as an escape from the hard times of the Great DEPRESSION. Television lessened demand somewhat, but in the 1960s a small group of artists, such as Roy Lichtenstein, claimed that comics were true modern art. The tradition of the funnies continues with Peanuts, Garfield, and Doonesbury.

COMMUNICATIONS INDUSTRY

The size of the United States has always made it important to convey information as fast as possible. There was no real communications industry until after Samuel

▲ The "Peanuts" characters were originally called "Li'l Folks" by their creator, Charles Schulz. The strip appears in newspapers in more than 60 countries.

▼ Communications satellites such as Telstar use electronic equipment to increase the strength of telephone signals.

157

Some Important Dates in History of American Communication

1673	The first regular mail service in the colonies begins between Boston and New York City.
1704	The *Boston News-Letter* is the first regularly produced newspaper in the colonies.
1844	Samuel F. B. Morse sends the first telegraph message from Washington, D.C., to Baltimore, Maryland.
1858	The first successful transatlantic telegraph cable is laid.
1860	The Pony Express begins.
1861	The first transcontinental telegraph service is completed at Salt Lake City, Utah.
1876	Alexander Graham Bell patents the first telephone.
1918	The first scheduled airmail service begins between Washington, D.C., and New York City.
1919	The Radio Corporation of America is established.
1946	Start of the television boom in the United States. By 1960, almost every household will own a television set.
1965	America launches the Early Bird satellite over the Atlantic to relay telephone and television signals between the U.S. and Europe.
1980	*The Columbus Dispatch* of Columbus, Ohio, becomes the first electronic newspaper. It can transmit some of its contents directly to office and home computers.
1980s	Satellite broadcasting widens the choice of television channels and programs.

The speed of communication has increased enormously over the past hundred years. It has been estimated that within 35 minutes after the assassination of President John F. Kennedy in 1963, more than 90 percent of the U.S. population had received the news. It took over eight months for the same proportion of the public to learn of President Abraham Lincoln's assassination in 1865.

MORSE invented the telegraph in 1837. Alexander Graham BELL's telephone, invented in 1876, took instant communications a step further. The first long-distance telephone lines between New York City and Chicago were opened in 1892.

This century has seen these inventions develop into multimillion-dollar industries. New developments in electronics, such as computers and microchips, make communications systems cheaper and more efficient.

Broadcasting, which includes RADIO and TELEVISION, is a branch of communications. Cellular telephones, used in automobiles, ships, and airplanes, broadcast using radio waves. And early in the next century, communications experts expect that videophones will allow people to see each other on television screens while they talk on the telephone.

▶ *Fiber-optic technology was introduced in 1980. It is the latest development in communications. Telephone messages travel on laser beams along fine strands of glass.*

158

COMMUNITY COLLEGES

Community colleges are also known as "junior colleges." Most of their study programs last two years. These colleges provide training in a number of fields, such as accounting, bookkeeping, computing, laboratory analysis, nursing, and secretarial work. Instead of going to a four-year college, some high school graduates may choose to go to a community college, where they can obtain associate of arts (A.A.) or associate of science (A.S.) degrees. If such students then decide to go on and study for a full bachelor's degree, they can often transfer the credits they earn at a community college toward a degree at a four-year college.

> The first public junior college was Joliet Junior College, established in 1901 in Joliet, Illinois, partly as a result of the influence of the educator William Rainey Harper. He is commonly regarded as the father of the junior college.

COMPUTER INDUSTRY

The computer industry is one of the largest and fastest-growing sections of the U.S. economy. Early computers, used in universities and scientific companies since World War II, were bulky and expensive. New developments in microelectronics changed the industry in the 1970s. Computers became smaller and less expensive. More important, the new computers could hold hundreds of times the amount of information.

The 1980s saw the real boom in computers. By the end of the decade more than $50 billion worth of computers were being sold each year in the United States. Companies such as Apple and IBM also opened

▲ Powerful microscopes are needed to examine the circuitry on a silicon microchip, the miniature coding inside electronic equipment. The technician wears protective clothing to prevent particles from his body from getting on the chip.

▶ *Photographs of a computer circuit board are magnified hundreds of times for checking. A broken element the thickness of a human hair can cause a computer to fail.*

Some of the Major Computer Companies in the U.S.

Mainframe Computers
1. IBM
2. Unisys Corp.
3. Amdahl Corp.
4. Cray Research Inc.

Minicomputers
1. IBM
2. Digital Equipment Corp.
3. Hewlett-Packard
4. Wang Laboratories

Microcomputers
1. IBM
2. Apple Computer Inc.
3. Compaq Computer Corp.
4. Tandy Corp.

up the market for personal computers (PCs). There are now more than 40 million PCs in use in the United States. Half of these are for home use; most of the rest are used for work. Annual spending on PCs rose from $3.1 billion in 1981 to $25 billion in 1989.

CONDOR

The California condor, a type of VULTURE, is one of the world's largest flying birds. It is about 50 inches (130 cm) long, and its wingspan can be as much as 10 feet (3 m). Once, condors were found all along the west coast of North America. But today, the species is in danger of becoming extinct (dying out) and is protected by law. As of mid-1990, there were only 40 California condors.

In the wild, condors usually eat the carcasses of dead animals. But sometimes they kill small animals.

▼ *A pair of condors nests only once every two years and lays only one egg. In hopes of ensuring successful breeding the 40 remaining condors are being held in captivity. There are plans to return them to their natural habitat in 1992.*

CONFEDERATE STATES OF AMERICA

The Confederate States of America, or Confederacy, was the name adopted by the Southern states that seceded (withdrew) from the United States just before the start of the CIVIL WAR in April 1861. These states seceded from the United States because they thought that the country's new Republican president, Abraham LINCOLN, would halt the expansion of slavery, thus threatening the Southern way of life.

Jefferson DAVIS was elected president of the Confederacy. Originally based in Montgomery, Alabama, the government later made Richmond, Virginia, its capital. The Confederacy's constitution was similar to that of the United States, but it gave more power to individual states and protected the system of slavery.

The First Members of the Confederate Cabinet	
President	Jefferson Davis
Vice president	Alexander H. Stephens
Secretary of state	Robert Toombs
Secretary of the treasury	Christopher Memminger
Secretary of war	Leroy P. Walker
Secretary of the navy	Stephen R. Mallory
Postmaster general	John H. Reagan
Attorney general	Judah P. Benjamin

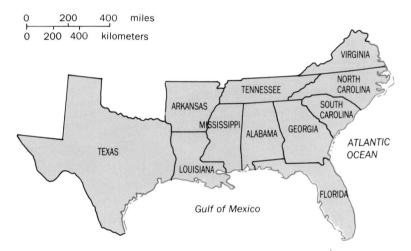

▲ The Confederacy was formed in February 1861 by South Carolina, Alabama, Florida, Georgia, Louisiana, and Mississippi. Texas joined in March, while Arkansas, North Carolina, Tennessee, and Virginia joined soon after the start of the war.

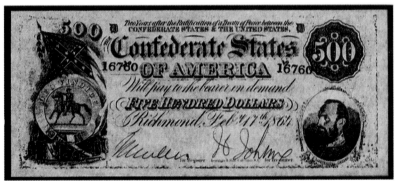

President Lincoln refused to accept the new nation, and war broke out between the Union and the Confederacy on April 12, 1861. The relative weakness of the Confederate government was to prove a drawback in conducting the Civil War. Jefferson Davis often had

▲ The Confederacy issued so much currency — $1.3 trillion worth — that inflation soared. By 1865, a pair of shoes cost as much as a soldier's wages for the entire four-year war.

Today the average member of Congress is in his or her fifties, the number of younger members having increased in recent years. The U.S. Congress is served by a larger staff than any other legislature in the world. There are more than 7,500 staff employees who work for members of the House of Representatives, and more than 3,600 for the senators. House and Senate committees also employ more than 3,000 staff. Other staff members bring the total serving Congress to more than 23,000.

problems getting the soldiers and equipment he needed from the individual states.

The Confederacy ended when Union troops captured President Davis a month after General Robert E. LEE surrendered at Appomattox on April 9, 1865.

CONGRESS OF THE UNITED STATES

The Congress is the lawmaking, or legislative, branch of the United States GOVERNMENT. The laws it passes apply to everyone in the country. Congress meets in the Capitol Building in Washington, D.C.

Congress is made up of the Senate and the House of Representatives. There are 100 senators, two for each state. Senators are elected for terms of six years. There are 435 representatives, each of whom is elected for a term of two years. Representatives are elected according to how many people live in a state; every state has to have at least one. The states with large populations, such as California, can have as many as several dozen.

The vice president of the United States serves as president of the Senate during the sessions. The vice president is not actually a member of the Senate, but if there is a tie vote, the president of the Senate then has the right to cast the deciding vote. The House of Representatives is headed by the speaker of the House. This important representative is chosen from the party that has the most members in the House.

Bills must be approved in both houses before going to the president of the United States for final approval. All bills that deal with finance and taxation must be introduced in the House of Representatives. The president can request military action, but only Congress (both houses sitting in a joint session) can declare war.

▼ *Committees in both houses discuss bills (proposed laws) in detail. Their reports save discussion time in Congress and help senators and representatives form opinions for voting. Sometimes nearly two years may pass before a bill becomes law.*

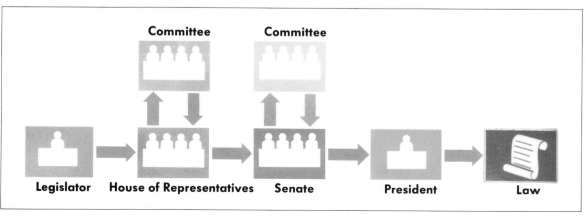

Committee Committee

Legislator House of Representatives Senate President Law

◄ *A lumberjack uses a back-cut technique to fell a Douglas fir. This valuable conifer accounts for one fourth of all lumber in the United States.*

▼ *The redwood is the tallest tree in the world. One California specimen was more than 375 feet (112 m) tall.*

Coast redwood

CONIFER

A conifer is a TREE or shrub that bears cones. Seeds and pollen are produced on the cones. Most conifers are evergreen and have needle-shaped leaves. Common North American conifers include firs, cedars, spruces, redwoods, yews, cypresses, junipers, larches, pines, and hemlocks.

The tallest type of conifer in the world is the SEQUOIA, or redwood, which grows in California and Oregon. Another conifer, the BRISTLECONE PINE, found in California and Nevada, is the oldest tree in the world.

Conifer forests, especially those in Oregon and Washington, provide lumber, wood pulp for papermaking, and other products. Douglas fir is the most valuable conifer commercially grown in North America.

▼ *A conifer cone does the same job as fruit or berries on other types of trees. Each scale has a seed at its base.*

▼ *The cones of a white spruce are usually grouped about 4 inches (10 cm) from the tip of the branch.*

Mature female cone of the giant sequoia

Mature female cones of the Sitka spruce

Mountain laurel

American robin

White oak

▶ *Sea captains' houses and shops line the harbor front at Mystic Seaport. New England's 19th-century whaling fleets set sail from ports such as Mystic.*

Connecticut is one of the NEW ENGLAND states. It is located on the northeastern seaboard, between NEW YORK State, MASSACHUSETTS, and RHODE ISLAND. It is one of the most historic states in the country, as well as one of the most important industrially. It is also one of the smallest states (only Delaware and Rhode Island are smaller). Connecticut is a popular vacation area. Its sandy beaches and small towns, many with fine colonial buildings, attract many visitors.

Connecticut was one of the first areas of the United States to be settled. The first Europeans arrived as early as 1614. By the mid-1600s, English settlements had been established in many parts of Connecticut. Connecticut played an important role in the American REVOLUTION. After the war, in 1787, delegates from

Connecticut
Capital: Hartford
Area: 4,872 sq mi (12,618 km²). Rank: 48th
Population: 3,295,669 (1990). Rank: 27th
Statehood: Jan. 9, 1788
Principal rivers: Connecticut, Housatonic, Thames
Highest point: Mt. Frissell, 2,380 ft (725 m)
Motto: *Qui Transtulit Sustinet* (He Who Transplanted Still Sustains)
Song: "Yankee Doodle"

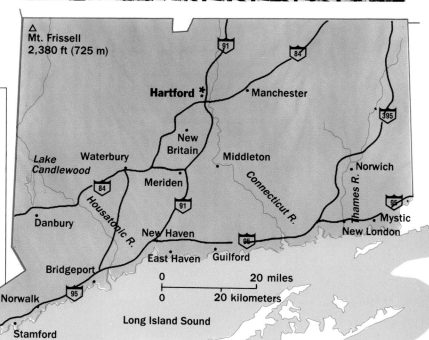

Connecticut played an important part in drawing up the U.S. CONSTITUTION. They proposed a solution, or compromise, known as the Connecticut Compromise, under which all states would have equal representation in the Senate but representation based on population in the House of Representatives. In 1788, Connecticut became the fifth state to sign, or *ratify*, the Constitution.

Through the 1900s, Connecticut grew to become an important industrial as well as agricultural state. Today, there are many major industrial plants and centers throughout the state. The state capital is Hartford. It is one of the leading centers in the country of the insurance business. Because the southern half of the state is close to New York City, many people who work in New York live in Connecticut, commuting to work every day.

▲ *The elegant state capitol building in Hartford was built in 1879. It contains mementos of the Revolutionary War.*

▼ *This traditional bridge crosses the Housatonic River in western Connecticut. Covered bridges kept rain and snow off travelers.*

Places of Interest

- Whitfield House, Guilford, was built in 1639 and is the oldest stone house in New England. It is just one of many colonial buildings that can be visited.
- Mark Twain Mansion, Hartford, was home to the author of *Tom Sawyer* for some years. It contains many personal belongings of the Twain Family.

- Mystic Seaport, Mystic, is a reconstruction of a whaling village of the 1800s. Today hundred-year old ships are moored in the harbor.
- Shore Line Trolley Museum, East Haven, exhibits trolleys that date from the late 1800s. Visitors may ride on some of the exhibits in the museum.

▲ *Solar panels use sunshine to heat water and provide electricity. They help conserve fuels that would do the same job.*

▲ *Mountain firs and rare wildflowers are protected in Mount Rainier National Park in Washington State.*

▶ *This mountain of scrap metal in Long Beach, California, will be melted down for recycling.*

CONSERVATION

Conservation means the protection and wise use of natural resources. Natural resources are materials found in nature that are useful or necessary to people.

More natural resources are being used than ever before. Some resources, such as *fossil fuels* (coal, natural gas, and oil) and minerals (such as iron and copper), cannot be replaced once they are used up. It is important to avoid wasting these *nonrenewable resources*. For example, driving smaller cars uses less gasoline. Using solar energy instead of fossil fuels to heat buildings is another example of conservation. Where possible, minerals should be *recycled*. Aluminum cans, for example, can be melted down and used to make new cans.

Other resources—such as water, farmland, and forests—*can* be renewed. But here, too, careful conservation is needed. For example, preventing forest fires and recycling paper saves trees, and replanting logged areas with young trees provides trees for the future.

As well as the careful use of natural resources, conservation also means ENVIRONMENTAL PROTECTION and avoiding POLLUTION. In the United States, the Departments of Agriculture, Energy, and the Interior supervise such aspects of conservation as oil production, land management, mining, soil conservation, and the forest service. The U.S. Environmental Protection Agency is also involved in conservation. But every citizen has a duty to use natural resources responsibly.

CONSTITUTION OF THE UNITED STATES

The U.S. Constitution is "the supreme law of the land." It was written in 1787 at a convention held in Philadelphia. The 55 delegates attending became known as the Founding Fathers. They included James MADISON, George WASHINGTON, and Benjamin FRANKLIN. The Constitution replaced the ARTICLES OF CONFEDERATION. After being ratified (approved) by nine states, it went into effect on June 21, 1788. By 1790, the four other states had ratified it.

The Constitution sets out a *federal* system of government. This means that there is a national (federal) government and also state governments.

The Constitution also states that the United States is a *republic*. It has a PRESIDENT elected by the people. There is also a CONGRESS to make the laws, and a SUPREME COURT, the highest court in the land. The Founding Fathers ensured that there was a system of "checks and balances" between these three branches of government.

In 1791 a BILL OF RIGHTS was added to the Constitution. This took the form of ten amendments that set out the rights of individuals. Since then, 16 more amendments have been added.

▲ *The Declaration of Independence, Constitution, and Bill of Rights are on display in the National Archives in Washington, D.C.*

CONSTITUTION ACT

The Constitution Act of 1982 revised the Canadian Constitution. Until that year, the BRITISH NORTH AMERICA ACT of 1867 served as Canada's constitution. Even though Canada has long been an independent country, the British North America Act could be amended only by the British Parliament. In 1982, however, the British Parliament passed the Canada Act. It gave Canada the right to change its own constitution. The Constitution Act of 1982 is part of the Canada Act. One addition is the Charter of Rights and Freedoms, which is similar to the American BILL OF RIGHTS.

CONSTITUTION, U.S.S.

The famous warship U.S.S. *Constitution* was nicknamed Old Ironsides for its ability to withstand enemy fire. Launched in Boston in 1797, it was one of the first frigates built for the U.S. Navy. It measured 204 feet (62 m)

The Constitutional Convention, which wrote the U.S. Constitution, was attended by 55 delegates representing 12 states. Rhode Island did not attend. Thirty-four of the delegates were lawyers; most of the others were merchants or planters. The great majority of the delegates were young men in their twenties and thirties. At 81, Benjamin Franklin was the oldest of those present.

▶ *The 44-gun U.S.S.* Constitution *remains on active duty. On each Independence Day it is taken on a "tour of duty" around Boston Harbor.*

Oliver Wendell Holmes, Sr., wrote the famous poem "Old Ironsides" when he heard about plans to scrap the U.S.S. Constitution. Published in 1830, the poem became popular across the country and helped preserve the ship as a national monument. It also gave the ship its nickname.

in length and carried 44 guns. It carried a crew of 80 sailors.

The *Constitution* first distinguished itself in 1803–1804, in the war against the Barbary pirates who controlled Tripoli (Libya). During the WAR OF 1812 it won several victories over British ships. In 1829 the *Constitution* was declared unseaworthy. Plans to scrap it were abandoned, and the ship, restored in 1927–1931, is now docked on the Charles River near Boston.

▼ *Steel girders form the skeleton of skyscrapers such as this one in Philadelphia. Construction workers use bolts to fasten girders to other girders and concrete floors.*

CONSTRUCTION INDUSTRY

The construction industry is one of the largest industries in the United States. More than 5 million people are employed in some form of construction. There are three

main types of construction. Heavy construction sees that the biggest projects, such as hydroelectric dams and other power plants, are built. The federal government and state governments, or some of the largest corporations, pay for these projects, which cost many millions of dollars. Highway construction is another large area, again funded by government. The third type, general construction, can vary in size from skyscrapers and large hotels to private houses. Total annual earnings for the construction industry come to more than $200 billion. Most construction workers belong to unions.

CONSUMER PROTECTION

Consumer protection is the idea of protecting the general public, which *consumes* (buys and uses) goods, from dangerous products and misleading advertising. This idea goes back to the beginning of the 1900s, when bad business practices were exposed by writers such as Upton SINCLAIR, who risked his life exposing the meat-packing industry. Government legislation during the DEPRESSION of the 1930s sought to protect small investors. The modern consumer movement began in the 1960s, with the crusading work of reformers such as Ralph NADER.

Consumer protection is now ensured at three levels. Most important are the government agencies such as the Food and Drug Administration, the U.S. Department of Agriculture, and the Federal Trade Commission. Many industries monitor themselves through the Committee of Better Business Bureaus or local Chambers of Commerce. Finally, private individuals and organizations, such as the Consumer Federation of America, look after the public interest.

CONTINENTAL CONGRESS

The Continental Congress was a group of delegates from the 13 American colonies that made the decision to declare independence from Britain and served as the young nation's first government. The First Continental Congress met in 1774 in Philadelphia. It met in response to the Intolerable Acts, which the British Parliament had passed to punish Massachusetts for the BOSTON TEA PARTY and to assert British power; one of these acts had closed Boston Harbor. The Congress

▲ Construction workers repair cable car tracks on a San Francisco street. Transportation and maintenance contracts can be worth millions of dollars to construction companies.

In 1938 an act was passed empowering the Food and Drug Administration to test the safety of all new drugs before they are placed on the market. Then, during the 1950s and 1960s, safety standards were set up to cover many products, including household chemicals, toys, flammable fabrics, and motor vehicles.

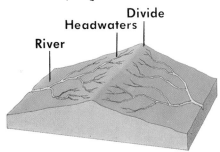

▲ The members of the First Continental Congress represented the interests of American colonists but made no move toward independence. British flags and banners hung over their debating chamber.

▼ The Continental Divide is often called "America's Watershed" because it feeds so many rivers. Melting snow from the mountains fills the headwaters of the rivers each spring.

Divide
Headwaters
River

passed a declaration of personal rights, petitioned the king to consider their grievances, and called for a boycott of British goods.

When the Congress met again in 1775, Britain had increased its repressive measures, and fighting had broken out at LEXINGTON AND CONCORD, Massachusetts. Congress adopted the New England militia as the "Army of the United Colonies," with George WASHINGTON as its commander. When further petitions to the king proved useless, the delegates resolved to separate from Britain. On July 4, 1776, they adopted the DECLARATION OF INDEPENDENCE.

The Congress continued to function as the national government throughout the American REVOLUTION and after it, under the ARTICLES OF CONFEDERATION, until the CONSTITUTION was adopted.

CONTINENTAL DIVIDE

The Continental Divide, or Great Divide, runs north–south along the crest of the Rocky Mountains. Its name comes from the fact that all the rivers and streams on the west side of the crest run west into the Pacific Ocean, and all the rivers and streams on the east side of the crest flow east into the Atlantic Ocean or one of its arms, such as the Gulf of Mexico. In other words, this is the highest point of the United States, one that "divides" most of the country's major natural waterways.

Calvin Coolidge was the 30th president of the United States. He served during the period of great prosperity between WORLD WAR I and the Great DEPRESSION which began with the stock market crash of 1929. A cautious, thrifty man, he was famous for using few words and was nicknamed Silent Cal.

Coolidge believed that government should interfere as little as possible in private business. The nation was very prosperous as this time. This was also the time of PROHIBITION, when the sale of alcoholic beverages was banned. Organized crime flourished, and Coolidge could not control it.

A Republican, Coolidge had been vice president under Warren G. HARDING. He became president when Harding died in office in 1923. Coolidge was visiting his father in Vermont when he learned of Harding's death. Coolidge's father, a notary public, swore him in.

Coolidge's first task was to clean up the corrupt administration he had taken over from Harding. His honesty and common sense were much admired, and in 1924, Coolidge was elected president with a very large majority. During his administration, Coolidge cut taxes and reduced government spending. He vetoed payment of a bonus to war veterans, but Congress passed the measure over his veto. He also vetoed bills to give financial aid to farmers, after a severe drop in farm prices. Coolidge did not take much interest in foreign affairs and was against the United States joining the League of Nations. At the end of his term in office he was very popular but refused to run for reelection in 1928.

▲ *President Coolidge opened the 1925 World Series. "Silent Cal" once spoke only four words during a baseball game: "What time is it?"*

(John) Calvin Coolidge
Born: July 4, 1872, in Plymouth Notch, Vermont
Education: Amherst College, Massachusetts
Political party: Republican
Term of office: 1923–1929
Married: 1905 to Grace Anna Goodhue
Died: Jan. 5, 1933, in Northampton, Massachusetts

▲ *James Fenimore Cooper began writing after boasting to his wife that he could write a better book than the novel she was reading.*

▲ *Aaron Copland conducted his own works in some of the first recordings of symphonic music.*

One of John Singleton Copley's most famous paintings is *Watson and the Shark,* now in the Museum of Fine Arts, Boston. It shows a young man being attacked by a shark while his friends try to aid him. Copley actually saw this event in Havana harbor.

COOPER, James Fenimore

James Fenimore Cooper (1789–1851) was born in Burlington, New Jersey, but spent most of his life in New York State. Cooper wrote many novels, some of which drew on his five years in the Navy. His most famous books are a series called *The Leatherstocking Tales*—including *The Deerslayer*, *The Pathfinder*, and *The Last of the Mohicans*. These tell of a frontiersman, Natty Bumppo, who lived among the Indians, and tales of people who settled the new country. Cooper also wrote a great deal about the values of American society.

COPLAND, Aaron

Aaron Copland (1900–1990) was one of the most famous American composers of this century. He studied in New York City and in Paris. Some of his earlier works were influenced by European music. Later he used American folk music and JAZZ in his compositions. The quality of Copland's music did much to raise the standing of American music in international circles. He wrote ballets based on American folklore, such as *Billy the Kid* and *Appalachian Spring*, as well as works to be performed by a full orchestra. Copland wrote a number of books on music, especially to encourage understanding of modern music.

COPLEY, John Singleton

John Singleton Copley (1738–1815) was a great painter during America's colonial period. He painted portraits of many colonial leaders. Copley completed his first signed painting when he was only 15 years old. But his real fame dates from 1766, when his portrait of his brother, *The Boy with Squirrel*, was sent to London and highly praised. Copley's mixed loyalties in the days after the Boston Tea Party made him a traitor in many patriots' eyes. In 1775, Copley moved to London where he developed his vivid and colorful style of portraits. He also painted many historical subjects. (See ART.)

CORN

Corn is the most important cereal crop in North America. It was cultivated by the Indians for centuries before

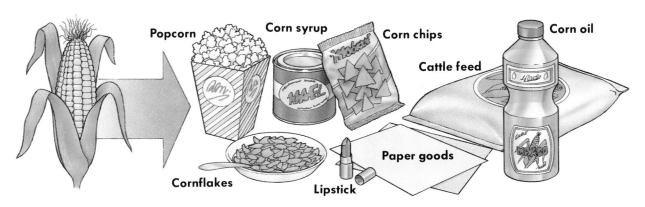

Popcorn
Corn syrup
Corn chips
Corn oil
Cattle feed
Cornflakes
Lipstick
Paper goods

Christopher Columbus's men first sampled it. The United States produces almost half of all the corn grown in the world. About 60 percent of the crop is used as feed for livestock. The rest is used as food in the United States or is sold to other countries. Most corn is grown in the area known as the Corn Belt. This is made up of the states of Iowa, Illinois, and Indiana, western Ohio, and parts of Minnesota, Nebraska, Missouri, Kansas, and South Dakota. The United States produces more than 200 million tons of corn each year.

▲ *Corn kernels can be refined (taken apart) to obtain by-products like popcorn.*

The 4 Leading Corn-Producing States in the U.S. (in bushels)

Iowa   1,707,300,000

Illinois   1,535,000,000

Nebraska 953,600,000

Indiana   756,500,000

CORONADO, Francisco Vásquez de

Francisco Vásquez de Coronado (1510?–1554) led the first expedition to explore the American Southwest. He set out to discover the legendary "Seven Golden Cities of Cibola" and bring back the gold to New Spain (Mexico). The cities turned out to be merely the Zuni Indian villages, which the Spaniards captured. Coronado's main force reached as far north as Kansas. Two other units explored the Gulf of California and the Colorado River, including the Grand Canyon. Although he failed to find gold, Coronado added greatly to Europeans' knowledge of North America.

▼ *Some of Coronado's men went west to the Grand Canyon. They were the first Europeans to lay eyes on this natural wonder.*

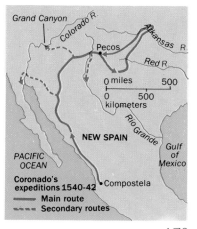

Grand Canyon
Colorado R.
Arkansas R.
Pecos
Red R.
0 miles 500
0 500 kilometers
Rio Grande
NEW SPAIN
PACIFIC OCEAN
Gulf of Mexico
Coronado's expeditions 1540-42
Compostela
—— Main route
- - - Secondary routes

CORPORATION

The corporation is the single most important type of business grouping in the United States. A corporation can own land, earn and spend money, and go to court just as if its members were one person. There are about 4 million corporations in the United States.

There are special rules governing corporations. For example, a corporation must be *chartered*, or incorporated, by the state or federal government. This forms a

The 10 Largest U.S. Industrial Corporations (by sales)
1. General Motors
2. Ford Motor
3. Exxon
4. IBM
5. General Electric
6. Mobil
7. Philip Morris
8. Chrysler
9. Du Pont
10. Texaco

▼ Indian tribes opposing the Aztecs helped Cortés reach Tenochtitlán, the Aztec capital.

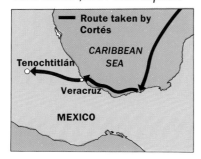

contract between the company and the government. The new corporation must also hold annual meetings and issue reports, so that its investors can study its spending and tax officials can assess corporate tax.

Many corporations sell shares of stock to investors, who are then part owners. This provides the money corporations need to expand. Enormous amounts of money are involved. Total corporate assets are more than $12 trillion.

Some of the first colonies, such as the Massachusetts Bay Colony and Virginia, were corporations. In the 1800s, corporations raised the millions of dollars required to build many of the nation's railroads. Some of today's richest corporations are General Motors, Ford, General Electric and Exxon.

CORTÉS, Hernán

Hernán Cortés (1485–1547) was one of the Spanish *conquistadores* (conquerors) of the Americas. He first sailed to the New World in 1504. He helped Spain conquer Cuba in 1511 and later became mayor of the town of Santiago. In 1519 he led an expedition of 600 men to Mexico and landed on the Yucatán peninsula.

▼ The Aztecs were very religious. When they first saw Cortés, they believed him to be a white-skinned god and welcomed him with gifts.

To prevent his men from deserting, he burned all but one of the party's 11 ships.

The Aztec civilization that Cortés found in Mexico was highly developed but politically weak. Cortés took advantage of this. With the help of an Indian princess, Malinche, he captured the Aztec emperor, Montezuma, and seized control of the capital of Tenochtitlán. Cortés was made governor of the colony of New Spain (Mexico). At home, however, Cortés had enemies who plotted his downfall. In 1540 he returned to Spain.

COTTON

Cotton is the soft white hairs, or fibers, that grow on the seeds of the cotton plant. After harvesting, the cotton fibers are separated from the seeds and spun into yarn. The yarn is generally woven into cotton fabric, which is used for clothing, sheets, and many other items.

Cotton is one of the world's most important crops. The United States is one of the leading producers, growing about 15 percent of the world's cotton. Most of the cotton is grown in the Cotton Belt, which stretches across the south from Florida to California. Texas is the main cotton-growing state.

The Indians grew cotton in many places, including the Southwest. The colonists cultivated it too. Later it was grown on plantations in the South. The cotton gin, invented in 1793 by Eli WHITNEY, increased production greatly. This machine separates the cotton fiber from the seed very quickly. Insect pests such as the boll weevil cause great damage to cotton crops.

▲ An Arizona cotton worker prepares raw cotton to be sucked into a yarn-spinning machine.

The 4 Leading Cotton-Producing States in the U.S. (in bales)	
Texas	4,650,000
California	2,950,000
Mississippi	1,750,000
Arizona	1,045,000

▼ Hundreds of field workers were needed to pick cotton in the 1800s. Mechanical pickers were not invented until 1940.

COUGAR

The cougar is North America's largest cat. It can grow to 5 feet (1.5 m) and have a 3-foot (1-m) tail. The cougar, which is also called the puma or mountain lion, is most common in the western United States and in northwestern Canada. But it can also be found in other parts of the continent. It prefers a rocky habitat and sparse woodland, particularly in the mountains. The eastern cougar is an endangered species.

The cougar is a carnivore, or meat eater. It preys on many animals, including deer, cattle, birds, mice, and rabbits. An expert climber, the cougar may lie in wait for its prey for hours before pouncing on it from above.

▲ Cougars save their energy for hunting. They will sometimes sleep up to 22 hours a day digesting their last kill.

▶ Dolly Parton is one of country music's biggest stars. She is a songwriter as well as a singer.

In 1925, radio station WSM in Nashville, Tennessee, began broadcasting a weekly hillbilly music show named the *Grand Ole Opry*. The first star of this show was "Uncle" Dave Mason, who sang 19th-century country ballads. Roy Acuff joined the show in 1938, and during the 1940s the *Grand Ole Opry* was broadcast nationally over NBC radio. By 1950 it had become a supershow with over a hundred performers. The *Grand Ole Opry* was largely responsible for Nashville becoming the center of the country music industry.

COUNTRY MUSIC

Country music has its roots in rural mountain music, especially from the southern United States. In the 1920s many new U.S. radio stations began playing rural music, and it became widely popular. In 1925 the *Grand Ole Opry* was first broadcast on radio. The Carter Family and Jimmy Rodgers were among the first of these country musicians. Gradually the music changed. By the 1930s western music had developed, sung by film-star cowboys such as Gene Autry. Another variation was honky-tonk, made famous by such musicians as Bob Wills and Ernest Tubb. Bluegrass music, originating in Kentucky, was developed by the Monroe Brothers and later made famous by Flat and Scruggs.

Country music had become big business by the 1950s and 1960s, with Nashville, Tennessee (home of the *Grand Ole Opry*), its capital. But by the late 1960s country music had gotten closer and closer to pop music. A number of musicians reacted against this and began producing country music more like the original sound. These "new country" musicians included Emmylou Harris, the Judds, Ricky Skeggs, George Strait, and Randy Travis.

COURTS *See* Government of the United States; Laws and Legal System

COWBOY

For many Americans, cowboys occupy a central role in United States history. They represent the brave frontier spirit that tamed the West. Thousands of films, television programs, and books have celebrated their deeds in the Wild West. In fact, most cowboys led monotonous, uncomfortable lives. But without cowboys, the West would have been much harder to settle.

Cowboys thrived from about 1865 to 1885. Later, when the new railroads were used to transport cattle and ranches were fenced in with barbed wire, no more than a handful of cowboys were needed. The main job of cowboys was to look after the huge herds of cattle that roamed across Texas and other parts of the Southwest and West. The cowboys rounded up the cattle, usually in the spring, and drove them north to towns

Stetson · Bandanna · Chaps · Texas saddle · Spurs · Rifle · Boots

▲ The clothes that a cowboy wore were designed for a life in the dusty prairie. The bandanna, for example, could be worn over the mouth and nose to filter dust and the smell of cattle.

Most cowboys came from the South, and many of them had fought in the Civil War. About a third of them were blacks or Mexican Americans.

◀ Young cattle are branded before they are turned loose to graze. Each ranch has a different brand, with symbols or initials to identify the cattle owner.

Between 1865 and 1880 cowboys drove at least 3.5 million cattle in herds of between 1,500 and 3,000 from southern Texas to towns in Kansas and Nebraska and to ranges in Wyoming, Montana, and elsewhere. Working up to 20 hours a day, the cowboy drove the animals from one watering hole to the next. For this hard and dirty work he earned between $25 and $40 a month.

▶ Coyotes have excellent eyesight and can run as fast as 40 miles per hour (65 km/hr).

▼ Cranberries are grown commercially in bogs, which are like shallow marshes. Farmers flood the bogs each winter to protect the plants from the extreme cold.

such as Abilene and Dodge City, Kansas, where they could be transported east by railroad. Cowboys had to be skillful riders—they might need to spend days at a time on horseback—and be able to use a rope called a *lariat* to rope individual cattle. All cowboys owned a saddle, but few had their own horses; these usually belonged to the ranch owners. The toughest part of a cowboy's life was a trail drive, when the cattle had to be taken north. Some trail drives were up to 1,000 miles (1,600 km) long.

COYOTE

The coyote is a type of wild dog. It is closely related to the wolf and is sometimes called the prairie wolf. The coyote is most common in the prairies of the western United States, but it is found all over North America, even as far east as New England. Smaller than a wolf, it is about 3 feet (1 m) long, not counting the tail. The coyote's long howl can often be heard at night.

Coyotes spend most of their time hunting. They used to follow BISON and PRONGHORNS. Today they hunt smaller animals, such as rabbits, birds, rats, frogs, and occasionally domestic animals. They also eat the remains of dead deer and other large animals. Coyotes usually hunt alone.

CRANBERRY

A relative of the blueberry, the cranberry is traditionally served as a sauce or relish with turkey at Thanksgiving and Christmas dinners. Cranberries are also used in pies and in drinks. The American, or large, cranberry grows wild in the northeastern United States. It is cultivated in Massachusetts, New Jersey, Wisconsin, Oregon, and Washington. The small cranberry, which has smaller fruit, grows in wild marshy ground in northern North America. More than 94,000 tons of cranberries are produced every year in the United States.

CRANE, Stephen

Stephen Crane (1871–1900) was a journalist and a writer. In his early twenties, Crane wrote newspaper articles about slum life in New York City during the 1890s. His first novel, *Maggie: A Girl of the Streets*, continued this theme. Crane also wrote about war. He saw this not as romantic or heroic but as brutal and cruel. His most famous work, *The Red Badge of Courage*, tells the story of a Union soldier in the Civil War. Later, Crane traveled to Europe to work as a war correspondent. He died there of tuberculosis at the age of only 28.

Stephen Crane was an adventurous reporter. In 1897, during a gun-running expedition to Cuba, he was shipwrecked and spent two days in an open boat with three other men. He wrote about this experience in one of his finest short stories, *The Open Boat*, published in 1898.

CRAZY HORSE

Crazy Horse (1849?–1877) was a great leader and war chief of the Oglalas, a band of the Teton SIOUX who lived in South Dakota and other parts of the northern plains. Crazy Horse fought against whites who tried to settle on Indian lands and against the army's efforts to force the Indians onto reservations. In 1876 he fought alongside SITTING BULL at the Battle of the Little Bighorn, better known as "Custer's Last Stand." Crazy Horse finally surrendered to the U.S. cavalry in May 1877. He was killed trying to escape in September of that year. Today a large sculpture of Crazy Horse is being created in South Dakota as a memorial.

▼ *Poundmaker, a famous Cree chief, joined the rebellions led by Louis Riel in Canada during the 1880s. They were defeated in Saskatchewan in 1885.*

CREES

The Cree INDIANS are a North American tribe. There are two groups of Crees, the Woodland Crees from the northern regions of Canada and the Plains Crees. The Plains Crees migrated south (some into the northern United States) after the spread of the horse, which made hunting buffalo much easier. During the 1600s the Crees in Canada worked with French fur traders. Some of them intermarried. Their descendants are called Métis. Today there are fewer than 3,000 Crees.

▲ *Images of the sun, which the Creek Indians worshiped, were turned into abstract designs on their pottery.*

CREEKS

The Creek INDIANS were one of the largest and most powerful tribes of the southeastern United States. They lived in what is now Georgia, Alabama, and northern Florida. Together with the CHEROKEES, Chickasaws, CHOCTAWS, and SEMINOLES, they formed a group that the white settlers called the Five Civilized Tribes. In 1813–1814 the Creeks, under TECUMSEH, fought against the new settlers. This was known as the Creek War. They were crushed by Andrew JACKSON, who took 23 million acres of their lands. In the 1830s they were moved west to Indian Territory. They suffered much hardship, and in 1901 a Creek Indian led the Snake Uprising to fight against unjust land distribution. Today there are about 13,000 Creeks.

CRIME

Crime is one of the biggest problems facing the United States. There are 20,000 murders each year in the United States, and in 1988 there were more than 1.5 million violent crimes. Despite these high figures, violent crimes decreased slightly between 1978 and 1988. At the same time, property crime, such as break-ins and vandalism, has been increasing, sometimes as fast as 10 percent per year. People who do not declare all their taxes or who defraud people in business are committing a "white-collar" crime.

People disagree about the best ways to prevent crime. Some argue that the death penalty is a deterrent—a way of making people afraid to commit a murder. Others argue that rehabilitation—teaching criminals how to become better citizens—is the answer. Apart from local and state police forces, the most famous anti-crime organization in the United States is the FEDERAL BUREAU OF INVESTIGATION (FBI). It fights all types of crime, including organized crime, illegal gambling, drug dealing, and blackmail.

Most common crimes in the United States
Robbery 3.8%
Aggravated assault 6.3%
Motor vehicle theft 9.6%
Burglary 24.0%
Rape 0.6%
Murder 0.2%
Larceny-theft 55.5%

▲ *The most common crimes committed in the United States. In some states, serious crimes are punishable by death.*

CROCKETT, Davy

Even in his own lifetime, the frontiersman David Crockett (1786–1836) was something of a legend. He had little formal schooling. Instead, he learned the skills of life on the frontier, such as hunting bear and raccoon.

In 1813 he joined the army and fought under Andrew JACKSON against the CREEK Indians. He later was a member of the Tennessee state legislature and served several terms in the U.S. Congress.

Crockett's early association with Andrew Jackson came to an end in the late 1820s, and he was taken up by the new Whig Party. The Whigs built up his image as a folk hero, as a counter to President Jackson's appeal.

After his political career ended in 1835, Crockett went to Texas, which had recently declared its independence from Mexico. Crockett was one of the men who fought to defend the Alamo when Mexican soldiers laid siege to it on February 23, 1836. He and all the other defenders, including James BOWIE, were killed in the Mexicans' final assault on March 6, 1836.

▲ Davy Crockett used his rifle as a club when he ran out of ammunition at the Alamo. He had been in Texas only two weeks when he was called into battle there.

▼ Bing Crosby was modest about his talent. He once said that he was "just another guy who likes singing in the shower."

CROSBY, Bing

Harry Lillis "Bing" Crosby (1904–1977) was a movie star known around the world for his easy charm and casual, "crooning" style of singing. Many regard him as one of the most talented entertainers of the 20th century. He began his career as a singer with dance bands, including that of Paul Whiteman, the "King of Jazz." In the 1930s, Crosby began making movies. Most of his films were comedies and musicals, although he could also be a serious actor. Crosby made many records as well; the most famous was "White Christmas," which sold 30 million copies. In 1944 he won the Academy Award as best actor for *Going My Way*.

▲ Crow medicine men prepared cures for the tribe and also helped in religious and magical ceremonies.

► Shrimp are small crustaceans. This banana shrimp, found in Hawaii, has a delicate, striped body.

CROWS

The Crows, a nomadic INDIAN tribe of the Great Plains, lived mainly in Montana, around the Yellowstone River. They were hunters of bison. When the United States began to expand, the Crows fought the white settlers who came to the northwest along the Oregon Trail. They soon saw that they could not win in the end and made peace with the army. The Crows fought with the whites against other Indian tribes. In 1876 they helped to defend the troops of General Crook at the battle of Rosebud Creek. Crook's troops had been attacked by Sioux and Cheyenne warriors under CRAZY HORSE.

In 1877 the Crows and the army tracked down the NEZ PERCÉ Indians on their march toward Canada. Today about 3,500 Crows live on a reservation in Montana.

CRUSTACEANS

A crustacean is an animal that has a hard shell and no bones. It also has many jointed legs. Most crustaceans live in the water, but some, such as wood lice, live on land. Some crustaceans, called shellfish, are popular foods. These include LOBSTERS AND CRABS, crayfish, and especially shrimp. Shrimp are the most valuable fishing catch in the United States, which is the world leader in shrimp production. Shrimp are found in both salt water and fresh water. The main shrimp-producing states are Alaska, Florida, Louisiana, and Texas. Large species of shrimps are often called prawns.

The crayfish is similar to the lobster, but it is smaller and lives in fresh water. Most of the world's crayfish come from Louisiana.

Barnacles and water fleas are also crustaceans.

Many crustaceans are very sensitive to natural and industrial pollution. One type of natural pollution, a type of algae called "red tide," can wipe out shellfish beds in just a few days.

CUBAN MISSILE CRISIS

The world held its breath for a whole week in October 1962. President John F. KENNEDY had received Air Force photographs showing that the Soviet Union was building missile launch sites in Cuba. The nuclear missiles could reach and destroy many U.S. cities. On October 22, after a secret meeting with his Cabinet, the president ordered a naval blockade of Cuba, demanding that the Soviet Union remove the missiles. On October 24, Soviet Premier Nikita Khrushchev angrily threatened to fight this act of "piracy."

Days passed, and neither side gave in. The United States made plans to invade Cuba, and the world braced itself for nuclear war. Finally, on October 28, Khrushchev agreed to remove the missiles and destroy the launch sites if the United States agreed not to invade Cuba. The crisis was over.

The high-flying U-2 aircraft was responsible for supplying the United States with accurate photographs of Soviet missile sites in Cuba during the Cuban missile crisis. This remarkable plane could fly at a height of about 90,000 feet (27,000 m). From this great height it could take very detailed pictures of ground installations. The U-2's job has now been taken over by satellites.

CURRIER AND IVES

In the mid- to late-1800s the firm of Currier and Ives published thousands of printed pictures showing scenes of American life. The business was started in New York in 1835 by Nathaniel Currier (1813–1888). In 1857 his bookkeeper, James Ives (1824–1895), who was also an artist, became a partner. The pictures were drawn by various artists, printed by lithography, and colored by hand. The subjects included sports events, frontier life, Mississippi River steamboats, great disasters, and other historic events. Between 1840 and 1890 more than 7,000 different pictures were produced.

Currier and Ives prints were not sold as great art, but they were very popular. Many of them sold for as little as 15 cents. These prints are now rare and costly. The prints often depicted current events. In 1840, three days after the burning of the steamship *Lexington*, Currier's artists and lithographers published a thrilling picture of the burning ship.

◀ Currier and Ives lithographs often celebrated great events. In 1881, Nathaniel Currier honored the yacht America, which 30 years before had won the race that later became known as the America's Cup.

▼ *During the Civil War, George Armstrong Custer was promoted briefly to the rank of brigadier general. He was only 24. Some historians blame this early success, and Custer's own vanity, for his downfall.*

▼ *The 2,000 Indians who defeated Custer at Little Bighorn were led by Crazy Horse and Sitting Bull. "Custer's Last Stand," as it came to be known, probably lasted less than an hour.*

CURTISS, Glenn Hammond

Glenn H. Curtiss (1878–1930) was a pioneer of the U.S. aviation industry. As a boy, an interest first in bicycles and then in motorcycles led him to design and build airplane engines. In 1908 he began building airplanes as well. In 1910, Curtiss became the first person to fly from Albany, New York, to New York City. Curtiss then designed airplanes for the U.S. Navy. During World War I, his factories produced thousands of planes. After the war, one of his seaplanes became the first airplane to fly the Atlantic Ocean.

CUSTER, George

George A. Custer (1839–1876) was an American cavalry officer. After the Civil War, where he served in the Union army, Custer was sent west with the 7th Cavalry to help subdue the Plains Indians. In 1874 he led an expedition that discovered gold in the Black Hills, in Dakota Territory. This area had been guaranteed to the Indians. But the U.S. government issued an order stating that any Indians who had not moved onto reservations by January 31, 1876, would be considered hostile.

The Indians may not have received the order, and they gathered that spring as usual for their hunting, near Little Bighorn, in Montana. Custer was ordered to go there and await General Alfred Terry's forces. Instead, he ordered his men to attack on June 25. Custer and all of his 265 soldiers were killed.

DAIRY INDUSTRY

The dairy industry produces milk from cows. It also processes and markets this milk, as well as milk by-products such as butter, cream, ice cream, and cheese. There are almost 170,000 dairy farms in the United States. They produce 17 billion gallons (64 billion liters) of milk every year. Dairying is a sophisticated industry that makes wide use of the latest agricultural technology. This helps it to meet the enormous demand for milk products while keeping its costs low, and to ensure that its products are always fit for humans to eat and drink. Strict regulations cover the way cows are kept, the food they eat, and the barns they live in. Wisconsin, California, New York, Minnesota, and Pennsylvania are the leading dairy states. The size of dairy farms varies enormously. Some have almost 1,000 cows, but most have fewer than 50. Most cows can produce around 1,500 gallons (5,677 liters) of milk a year.

DAKOTA INDIANS *See* Sioux

▲ Strict health laws govern the bottling of milk. More than 17 billion gallons (64 billion liters) are produced in the United States each year.

DALLAS

Dallas is the second largest city in TEXAS and one of the largest cities in the country. Over a million people live in Dallas. Located in the northeastern part of the state, it is a busy, bustling city. There are many spectacular high rises and elegant shops in its downtown area. The 72-story InterFirst Plaza building and the 50-story Reunion Tower are the best-known city landmarks.

Dallas was founded in 1841 and quickly became a

◄ The modern Dallas skyline reflects the building boom of the 1970s and early 1980s. During that time the population of Dallas rose by more than 20 percent.

> **Since a dam blocks the passage of fish, many dams have stepped pools at their sides that allow the fish to bypass the dam.**

major transportation and trading center. But it wasn't until after 1940 that Dallas became anything like today's huge city. Between 1940 and 1970, its population tripled. Oil is the city's major business, but there are numerous important manufacturing industries based here, too. Dallas is also a major cotton market. President John F. KENNEDY was assassinated in Dallas on November 22, 1963.

DAMS

A dam is a barrier built across a river or stream to control the flow of the water. This is done for a number of reasons. Dams stop flooding. They create reservoirs that hold a water supply for household and industrial use. And they provide water for the irrigation of farmland. The water stored in a dam's reservoir can also be used to create HYDROELECTRIC POWER.

There are many dams in the United States. One of the largest dam projects was the Tennessee Valley Authority (TVA). The authority built several dams along the Tennessee River. These created large lakes and helped to control the water supply.

The New Cornelia Tailings Dam, Arizona, is the second largest earth-fill dam in the world. The Fort Peck Dam, which is 4 miles (6.4 km) long, spans the Missouri River in Montana. The Grand Coulee across the Columbia River in the state of Washington is the largest concrete dam in the United States. It supplies water for irrigation. It also provides more hydroelectric power than any other source in the country.

The 7 Largest Dams in the U.S. (by volume)	
Dam	Location
New Cornelia Tailings	Ten Mile Wash, Arizona
Fort Peck	Missouri River, Montana
Oahe Tailings	Missouri River, South Dakota
Oroville	Feather River, California
San Luis	San Luis River, California
Garrison	Missouri River, North Dakota
Cochiti	Rio Grande, New Mexico

▶ Hoover Dam, on the Arizona-Nevada border, backs up the Colorado River to create Lake Mead, the largest artificial lake in the United States. The dam was finished in 1936 after three years of construction costing $120 million. It provided many jobs during the worst years of the Depression.

DANCE

▲ The Apache round dance is a ritual celebrating tribal history and famous battles.

Dance is probably the oldest of all art forms. Since ancient times, people have danced for many reasons: as recreation, as a courtship ritual, as entertainment, to tell a story, and as an act of worship. Religious dance is still part of the culture of some American Indian tribes.

Many different dance traditions have flourished, and some have originated, in North America. During Colonial times, American society danced the minuet and refined forms of English country dances; in the 19th century it took up a new European dance, the waltz. On the frontier, square dancing became a popular social activity. In this century Americans have created such dances as the Charleston, the jitterbug, and the twist. Many modern ballroom dances, however, like the rhumba, tango, and cha-cha, come from Latin America.

◄ Merce Cunningham's troupe has led modern dance into a new era of free expression.

▼ Dance routines by Fred Astaire and Ginger Rogers were the highlights of many movie musicals in the 1930s and 1940s.

American stage and film musicals have nourished a variety of dance styles, from solo tap dancing (originally developed by black Americans) to lavish numbers based partly on BALLET. And classical ballet itself has a huge following. Some American ballet companies, such as the New York City Ballet and the Dance Theater of Harlem, are among the best in the world.

As a reaction against the formality of ballet, some American dancers have developed freer styles, known collectively as "modern dance." Pioneers of modern dance include Isadora DUNCAN and Martha GRAHAM.

▼ Bette Davis was furious when Vivien Leigh was chosen to play Scarlett O'Hara in Gone With the Wind. Instead, her studio offered her the lead role in Jezebel. This gave Bette Davis the chance to play a similar strong southern heroine. The Oscar that she won helped make up for her earlier disappointment.

▼ Jefferson Davis's birthday, June 3, is a public holiday in seven southern states. The date is also known as Confederate Memorial Day.

DARROW, Clarence

Clarence Darrow (1857–1938) was a brilliant criminal defense lawyer. He also fought for many causes during his career, including freedom of expression and the abolition of the death penalty. Born in Ohio, he practiced mainly in Chicago. During the early part of his career he successfully defended several labor leaders; later, he turned to criminal cases. Darrow is perhaps best known for his role in a case he lost: the trial of John Scopes. In 1925, Scopes was tried for teaching evolution in Tennessee. At the time, this was against the law. Darrow's eloquent defense of Scopes was one of the most dramatic in U.S. legal history. Darrow wrote his autobiography, *The Story of My Life*, in 1932.

DAVIS, Bette

Born in Lowell, Massachusetts, the actress Bette Davis (1908–1989) was one of the great stars of motion pictures. She often played women who were strong and determined, including *Jezebel*, for which she won her second Oscar in 1938. She won her first in 1935 for her role in *Dangerous*. Perhaps her greatest role was as Margo Channing in *All About Eve* in 1950. In the 1960s she starred in a number of horror films, including *Hush, Hush, Sweet Charlotte, Whatever Happened to Baby Jane?*, and *The Nanny*.

DAVIS, Jefferson

Jefferson Davis (1808–1889) was the only president of the CONFEDERATE STATES OF AMERICA. He was born in Kentucky and grew up in Mississippi. Davis was first elected to the U.S. House of Representatives in 1845. Later he served as a U.S. senator from Mississippi and as secretary of war under President Franklin PIERCE.

Davis took a moderate line in the dispute between North and South. He was not in favor of secession, but he thought that states had a constitutional right to secede if they wished. He also supported slavery. After Abraham LINCOLN was elected president in 1860, Mississippi was among the states that seceded and formed the Confederate States of America. In February 1861, Davis was named president of the Confederacy.

After the South was defeated, in 1865, Davis was captured by Union troops and charged with treason. He spent two years in prison, but the case was never brought to trial. His last years were spent in Mississippi.

D DAY

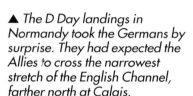

June 6, 1944, called "D Day," was the date of the Allied invasion of German-occupied France in WORLD WAR II. A combined British, American, Canadian, and Free French force crossed the English Channel and landed on the coast of Normandy. Some 176,000 troops took part in Operation "Overlord," making it the largest invasion force in history.

The forces were commanded by the American General Dwight D. EISENHOWER. The five landing beaches—called Utah, Omaha, Gold, Juno, and Sword—were spread along a 40-mile (65-km) stretch of the Normandy coast. The worst fighting took place at Omaha Beach, where 2,000 Americans lost their lives. However, by the end of D Day the Allies controlled all five beaches.

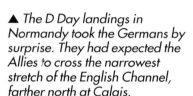

▲ The D Day landings in Normandy took the Germans by surprise. They had expected the Allies to cross the narrowest stretch of the English Channel, farther north at Calais.

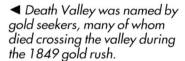

◀ Death Valley was named by gold seekers, many of whom died crossing the valley during the 1849 gold rush.

▼ The lowest part of Death Valley is the lowest piece of land in the Western Hemisphere.

DEATH VALLEY

Death Valley is a desert in southeastern California. It is about 140 miles (225 km) long. It forms part of the much larger Death Valley National Monument. Its lowest part is Badwater, 282 feet (86 m) below sea level. Movements in the earth's crust created Death Valley. These forced the surrounding lands up and forced down the area between them. Death Valley is extremely hot and receives almost no rain. In 1913 the highest temperature ever recorded in the United States was in Death Valley, a searing 134°F (57°C). Few plants and animals can live in these arid conditions.

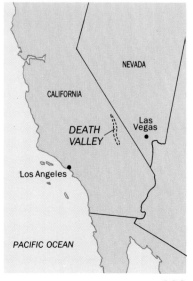

The Declaration of Independence was written almost entirely by Thomas Jefferson. Only two passages in Jefferson's draft were rejected by the Congress — a very strong denunciation of the slave trade and an impolite reference to the English people.

▶ The Declaration Committee, a Currier and Ives print, was a popular memento of the U.S. Centennial in 1876, held to mark the 100th anniversary of the signing of the Declaration of Independence.

▼ The Declaration was read out at state houses within days of its signing. Most of the public was wildly in favor of it.

DEBS, Eugene V.

Eugene V. Debs (1855–1926) was a labor and political leader. Born in Terre Haute, Indiana, he began working for the railroads while still in his teens. Debs joined the Brotherhood of Locomotive Firemen and in 1893 formed the American Railway Union. A year later he was jailed after involvement with a strike. While there, he became a socialist. He ran for president as a socialist five times. His 1920 campaign was run from prison, to which he had been sent after his outspoken opposition to war during World War I.

DECLARATION OF INDEPENDENCE

The Declaration of Independence marked the birth of the United States. It was adopted on July 4, 1776, by representatives of the 13 colonies attending the Second Continental Congress. This was held in Philadelphia, at the Pennsylvania State House, which became known as INDEPENDENCE HALL. Messengers carried copies of the Declaration to different states. It was later signed by the 56 delegates to the Congress. July 4 is still celebrated as the nation's birthday.

The document was drafted by Thomas JEFFERSON. He was assisted by John ADAMS, Benjamin FRANKLIN, Robert Livingston, and Roger Sherman. The Declaration proclaimed that the 13 British colonies in North America were no longer under British rule. It also said that although they were independent states, they were also united.

The first part of the Declaration sums up the rights of all people. It states that all men are born equal—that is, they all have the same rights. It also says that governments exist to protect each citizen's right to life, liberty, and happiness. The rest of the document lists the colonies' grievances against King George III of Britain.

Written on parchment, the Declaration of Independence can be seen in the National Archives building in Washington, D.C.

DECORATIONS AND MEDALS

The Purple Heart is the oldest U.S. military medal. George Washington issued the first three in 1782, and the medal still bears his profile. This award is for being killed or wounded in action. A member of any branch of the armed forces can receive the Purple Heart, as well as other medals such as the Silver Star and Bronze Star. Other medals, such as the Distinguished Flying Cross (Air Force) and the Distinguished Service Cross (Army), can be issued by only one branch. The highest military award is the Medal of Honor. This can be awarded to any military person and honors bravery and risk of life to help others.

The government also recognizes the value of great actions in peacetime. The highest nonmilitary award is the Presidential Medal of Freedom. It honors important contributions to the interests of the United States or the cause of world peace.

DEER

Deer are animals that chew the cud and have *cloven* hoofs (hoofs that are divided in half). The males usually have antlers. No other animal has antlers. Deer eat

▲ The original Purple Heart was called the Badge of Military Merit. It honored bravery in the Revolutionary War. This modern version, established in 1932, is awarded to members of the armed forces who have been killed or wounded in action.

▼ Deer antlers develop each year from tender stumps, covered in a layer of soft, hair-covered skin, to fully grown branches. The four stages show the period from spring to fall.

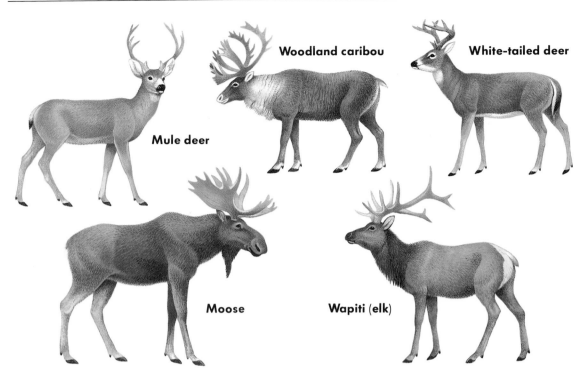

Woodland caribou

White-tailed deer

Mule deer

Moose

Wapiti (elk)

▲ *Deer of North America. Male deer, or stags, use their antlers mainly for fighting one another. Speed is a deer's greatest defense against predators. A white-tailed deer can run at 40 miles per hour (64 km/hr). Even the moose, which can weigh nearly a ton, can reach speeds of up to 20 miles per hour (32 km/hr).*

leaves, fruit, grass, and sometimes moss, bark, and twigs.

The largest deer in the world is the MOOSE. It lives in Alaska, northern Canada, the Great Lakes region, New York, Montana, and Idaho. The male moose has massive antlers. The male wapiti, or elk, also has spectacular antlers. It was once found from central Canada to New Mexico but now lives only in the northern part of this range.

The white-tailed, or Virginia, deer is the most common deer in North America. It is found in forests and open country through most of the United States from the Atlantic coast to the Rocky Mountains, as far south as Mexico. A close relative, the black-tailed, or mule, deer, lives in the western United States.

The CARIBOU is the North American reindeer. It is found in Canada and Alaska. Both the female and the male have antlers. Herds of caribou migrate from summer ranges to winter ranges.

The Department of Defense employs about 2 million men and women on active duty and about 1 million civilian employees. It takes more than one fourth of the total U.S. annual budget.

DEFENSE, DEPARTMENT OF

The U.S. Department of Defense was set up in 1949 as a way of centralizing the three main branches of the armed forces. It is part of the executive branch of the federal GOVERNMENT. The secretary of defense is a Cabinet member. The Army, Navy, and Air Force make up the three military departments of the Department of Defense. Each of these services is led by a chief of staff. Together these three are known as the Joint Chiefs of Staff (JCS). Their job is to meet with and advise the secretary of defense and the president.

Important military orders begin with the president, who is commander in chief of the armed forces. They are passed on to the secretary of defense and then to the JCS. This elaborate system ensures that civilians, represented by the president and the secretary of defense, have ultimate control over military action. The responsibility is great. The Department of Defense has an annual budget of about $300 billion, or 28 percent of the federal budget. With the apparent end of the COLD WAR in 1990, it is expected that this percentage will decrease in the years ahead.

▼ *The five-sided Pentagon in Washington, D.C., is the headquarters of the Department of Defense. Covering 29 acres (12 ha), it is one of the world's largest office buildings. More than 20,000 people work in the Pentagon.*

DE FOREST, Lee

Lee de Forest (1873–1961) was a pioneer of the early days of radio. In 1907 he invented a vacuum tube known as a *triode*. Because of its ability to boost, or amplify, weak electrical signals, the triode played a crucial role in the development of long-distance radio. De Forest resoundingly demonstrated its success in 1910, when he broadcast a concert from the Metropolitan Opera House in New York City. He also worked for the U.S. Navy. His early naval radio stations revolutionized communications at sea. Later, he did important work on sound waves, paving the way for talking pictures.

Lee de Forest took out more than 300 patents on radio and electronic devices. But the one invention that some people say was as great as the invention of radio itself was the vacuum tube called a *triode* or *audion*. Before this invention, the only radio signals were the "dot-dash" of Morse code.

DELAWARE

Peach blossom

Blue hen chicken

American holly

442 ft (135 m)

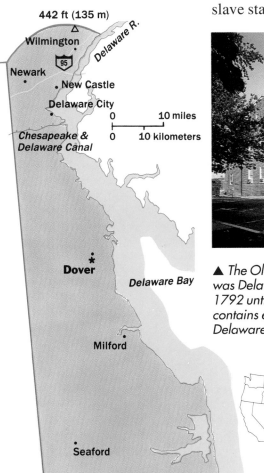

Wilmington

Newark

New Castle

Delaware City

Chesapeake & Delaware Canal

0   10 miles

0   10 kilometers

Delaware R.

95

Dover

Delaware Bay

Milford

Seaford

Delaware lies on the Atlantic coast between Maryland, Pennsylvania, and New Jersey. It is the second smallest state (only Rhode Island is smaller). It is also the oldest state. On December 7, 1787, Delaware became the first state to ratify, or approve, the new U.S. Constitution. Delaware's nickname, The First State, commemorates this historic action.

The region occupied by Delaware was one of the first to be visited, and later settled, by Europeans. Henry HUDSON, an Englishman, reached it in 1609. The following year, another Englishman, Samuel Argall of the Virginia Colony, also reached it. He named the bay he found for Lord De La Warr, governor of Virginia. Delaware was settled by both the Swedish and the Dutch, but by 1664 it had become an English colony. Delaware played a small but significant role in the American REVOLUTION. Later it fought on the Union side throughout the CIVIL WAR even though it was a slave state.

▲ The Old State House, in Dover, was Delaware's capitol from 1792 until 1933. Today it contains exhibits relating to Delaware's history.

Places of Interest

● Fort Delaware stands on Pea Patch Island and can only be reached by boat from Delaware City. It was used as a prison during the Civil War.

● Hagley Museum and Eleutherian Mills, near Wilmington, features the original powder mills of Éleuthère Irénée du Pont as well as models showing the development of industry in Colonial America.

● The town of New Castle contains many interesting colonial buildings, cobblestone streets, and an old village green.

● Henry Francis Du Pont Winterthur Museum, near Wilmington, houses a collection of Early American furniture, china, and silver dating from 1640 to 1840.

Delaware today is an important business area. The state's favorable laws governing registered companies have led almost 200,000 U.S. companies to establish themselves here, even though many trade in other areas of the country. Numerous law firms in particular are registered in Delaware. Few industries are based in the state. The most important are in the chemical business, especially in Wilmington, Delaware's largest city. Farms cover much of the state, especially the fertile plains that stretch inland across southern Delaware. The sandy beaches of the southeastern coast of the state draw many summer vacationers.

Delaware
Capital: Dover
Area: 1,932 sq mi
(5,005 km²). Rank: 49th
Population: 668,696
(1990). Rank: 46th
Statehood: Dec. 7, 1787
Principal rivers: Delaware,
Mispillion, Nanticoke
Highest point: Centerville,
442 ft (135 m)
Motto: Liberty and
Independence
Song: "Our Delaware"

◄ *Delaware's only major city, Wilmington, is within 10 miles (16 km) of New Jersey, Pennsylvania, and Maryland. It is the center of Delaware's chemical industry.*

▼ *The Brandywine Valley in northern Delaware is the highest region of the state.*

The First Democratic Donkey

▲ *The donkey first appeared as the Democratic Party symbol in this 1870 political cartoon by Thomas Nast. The donkey was meant to represent only a faction of the party, but the Democrats adopted it as the party mascot.*

DEMOCRATIC PARTY

The Democratic Party is one of the two major POLITICAL PARTIES in the United States. The beginnings of the Democratic Party were in 1792, when supporters of Thomas JEFFERSON formed the Democratic-Republican Party. They believed in states' rights and government by the people. In the 1830s it became known as the Democratic Party.

In 1860, after nearly 60 years of being in office, the party split over the issues of states' rights and slavery. For the next half century, there was only one Democratic president, Grover CLEVELAND. In 1896 the party split between supporters of gold coins and silver. The Democrats won in 1912 and 1916 with Woodrow WILSON, then not again until 1932, with Franklin D. ROOSEVELT. He was followed by Harry S. TRUMAN. The next Democratic victory was in 1960, when John F. KENNEDY was elected president. Lyndon B. JOHNSON succeeded him, serving from 1963 till 1969. Since Jimmy CARTER was elected in 1976, the Democrats have not won a presidential election.

DEMPSEY, Jack

Jack Dempsey (1895–1983), whose real name was William Harrison Dempsey, was heavyweight BOXING champion from 1919, when he beat Jess Willard, to 1926, when he lost to Gene Tunney. In 1927, Dempsey fought Tunney again. This time Dempsey knocked Tunney down, but the referee didn't start counting Tunney out until Dempsey got to the neutral corner. As a result, Tunney was able to get up at the count of 9. He went on to win the fight. This "long count" became one of the most famous incidents in boxing history.

▼ *Denver's bustling commercial center is located only 10 miles (16 km) east of the Rocky Mountains. The Great Plains lie on the other side of the city.*

DENVER

COLORADO's capital, Denver, is known as the Mile-High City because the state capitol is exactly 5,280 feet (1,610 m) above sea level. Denver is located on the western edge of the Great Plains. It is the industrial, commercial, and transportation center of the Rocky Mountain region and has a population of over 467,000. Denver's most important employers are the state and federal governments. It is also the site of a federal mint.

DEPRESSION, GREAT

The Great Depression was a severe economic slump that occurred in the United States, and later in other countries, in the 1930s. It was triggered by the stock market crash of 1929, when share prices plunged.

The sudden drop in prices affected almost every part of the economy. Many farmers, for example, now received so little for their crops that they were unable to pay their debts. Many lost their farms. The reduced demand for goods and services forced most businesses to lay off some of their employees. By 1933, the worst year of the Depression, 12 million Americans were unemployed—about one quarter of the work force. Many unemployed, homeless people took shelter in shantytowns, managing to keep alive through odd jobs, charity, and begging.

Among the many businesses that failed were thousands of banks. There was no federal deposit insurance, and when people feared that a bank was in trouble they would rush to withdraw their savings. With all its assets wiped out, the bank would be forced to close.

For the first two years of the Depression, the government took little direct action, believing that the economy would recover naturally. Then the election of Franklin D. ROOSEVELT as president brought the NEW DEAL. This was a set of laws designed mainly to ease the worst of the poverty, provide support for the banks, and create new jobs. This helped considerably. But it was not until 1939, when the outbreak of WORLD WAR II gave an enormous boost to heavy industry, that the Depression came to an end.

The Great Depression changed the way the public and the government viewed the U.S. economy. Before the Depression, people looked to bankers and business executives as the leaders of the nation's economy, and the government kept federal involvement to a minimum. After the stock market crashed, the public lost faith in the business tycoons and looked to the government to solve the crisis. Since then the government has been more involved in the way the economy is run.

◄ The New Hope Mission in New York City, and thousands like it around the country, gave food to the poorest families during the Depression.

During the Depression the total earnings of everyone in the country fell by half. Top stenographers in New York saw their pay drop from $35.45 a week to $16. There were more than 85,000 business failures. The Depression years saw a burst of union organizing. Total union membership rose from about 3 million to over 10 million in 1941. In other countries the Depression had an even more profound effect. It strengthened the hold of Adolf Hitler in Germany and added to the tensions that led to World War II.

DESERTS

Elf owl

Pack rat

Saguaro cactus

Night-blooming cereus

Bobcat

Jumping cholla

Scorpion

Kangaroo rats

Barrel cactus

Jackrabbit

Rattlesnake

Collared lizard

Prickly pear

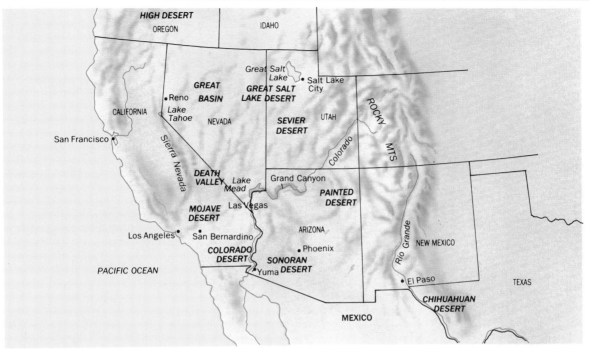

▲ *Most deserts in the United States are located west of the Rocky Mountains.*

■ **Desert areas of the United States**

Sometimes several inches of torrential rain might fall in desert areas within a few hours, but usually rain falls only at very long intervals. Records at Iquique in the Atacama Desert of northern Chile showed no rain at all for a period of four years. Death Valley in California has an average annual rainfall of only 1.5 inches (38 mm) compared with New York City's 42 inches (1,067 mm).

A desert is a barren region of limited rainfall. The soil is too dry for many plants to grow. There are large desert regions in the western United States and in Mexico. They are caused by mountains to the west that block moist air moving in from the Pacific Ocean. Conditions in many deserts are extreme, usually with hot days and cold nights. DEATH VALLEY, in California, is one of the hottest places in the world during summer. Temperatures there have been known to soar to over 130°F (54°C). A "cold desert," such as that in northern Canada and Alaska, is a place where the barrenness is caused by low temperatures.

Deserts are not always covered in sand dunes. Much of North America's largest desert region, the Great Basin, is high, dry sagebrush country.

North American deserts have more plants than other deserts in the world. These include many kinds of CACTUS and the famous Joshua trees, which are found in the MOJAVE and other deserts of the Southwest.

Some animals have adapted to desert life in North America. Birds include the roadrunner, cactus wren, and sage hen. Other desert animals include the Gila monster, kit fox, collared peccary, and kangaroo rat. Tiny insects live in some desert ponds. They are dormant (temporarily inactive), some times for months, until some rainfall creates a tiny pond in which they reproduce.

Some deserts are rich in minerals and other natural resources. Uranium and copper, for example, are mined in North American deserts. If irrigated (artificially watered), deserts can be made suitable for farming. Part of the Colorado River has been used to irrigate areas of the Sonoran Desert to produce fertile farmland.

De Soto arrived at the Mississippi River at what is now the border between Mississippi and Arkansas.

DE SOTO, Hernando

The Spanish *conquistador* (conqueror) Hernando de Soto (1500?–1542) explored the southeastern part of what is now the United States and discovered the Mississippi River.

Between 1516 and 1536, de Soto took part in various expeditions in Central America and Peru. His last and most important expedition took him to the lands north of Mexico where he hoped to find gold. He arrived in Florida in 1539, with 1,000 men, and began a three-year-long exploration that took him as far north as Tennessee and as far west as Oklahoma. He died of a fever and his body was sunk in the Mississippi.

DETROIT

Detroit, Michigan, is a major manufacturing center and the country's leading automobile-producing city. It is one of the largest cities in the country, with a population of more than 1 million. The city is also a major port and transportation center. It lies on the Detroit River, in southeastern Michigan, facing Canada across the river. Detroit was founded by a Frenchman, Antoine CADILLAC, in 1701. It quickly became a leading center of the fur trade. In the early years of this century, Detroit became the headquarters of the automobile industry. Thereafter, it grew rapidly. Almost 60 percent of the

▼ Older buildings, such as Christ Church, are dwarfed by Detroit's Renaissance Center. Four 39-story office towers flank a 73-story hotel.

population is black, and the city has suffered from racial tensions for many years. These are often worst when economic conditions are also poor.

DEWEY, George

George Dewey (1837–1917), an American naval officer, was a hero of the SPANISH-AMERICAN WAR. Dewey graduated from the U.S. Naval Academy at Annapolis in 1858 and, as a young officer, fought in the CIVIL WAR. When the Spanish-American War broke out in 1898, Dewey was a commodore. He was in charge of the six ships that formed the Asiatic Squadron. Dewey and his fleet sailed from Hong Kong to Manila in the Philippines. In spite of being outnumbered, he destroyed ten ships of the Spanish fleet and seized the harbor. Not one American life was lost in the battle. Dewey was made an admiral of the navy the following year.

▲ The educator John Dewey believed that knowledge came from dealing with new experiences. He argued that students should learn from experiments, rather than by memory.

DEWEY, John

John Dewey (1859–1952) was a philosopher and educator who strongly influenced educational practices in the United States. He believed that intelligence needed to be stimulated by new and different problems if people, especially young people, were to develop their full potential. Earlier education had often focused on teaching largely by memory. Dewey called on educators to set problems that would challenge children and make them think for themselves. He believed, too, that education should aim to do more than instill knowledge: it should also ensure the moral development of children.

▼ Emily Dickinson believed it was the poet's duty to produce "amazing sense from ordinary meaning." Her poems are considered among the greatest in American literature.

DICKINSON, Emily

Emily Dickinson (1830–1886) was a famous American poet. Born in Amherst, Massachusetts, she grew up in a prosperous, educated family. Her father was a lawyer and congressman. Her home was strict and rules were rigid. She rarely left it. She created her own world in her poetry. Only about ten of 1,800 poems she wrote were published during her lifetime; the rest appeared over many years only after her death in 1886. Dickinson's poems are short and simple, but they are full of passion. She tended to use single, sharp images. Many of her poems were about feelings and nature.

▼ The Allosaurus was a carnivore (meat eater).

◄ Scientists called paleontologists can piece together complete dinosaur skeletons from just a few bones.

During the early part of the age of the dinosaurs, 200 million years ago, the continents were all joined together in one great land mass. This is why dinosaurs have been found on every continent except Antarctica. Remains of about 300 different species of dinosaurs have been found, but some of these are known only from a single tooth or a small bone fragment.

▼ The Stegosaurus ate mostly plants. Its armor plates and spiked tail were good defenses against attack.

DINOSAURS

Dinosaurs were reptiles that lived for millions of years on most parts of the earth. The word dinosaur means "thunder lizard" in Greek. Dinosaurs died out mysteriously about 65 million years ago. We know about dinosaurs because people have discovered and preserved fossils, the remains of dinosaurs found in rock. Dinosaur fossils have been found all over North America, but the best finds have been in the western states and Canadian provinces. Some outstanding displays of dinosaur fossils are in the Dinosaur National Monument, on the border between Utah and Colorado.

In general, North American dinosaur fossils are similar to those found on other continents. This is because many of the continents were still attached to each other during the early part of the age of the dinosaur.

American dinosaur specialist Jim Jensen was examining an arm and shoulder bone in 1979 and found that they were from an undiscovered large species. He calculated that such a dinosaur, which he named Ultrasaurus, would be 100 feet (30 m) long and would weigh 143 tons, as much as the weight of 20 large elephants. That would make Ultrasaurus the largest animal that ever roamed the earth. It would have looked like a larger version of the more familiar Brachiosaurus.

◀ *Disneyland, in Anaheim, California, was the creation of Walt Disney (below). It opened in 1955.*

DISNEY, Walt

Walter Elias Disney (1901–1966) was a cartoon artist and a producer of cartoon films. He was born in Chicago and raised in Missouri. In 1923 he began to experiment with cartoon *animation*. Disney's "stars" became famous around the world—Mickey and Minnie Mouse, Donald Duck, and a host of others. *Snow White and the Seven Dwarfs, Cinderella, Fantasia,* and *101 Dalmatians* are just a few of the feature-length cartoons turned out by Disney's animation team. He later went on to produce nature films and TV programs. Two theme parks —Disneyland, in California, and Disney World, in Florida—pay tribute to Disney's creative genius.

► *The first Mickey Mouse cartoon, called Plane Crazy, appeared in 1928.*

© DISNEY

▼ *The fantasy atmosphere of Snow White and the Seven Dwarfs (1937) offered audiences an escape from the Depression.*

© DISNEY

American beauty rose

Wood thrush

Scarlet oak

▼ The Jefferson Memorial is built in the same architectural style that Jefferson used for his own home, Monticello.

The District of Columbia is the seat of the government of the United States. Since 1890 it has also covered the same area as the city of WASHINGTON, D.C. The Constitution provided that a tract of land be set aside for the new nation's capital. Congress authorized it in 1790. In 1791, George WASHINGTON himself chose the site of the new city, and he hired a French architect, Pierre Charles L'Enfant, to design it. It was to be built on land ceded by Maryland and Virginia. In 1800, the federal

Places of Interest

● The Capitol is the building where the U.S. Congress meets. Visitors to the Capitol can see Congress in action and enjoy the works of art that hang in the Great Rotunda.
● The White House was begun in 1792 and has been home to every U.S. president except George Washington.

● The Air and Space Museum has many interesting exhibits, including the Wright brothers' first airplane.
● The Washington Monument, Lincoln Memorial, and Jefferson Memorial pay tribute to three of America's great presidents.

government moved to the new city from Philadelphia. In 1846 the land given by Virginia was returned to that state. Confederate territory in the CIVIL WAR began just over the Potomac River, in Virginia.

Today Washington, D.C., is probably the most important center of government in the world. The WHITE HOUSE, the CAPITOL, and the SUPREME COURT are all located in the city.

District of Columbia
Area: 68.25 sq mi (176.75 km²)
Population: 609,909 (1990)
Principal river: Potomac
Highest point: Tenleytown, 410 ft (125 m)
Motto: *Justitia Omnibus* (Justice for All)

DOGS

In the United States, 128 breeds of purebred dogs are registered with the American Kennel Club, the organization of U.S. dog breeders. The breeds are divided into seven groups: sporting, hound, toy, working, herding, terrier, and nonsporting breeds. Seven breeds were originally developed in the United States. The first was the Alaskan malamute, bred by the Inuits (Eskimos) 3,000 years ago. Others are the American water spaniel, Chesapeake Bay retriever, American foxhound, black-and-tan coonhound, American Staffordshire terrier, and Boston terrier. Many pets are not purebred but are crosses between more than one breed. North American relatives of the dog are the COYOTE, FOX, and WOLF.

▼ *The names of North American dog breeds give a clue to why they have been called man's best friend. An Eskimo sled dog (above) is used to pull sleds in the Arctic.*

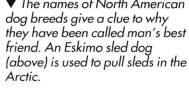

Newfoundland

American cocker spaniel

Black and tan coonhound

American foxhound

Boston terrier

▶ *The first Douglas DC-3s were built especially for American Airlines in 1935. The DC-3 soon became the world's most popular transport plane.*

The famous Douglas DC-3, the Dakota, carried 21 passengers at a speed of 192 miles per hour (309 km/hr) and accounted for most of the world's passenger traffic for many years. The DC-3 was modified for military use and named the C-47 during World War II. It was the mainstay of U.S. troop and cargo transport.

DOUGLAS, Donald W.

Donald W. Douglas (1892–1981) was an aircraft designer. In 1921 he founded the Douglas Aircraft Company, which became part of the McDonnell Douglas Corporation in 1967. Douglas planes include commercial transports, bombers, and jet airliners.

DOUGLAS, Stephen A.

Stephen A. Douglas (1813–1861) is remembered today mainly as the Democratic opponent of Abraham LINCOLN in a series of debates during their race for an Illinois Senate seat in 1858. An excellent speaker, he was especially eloquent in the causes of U.S. westward

▼ *Although Stephen A. Douglas was a short man, his powerful speaking voice and strong build gained him the nickname the Little Giant.*

expansion and "popular sovereignty." This was the principle that the people settling a territory should be allowed to decide for themselves whether or not to allow slavery.

Douglas won the 1858 senatorial election, but two years later he came in second to Lincoln in the presidential race. Douglas supported the new president, but he died soon after Lincoln's inauguration.

In addition to his prominent political career, Stephen A. Douglas was a wealthy land speculator around the Chicago area. He helped make that city a major railroad terminus.

DOUGLASS, Frederick

Born of a slave mother and a white father (whom he never knew), Frederick Douglass (1817–1895) became one of the most outstanding CIVIL RIGHTS leaders in U.S. history. As a child he was taught to read by a kindly white mistress; when the master forbade this, Frederick secretly continued his education on his own. In 1838 he escaped to the North. Here, his gift with words soon brought him to the forefront of the ABOLITIONIST movement. During the Civil War he was an adviser to President Abraham LINCOLN. Afterward, he worked for full civil rights for blacks and women and held several important jobs in the U.S. government. His autobiography is *Life and Times of Frederick Douglass*.

During the Civil War, President Lincoln's government passed a law that all able-bodied males aged 20 to 45 were liable for the draft unless they paid $300. This law caused many riots, especially in New York City. Workers, largely of Irish descent, battled with police and militiamen. There were about 1,000 casualties.

DRAFT

The draft, also called conscription, is a method of calling men for service in the armed forces. During the CIVIL WAR, the South was forced to draft soldiers beginning in 1862; the North followed in 1863. Before

▼ *Secretary of War Newton Barker drew the first draft number of World War I on June 27, 1918. About 2.5 million Americans were drafted over the remaining five months of the war.*

When Theodore Dreiser published his first book, *Sister Carrie*, in 1900, it sold only 456 copies. It was considered immoral, and the publisher refused to distribute or advertise it.

▼ The government's anti-drug efforts are aimed mainly at young people in the inner cities. This poster in Harlem, New York City, is part of the "Say NO to Drugs" campaign.

▼ W.E.B. Du Bois once described his civil rights beliefs as "the recognition of the principle of human brotherhood as a practical present creed."

the United States entered WORLD WAR I, the U.S. Army had only just over 125,000 men. A draft was started, and 2.5 million more soldiers were called up. During WORLD WAR II, 10 million of the 18 million U.S. soldiers were drafted. Two million men were drafted to fight in Korea, and about 1.75 million drafted soldiers fought in the VIETNAM WAR. The United States has had a volunteer army since 1973. But young men must register for the draft with the Selective Service System when they reach the age of 18.

DREISER, Theodore

The novelist Theodore Dreiser (1871–1945) is best known for two books, *Sister Carrie* and *An American Tragedy*. Dreiser earned a good living as a magazine editor. But he achieved little success as a writer until 1925, when *An American Tragedy* was published. This book, based on a real murder case, was hailed as a masterpiece. Dreiser had a pessimistic view of American society. His books often portray individuals who are helpless against this society.

DRUG ABUSE

The harmful use of mind-altering drugs is called drug abuse. Some people start to use drugs for a thrill or as an escape from stress or poverty. Sometimes these drugs are legal, such as alcohol, sleeping pills, or prescription drugs. In the 1960s a wide range of illegal drugs began to appear. Officials seize about $600 million worth of drugs each year, but many times that amount reach the country. The most dangerous are heroin and crack, a type of cocaine. Both are addictive and can lead to death from overdoses. Marijuana and amphetamines (mood lifters) are not physically addictive but can cause users to crave them and resort to crime to obtain them. Clinics and halfway houses, supported privately or by the government, help drug abusers "kick the habit."

DU BOIS, W.E.B.

W.E.B. Du Bois (1868–1963) was an important black-American leader and historian. He became the first black to obtain the degree of doctor of philosophy (Ph.D.) from Harvard University. Du Bois believed that black people must actively fight prejudice and injustice. In 1909 he was one of the founders of the NATIONAL ASSOCIATION FOR THE ADVANCEMENT OF COLORED PEOPLE (NAACP). After decades of work DuBois saw little progress and began to look for new solutions. He joined the Communist Party in 1961. Du Bois lived in Ghana for the last years of his life.

DUCHAMP, Marcel

Marcel Duchamp (1887–1968) was a French artist who moved to the United States in 1942. He dramatically expanded the frontiers of modern art—though even today many people believe Duchamp was a clever showman rather than a true artist. During his life, his works angered critics and the public. Duchamp maintained that art was whatever an artist said it was, however ridiculous. A well-known work is his *Mona Lisa*, a copy of the famous painting with a beard and mustache added.

DUCKS AND GEESE

Ducks and geese are birds that swim. They have webbed feet and flat bills. Ducks are smaller than geese and have shorter necks. Male ducks, or drakes, are usually more brightly colored than females. The male goose, or gander, has the same coloring as the female. Ducks

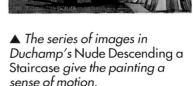

▲ The series of images in Duchamp's Nude Descending a Staircase *give the painting a sense of motion.*

▼ *Ducks and geese are migratory birds. Some will travel huge distances, even all the way from Alaska to Texas.*

Pintail

male

Canada goose

female

male

Common goldeneye

Mallard

Shoveler

female

male

female

male

209

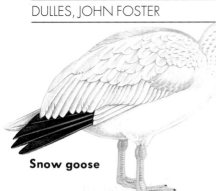
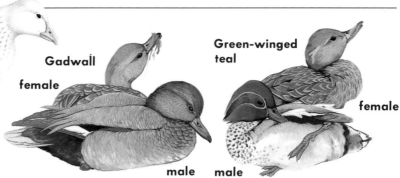

Snow goose

Gadwall
female

male

Green-winged
teal

female

male

▲ *The plumage colors of ducks and geese often act as camouflage. The snow goose is well suited to its Arctic home.*

spend more time in the water than geese, and their legs are set farther back.

Ducks and geese nest in the north and travel south in the winter. In North America, many species of ducks and several species of geese nest along the northern coast of North America. South of this Arctic region, the lakes and rivers of the spruce belt that runs from east to west across Canada and Alaska provide nesting grounds for millions of ducks. The marshes, ponds, and lakes of the northern prairies are also the main breeding grounds for enormous numbers of ducks. Many ducks and geese spend the winter on the east coast, and many millions more winter in the marshes and ponds of the California valleys.

DULLES, John Foster

John Foster Dulles (1888–1959) was secretary of state between 1953 and 1959 under President Dwight D. EISENHOWER. He helped formulate U.S. foreign policy during the COLD WAR. Dulles strongly opposed communism. He urged that the United States respond actively to Communist expansion. He even called for the "liberation" of countries of the Soviet bloc. Earlier, he had served as a U.S. delegate to the UNITED NATIONS and as a senator from New York.

DUNCAN, Isadora

▼ *Isadora Duncan caused a sensation dancing barefoot in loose tunics or Grecian-style robes. She again caused a sensation when she declared herself a Communist. Boston banned her from dancing there in 1922.*

Isadora Duncan (1878–1927) was a famous dancer. As a child in San Francisco, she decided that the movements of classical ballet were too stiff, too artificial. Later, in Europe, she saw artwork showing the ancient Greeks. She soon developed dances based on how she thought the Greeks had danced. She danced barefooted, had long, flowing hair, and wore flowing garments. And her dancing flowed too. She used very free movements, like the movements she saw in nature, such as rolling waves. Duncan's dancing helped launch modern dancing. She died in France, strangled when her long scarf was caught in the wheel of a car.

DU PONT, Éleuthère

Éleuthère Irénée du Pont (1771–1834) was a Frenchman who came to the United States in 1800 and founded a company that was to become world famous. In 1802, near Wilmington, Delaware, du Pont built a gunpowder plant, later known as E. I. du Pont de Nemours and Co. The company prospered, especially during the War of 1812. After du Pont's death, members of the family continued to run the business. The company expanded into a wide range of products, including plastics, chemicals, and synthetic fibers.

▲ Charles Duryea demonstrated the one-horsepower car that won the first U.S. automobile race. In February 1896 the Duryea brothers sold the first automobile in the United States.

DURYEA, Charles E. and J. F.

The Duryea brothers, Charles E. (1861–1938) and J. Frank (1869–1967), were trailblazers in the U.S. automobile industry. They built the first gasoline-powered automobile in the United States. This was demonstrated in Springfield, Massachusetts, in 1893. Two years later they won the first gasoline-powered automobile race, in Chicago, with a similar one-cylinder model. They invested some of their $2,000 prize in a workshop and set up the Duryea Motor Wagon Company that same year. Three years later Frank merged this company with the larger Stevens Arms Company. With more money and a larger factory he helped to design Stevens-Duryea cars, which were some of the first four- and six-cylinder automobiles.

▼ The conditions in the Dust Bowl caused terrible poverty for many farmers and their families. Many had to give up their livelihood and seek employment elsewhere. The story of one such family is movingly told in John Steinbeck's novel The Grapes of Wrath.

DUST BOWL

In the mid-1930s, a series of terrible dust storms swept across the southern Great Plains. This area, centered in Kansas, Oklahoma, Texas, New Mexico, and Colorado, became known as the Dust Bowl. In the 1930s the soil was dry because of a long drought. Hundreds of millions of tons of topsoil were carried off by the winds, destroying the land. Many people lost their farms. Improved farming methods brought some relief, but dust storms are still a problem in this region.

EAGLE

Eagles are large BIRDS OF PREY. Two species, the bald eagle and the golden eagle, breed in North America. The bald eagle is found nowhere else in the world. It ranges from Alaska to British Columbia and the western Great Lakes region and is also found in parts of the East. At one time it was found all over the continent, but it has become very rare. A type of sea eagle, it eats fish. The golden eagle lives in open country, mountainous regions, and prairies, from Alaska to Mexico. The numbers of both species have been reduced by hunting, and now they are protected by law.

Golden eagle

Bald eagle

▶ The bald eagle, the U.S. national symbol, is not really bald; it has white feathers on its head. Similarly, Mexico's national symbol, the golden eagle, is not really gold. It has just a few gold flecks on the back of its neck.

▼ "Gas is low" were the last words heard from Amelia Earhart before her plane disappeared over the Pacific.

EARHART, Amelia

Amelia Earhart (1897–1937) was a famous American aviator who broke several world flying records. She worked to open aviation to women. In 1928 she became the first woman to cross the Atlantic Ocean by air. This was as a passenger, but in 1932 she became the first woman to fly across the Atlantic alone. In 1935 she became the first woman to fly from Hawaii to California. In 1937 she and a navigator attempted to fly around the world. With less than one third of the journey to go, her plane disappeared in the Pacific Ocean. No trace of the plane or aviators has ever been found.

EARP, Wyatt

Wyatt Earp (1848–1929) was a legendary frontiersman and peace officer of the Old West. He worked as a stagecoach driver, a railroad construction worker, a gambler, a surveyor, and a buffalo hunter before becoming a lawman. In 1876 he became chief deputy marshal in Dodge City, Kansas. In 1879 he settled in Tombstone, Arizona Territory. Earp and his brothers participated in the famous "Gunfight at the O.K. Corral," in which they killed several suspected cattle rustlers.

EARTHQUAKES

The Earth's crust is made up of "plates" of rock. Huge pressures within the Earth push the plates against and over each other at the edges, which are known as faults. An earthquake occurs when two plates suddenly lurch against each other.

Most major quakes in the world have occurred in the earthquake "belt" that circles the Pacific. In North America, this belt runs along the west coast. The SAN ANDREAS fault runs through California from north to south. In the San Francisco Bay area, there are three more faults—the Hayward, Calaveras, and Sargent faults. They often have tremors, or small quakes.

A quake measuring 6.9 on the Richter scale (which

▲ The "Gunfight at the O.K. Corral" took place on October 26, 1881, in Tombstone, Arizona. Wyatt, Virgil, and Morgan Earp, and town dentist Doc Holliday killed four members of the Clanton gang.

▼ The older buildings of San Francisco's Marina district had no earthquake protection. They suffered the worst in the 1989 earthquake.

The Worst 20th-Century Earthquakes to Hit the U.S.

1906, April 18 San Francisco is destroyed by an earthquake. More than 500 people are killed or missing.

1933, March 10 An earthquake at Long Beach, California, kills 117 people.

1964, March 27 The strongest earthquake to hit North America strikes 80 miles (130 km) east of Anchorage, Alaska. It is followed by a tidal wave 50 ft (15 m) high. A total of 117 people are killed.

1989, October 17 An earthquake measuring 6.9 on the Richter scale hits San Francisco, destroying parts of the Bay Bridge and the Interstate 880. Nearly 100 people are killed.

▶ *In 1912, Eastman Kodak became one of the first companies to build a research laboratory. Before that, firms kept their products unchanged and hoped they would continue selling.*

▼ *The first amateur photographers sent their cameras, with exposed film inside, to this Eastman plant in Rochester, New York. In return they would receive a new loaded camera.*

records the magnitude, or strength, of an earthquake) hit the San Francisco area in October 1989. An elevated freeway and part of the Bay Bridge collapsed, as did many buildings.

Although many minor earthquakes have taken place in the region, the most damaging quake there was the 1906 San Francisco earthquake. During the quake, the land along the San Andreas fault lurched 21 inches (53 cm). It was one of the most devastating earthquakes ever.

EASTMAN, George

George Eastman (1854–1932) did more to bring photography within the reach of ordinary people than any other pioneer of photography. The company he founded in 1880, Eastman Kodak, is still one of the largest photographic businesses in the world. One invention of Eastman's — roll film — revolutionized photography. Before that, pictures could only be taken using cumbersome glass plates. By 1888, Eastman had produced his first all-purpose camera. It cost $25. By 1900 he was making a camera that cost only $1.

ECKERT, John P., Jr.

John Presper Eckert (1919–) and the physicist John W. Mauchly (1907–1980) created the first electronic digital computer. This machine, called ENIAC (*E*lectronic *N*umerical *I*ntegrator *a*nd *C*omputer), was made for the U.S. Army and completed in 1946. It weighed

60,000 pounds (27,000 kg) and almost filled a room 50 by 30 feet (15 by 9 m). Eckert and Mauchly formed their own computer manufacturing company. Over the next two decades they made many discoveries. Their research and work provided the basis for most of the computers that are in use today.

ECONOMY, U.S.

The U.S. economy is the most powerful in the world. Economists judge its performance by examining the Gross National Product (GNP), which is the total monetary value of goods and services produced annually. The U.S. GNP is about $5 trillion. SERVICE INDUSTRIES, worth about $800 billion each year, are the largest element, with MANUFACTURING close behind. Government spending comes to about $600 billion each year. Compared with some other countries, the U.S. government plays a smaller role in national economic affairs. The American free market system favors individuals or private companies.

Colonial America's economy was largely agricultural. Manufacturing took the lead in the 1800s, but in the past ten years service industries have been in first place.

▲ Traders at the New York Stock Exchange scramble to handle orders on a busy trading day. Stock market trading often reflects the health of the national economy.

Some Economic Terms

Boom is a time of fast economic growth. During a boom, unemployment is low and people have plenty of money.

Capitalism is an economic system where private individuals control most of a country's industries.

Consumer is anyone who buys goods and uses services.

Cost of living is the cost of buying the products and services that are used in everyday life.

Depression is a time when business activity is very low and unemployment is high.

National income is the total amount of money earned in a nation over a period of time.

Standard of living is a term used to describe the level at which a family or country lives.

▼ Mary Baker Eddy believed that the practice of medicine was not the route to healing. Healing could only begin when a patient had faith in God.

EDDY, Mary Baker

Mary Baker Eddy (1821–1910) was the founder of the CHRISTIAN SCIENCE religion. From childhood she suffered from a spinal illness that often prevented her from going to school. As an adult she was cured, temporarily, by a faith healer. After his death and the return

At the age of 12, Thomas Edison became a train boy, selling candy and magazines on the Grand Trunk Railroad. In his spare time, he experimented with chemicals in the baggage car. He even printed a newspaper on the moving train.

of her illness, she turned to the New Testament, and her reading and meditation on it produced a cure. She described her system of faith healing in a book called *Science and Health with Key to the Scriptures* (first published in 1875). Soon she had many followers, including Asa G. Eddy, whom she married. In 1879 she founded the First Church of Christ, Scientist, in Boston. In 1908, Mary Baker Eddy founded the highly respected *Christian Science Monitor*.

EDISON, Thomas Alva

Thomas Alva Edison (1847–1931) was perhaps the most successful inventor of all time. Though largely self-taught, he devised thousands of new and different machines. Many were improvements to existing inventions —Edison was primarily interested in helping improve the quality of people's lives, not in being a great inventor—but a number, such as the phonograph, were entirely original. His impact on the modern world was immense and recognized in his own lifetime.

Edison's interests knew no limits. Even as a boy in Ohio, he was interested in everything around him. His major work included perfecting the electric light; a new, more reliable typewriter; an improved version of the telephone; movie cameras; electric generators; and the dictaphone. To many, he personified the questing spirit of America. His laboratory in New Jersey is now a national monument.

▼ The hardworking Edison once decribed genius as "1 percent inspiration and 99 percent perspiration."

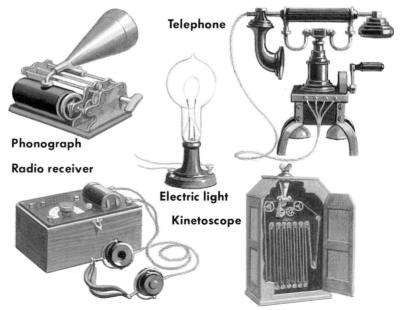

Telephone

Phonograph

Radio receiver

Electric light

Kinetoscope

▶ Thomas Edison showed his skill at improving other inventions as well as devising his own. His work improved the performance of the telephone and the radio receiver. The phonograph, electric light, and kinetoscope were his own creations.

EDMONTON

Edmonton is the capital and second largest city of the Canadian province of ALBERTA. Located on the North Saskatchewan River, it is the most northerly city in Canada and is known as the Gateway to the North. Edmonton began as a fur-trading post in 1795. Today it is an important center of Canada's oil industry. Most of Alberta's oil fields are within 100 miles (160 km) of the city. Edmonton is also a major distribution center for goods being transported to and from Alaska and the Canadian northwest. Downtown Edmonton is elegant and thriving, with large malls, parks, and high rises.

▲ The 3,000-acre (1,200-ha) Capital City Recreation Park is just across the river from downtown Edmonton.

◄ Most schools in the country had only one room and one teacher. Some children had to walk more than 10 miles (16 km) to get to school. The teacher had to teach children of all ages and grades. One-room schools existed well into this century.

EDUCATION

More than 58 million people are enrolled in all public (tax-supported) and private schools in the United States. Almost 46 million of this total attend elementary and secondary schools. The rest attend institutions of higher education—which is everything beyond high school. Public schooling is funded and controlled at the state and local level. The federal Department of Education provides mainly guidance and some money—about 6 percent of the total cost of $325 billion each year. Federal funds also pay for special programs for the handicapped and bilingual education.

A completed high school education is important for getting a good job, but more than 30 percent of high school students leave before graduation. States decide at what age students are allowed to leave school—

Public education in the United States takes place in more than 85,000 elementary and secondary schools, on which about $185 billion a year is spent. There are more than 3,200 private and public colleges, community and junior colleges, and universities, on which almost $125 billion a year is spent. Almost 90 percent of regular day-school students and almost 75 percent of students in higher education are in public institutions.

▶ *High schools offer a course of study that allows students to prepare for college or university. Vocational courses are also offered for students who intend to get a job when they graduate from secondary school.*

Some Important Dates in the History of U.S. Education

1635 The first secondary school in the colonies, The Boston Latin School, is opened.

1636 Harvard College (now Harvard University) is founded near Boston.

1647 Massachusetts passes a law that requires towns to establish public elementary and secondary schools.

1833 Oberlin College is the first U.S. coeducational college.

1852 Massachusetts is the first state to pass a law making school attendance compulsory.

1901 Joliet Junior College opens in Illinois. It is the country's oldest junior college.

1954 The U.S. Supreme Court rules that segregation by race in public schools is unconstitutional.

1965 Congress passes the Elementary and Secondary Education Act to improve education for children from low-income families.

1979 Congress establishes the U.S. Department of Education.

usually 15 to 16 years of age. More than 2.8 million students graduate from high school annually, and about 1 million from four-year colleges.

The curriculum—exactly what is taught—has changed greatly since the first American public schools more than 150 years ago. It was enough then to teach reading, writing, and arithmetic. The modern world calls for such subjects as computer science. And to enable the United States to compete better in the world economy, more schools are offering a wider variety of language courses, including Japanese. They are also offering courses in global studies, so that Americans can learn about other countries and cultures. At the same time, traditional nonacademic studies such as home economics and industrial arts continue to be important.

▶ *Here pupils from a New York City elementary school learn about their city. Field trips are an important part of education.*

◀ *On average, more than $4,000 is spent on every pupil in the United States each year. Some of this money goes toward simple items such as the dry cells needed to teach basic electricity. Computers and similar equipment cost much more.*

Some high schools even specialize in these subjects, which are also called vocational skills. These skills must keep pace with the changing machinery and technology the students must face. Another recent trend is the changing of the curriculums to reflect the contributions of non-European ethnic groups to American society.

Boys and girls in Colonial America had very different educations. Six- and seven-year-olds would learn the alphabet at the same school. After that boys would continue their "book learning" in the hope of attending college. Girls would stay at home to be taught domestic skills such as cooking and weaving.

EINSTEIN, Albert

Albert Einstein (1879–1955) was one of the greatest physicists of all times. He won the 1921 Nobel Prize for physics for his work on the photoelectron effect—the release of electrons by a metal that is struck by light. Einstein was born in Germany and went to school there and in Switzerland. In 1914 he became director of the Kaiser Wilhelm Institute in Berlin. In 1933, however, the Nazis came to power in Germany, and they took away Einstein's citizenship because he was Jewish. He then joined the Institute for Advanced Study in Princeton, New Jersey. He worked there for the rest of his life and became a U.S. citizen in 1940.

Einstein is best known for his general theory of relativity, which he published in 1916. This incorporated the work of many years and explained the way space, time, motion, mass, light, and gravitation are related. His theory also states that mass and energy are two forms of the same thing. This is the basic idea behind atomic energy. During the last 25 years of his life, Einstein continued his work on the theory of relativity. Sadly, he died before he felt that his work had been completed.

▼ *Albert Einstein was a brilliant scientist but could sometimes be an "absent-minded professor." Once he was found walking up and down a street in Princeton, New Jersey, where he lived, looking puzzled. He had forgotten his address.*

EISENHOWER, Dwight D.

Dwight D. Eisenhower
Born: Oct. 14, 1890, in Denison, Texas
Education: West Point Military Academy, New York
Political party: Republican
Term of office: 1953–1961
Married: 1916 to Mamie Geneva Doud
Died: Mar. 28, 1969, in Washington, D.C.

▶ *Eisenhower negotiated an end to the Korean War.*

▼ *During World War II, General Eisenhower made many of his decisions jointly with Britain's Field Marshal Montgomery.*

Dwight David ("Ike") Eisenhower (1890–1969) was elected president in 1952. Previously he had been Supreme Allied Commander during WORLD WAR II and the first Commander of the NORTH ATLANTIC TREATY ORGANIZATION (NATO) forces. His bravery, integrity, warmth, and sincerity made him enormously popular both before and after his election.

Elected on the Republican ticket, Eisenhower introduced a domestic program he called "Modern Republicanism." He introduced social welfare programs that included more social security benefits; government aid in building schools; and a new Department of Health, Education, and Welfare. In 1954 the Supreme Court ruled that racial segregation in public schools was unconstitutional. When violence broke out at some newly integrated schools in the South, Eisenhower sent troops into Little Rock, Arkansas, to enforce the law.

Eisenhower worked hard to achieve peace, and in 1953 he negotiated an end to the KOREAN WAR. But he also was firmly against communism. In 1954 he helped create the Southeast Asia Treaty Organization (SEATO) to prevent the spread of communism. In 1957 he promised military and economic aid to any Middle Eastern countries that asked for it, to help them resist Communist aggression. This became known as the Eisenhower Doctrine. The next year, he sent marines into Lebanon, after its president appealed for help. In 1961, Eisenhower broke off diplomatic relations with Cuba, which had become Communist under the dictator Fidel Castro.

ELECTIONS

Many government positions at local, state, and national levels are held by people who are chosen by voters in elections. The elections are held at intervals laid down by law, which vary depending on the position.

Nationwide, presidential elections draw the most attention. They are held every four years on the first Tuesday after the first Monday in November. Presidential candidates are nominated at national party conventions. The voting is done by delegates who are chosen, usually in *primary elections*, to represent their states. The candidates for each party then campaign throughout the nation to explain what they would do if elected. Finally, all registered voters in each state cast their ballot in the national election. The results of presidential elections are decided by the ELECTORAL COLLEGE. The candidate who wins the majority of the electoral votes is declared president.

▲ Modern voting machines have largely replaced the traditional ballots that voters marked in ink. Election results can now be known in hours rather than days.

ELECTORAL COLLEGE

The electoral college is a group of individuals who elect the president and vice president of the United States. Each state has a certain number of. electors. This number equals the number of the state's congressional representatives and senators combined. The electors meet in state capitals on the first Monday after the second Wednesday in December in presidential election years. They vote for whichever candidates, presidential and vice presidential, got the most votes in their state. On January 6 (or the next day, if January 6 is a Sunday), the president of the Senate announces the winners. This never comes as a surprise because the electors usually follow their states' voting patterns. The popular vote is often closer than the electoral vote because the electors use a winner-take-all system. In the 1988 election, George Bush got 48 million votes and 426 electoral votes. Michael Dukakis received 41 million votes but only 111 electoral votes. because he won in only ten states.

▼ Electric power plants must operate 24 hours a day. Any time when they are off — called downtime — is expensive for the power companies.

ELECTRIC POWER INDUSTRY

The electric power industry in the United States produces more electricity than any other country in the world and supplies the nation with energy. Electric

▲ *T. S. Eliot used diagrams and symbols to explain some of his work to students at Princeton University.*

▼ *Musicians were always loyal to "the Duke." Clarinetist Jimmy Hamilton (right), a top soloist, played with Ellington (left) for nearly 30 years.*

power is generated in large factories, called plants. About 57 percent of electric power comes from burning coal. Other sources are nuclear energy, natural gas, and hydroelectric plants. Hydroelectric power is usually produced in areas where there are few people, such as at the dams in Washington State, so long cables are used to take the electricity to big cities. Some oil is also burned to produce electricity. The demand for electricity in the United States continues to grow. Soon new ways of producing it will have to be found as many of the fossil fuels used today, such as coal and natural gas, will soon run out. Some electric companies have already started to experiment with solar and wind power to generate electricity.

Some electric companies supplying power are owned by state governments, but most (about 80 per cent) are owned by private investors.

ELIOT, T. S.

The poet, playwright, and literary critic Thomas Stearns Eliot (1888–1965) was one of the most important writers of the 20th century. He received the 1948 Nobel Prize for literature. Eliot was born in St. Louis, Missouri, but as a young man he settled in England and became a British citizen in 1927. Eliot's poetry deals mainly with the problems of living in a purposeless, modern world. Most of his poems, including *The Waste Land* and *Four Quartets*, are not easy to read. In a lighter vein, Eliot wrote *Old Possum's Book of Practical Cats*, which was later used for the musical *Cats*.

ELLINGTON, Duke

Edward Kennedy ("Duke") Ellington (1899–1974) was a jazz pianist, songwriter, and bandleader. He is considered one of the most important people in the history of JAZZ. He came to public attention in the late 1920s, when his band was playing in New York City at Harlem's famous Cotton Club. His band sound was unique in music. His song, "Take the A Train," was one of the best-selling records of the 1930s. He helped other musicians by changing the lineup of his band. A number of his works were composed to highlight solo jazz musicians. But he also wrote large works, some of which were religious, intended to be performed as concerts.

EL PASO

El Paso, with a population of more than 515,000, is the largest city on the Mexican border. It is located on the north bank of the RIO GRANDE in the extreme west of TEXAS. More than 30 percent of the country's copper refining takes place in El Paso. Clothing manufacture and the military also provide employment. Fort Bliss, located just northeast of the city, is the headquarters of the Army Air Defense Center. El Paso was founded by the Spanish in 1659. It began to grow from 1849, when the MEXICAN WAR established the Rio Grande as the U.S.–Mexican border.

▲ The El Paso Civic Center was built during the 1970s, when El Paso's population grew by more than 30 percent.

EMANCIPATION PROCLAMATION

Many people believe that the Emancipation Proclamation, issued on January 1, 1863, freed all the slaves in the United States. But this came after the CIVIL WAR, by the Thirteenth Amendment to the Constitution.

President Abraham LINCOLN opposed slavery, but he had been elected on a platform that promised not to interfere with slavery within the slave states. His primary aim was to save the Union. He first issued the Proclamation, in rough form, just after the Union victory at Antietam, in September 1862. It declared that all the slaves in the Confederacy were free (*not* those in the loyal border slave states, whose support Lincoln badly needed). At the time, of course, Lincoln had no power over the Confederate states. But nearly 200,000 of their slaves went north as free men and joined the Union army. The Proclamation also identified the Union's cause firmly with the fight against slavery.

▼ Ralph Waldo Emerson came from a long line of clergymen. Trained as a minister, he resigned in 1832 to become a writer and public figure.

EMERSON, Ralph Waldo

Ralph Waldo Emerson (1803–1882) was one of the most important American writers of the 19th century. He is best known for his essays written on such subjects as "Politics," "Friendship," and "Self-Reliance." These reveal Emerson's belief in a divine spirit within humans. His essay *Nature* affirms the power of nature to reveal spiritual truths (a philosophy known as *transcendentalism*). Many of Emerson's beliefs were shared by other American writers of the time such as Henry David THOREAU. Emerson also wrote poetry.

Some Endangered U.S. Animals and Plants

Mammals
Ocelot
Southern sea otter
Red wolf
Grizzly bear

Birds
California condor
Whooping crane
Ivory-billed woodpecker

Reptiles and Fish
American crocodile
Red-bellied turtle
Gila trout

Plants
Arizona hedgehog cactus
Dwarf bear poppy
Antioch Dunes evening primrose

▶ *Some native plants, such as the Knowlton's cactus, have become endangered as more people move to the southwestern states.*

▼ *The brown pelican can hold twice its body weight in its bill pouch. Pollution in the Gulf of Mexico threatens its fishing grounds.*

ENDANGERED ANIMALS AND PLANTS

These are species, or types, of animals and plants that will soon become extinct (die out) unless they are protected. Most are at risk because of people. Animals are often hunted and plants are collected so much that they disappear forever. More animals are trapped in the United States than in any country in the world except the Soviet Union.

Many species have been threatened because the growth of cities, agriculture, and industry has destroyed their *habitat* (the place where animals live naturally). POLLUTION has affected many species too. Pesticides in rivers collect in the bodies of fish, which are then eaten by birds. The pesticides make the birds' eggs break too easily. This is one reason why the osprey and southern bald EAGLE are endangered.

Federal and state laws protect wild animals and plants that are listed as endangered. They cannot be hunted, collected, bought or sold, or threatened in any way. Their habitats are protected in NATIONAL PARKS and wildlife refuges and by government controls over land use and pollution. Sometimes animals that are nearly extinct, such as the California CONDOR, are captured to be bred in captivity so that possibly one day they can be returned to the wild.

ENVIRONMENTAL PROTECTION

The environment is the surroundings in which people, animals, and plants live. Environmental protection means keeping our environment safe for the future.

In North America many measures are being taken to protect the environment. POLLUTION is controlled by

◄ *More than 35,000 tons of toxic petroleum were released in 1989 when the Exxon Valdez ran aground off the coast of Alaska. Environmental disasters such as this destroy much wildlife. Seabirds die when their feathers are soaked with oil.*

law, and CONSERVATION of NATURAL RESOURCES is encouraged. However, many people believe that more could be done.

ENDANGERED ANIMALS are protected by law. These are the types of animals that have been hunted so much by people that they are in danger of disappearing forever. NATIONAL PARKS and nature reserves protect wildlife in its natural environment. Plants and trees that are at risk are protected in much the same way.

The countries of the world cooperate in protecting the environment. A good example is the proposed Bering Land Bridge National Preserve, in the Bering Strait between Alaska and Siberia. This national park and wilderness preserve will be managed by the United States and the Soviet Union together.

EPISCOPALIANS

Episcopalians are members of the Episcopal Church, which is part of the worldwide Anglican Communion. Before the American REVOLUTION, Episcopalians belonged to the Church of England. The Revolution severed the ties between the Church in the United States and the Church of England. There are three Episcopal churches. The largest, the Episcopal Church, has over 2.5 million members. The other two churches are very small and together have only about 12,000 members between them. Episcopalians are Protestant. Their services are often based on those that were developed in the Church of England.

Some Important Dates in the History of U.S. Environmental Protection

1872 Yellowstone National Park, the first national park in the world, is established.

1899 The first important pollution law is passed making it illegal to dump any liquid waste (except from sewers) into navigable waters. This law was not enforced.

1903 Pelican Island, Florida, becomes the first federal wildlife refuge.

1916 Congress sets up the National Park Service.

1933 The Civilian Conservation Corps is set up to plant trees and perform other conservation tasks.

1966 The National Wildlife Refuge System comes into being.

1970 The Environmental Protection Agency is set up to guard against pollution.

1972 DDT is banned from general use as a pesticide because it is discovered that it poisons the food chain.

1973 The Endangered Species Act provides more protection for threatened animals and plants.

1990 The U.S. and 69 other countries agree to phase out CFCs (chlorofluorocarbons) by the year 2000. CFCs are one of the major causes of the destruction of the ozone layer.

▲ Leif Ericsson's accounts of a new land called Vinland seem to describe the east coast of North America.

According to old Icelandic stories called *sagas,* **Leif Ericsson and his men put ashore on a barren tableland of flat rocks backed by icy mountains. They then sailed south and finally landed on a shore where the land was green with trees and sweet "grapes." Ericsson named this place Vinland (Wineland), and they spent the winter there. The "grapes," which were probably cranberries or gooseberries, were used to make wine.**

▶ By providing a link with the Great Lakes and the Midwest, the Erie Canal made New York City the chief port of the U.S. east coast.

ERICSSON, Leif

Christopher COLUMBUS is hailed as the man whose explorations led to the permanent settlement of North America. But he was not the first European to reach the Americas. That achievement probably belongs to Leif Ericsson (about A.D. 980–1025), a Norseman, or Viking, originally from Iceland. Around the year A.D. 1000, he sailed west from Greenland with 35 men in search of a land said to have been seen by another Norseman. No one is quite sure where Ericsson made landings. Some say northern Newfoundland, where remains of a Norse settlement have been found. But Ericsson and his men are known to have spent the winter in this new land before returning to Greenland.

ERIE CANAL

The Erie Canal stands as one of the greatest engineering and construction feats in U.S. history. It was built between 1817 and 1825 to provide a waterway from the

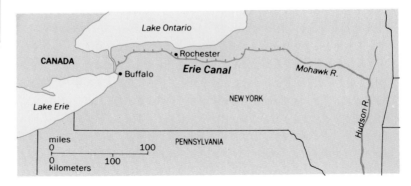

East to the GREAT LAKES. The canal runs 363 miles (585 km) from Albany on the HUDSON RIVER to Buffalo on Lake Erie. The original canal was 40 feet (12 m) wide and 4 feet (1.2 m) deep. This narrow and shallow design was chosen so that wide, flat-bottomed barges could be drawn by horses on either side of the canal. The $7 million cost to build the canal was quickly paid back by the canal fees paid by barges. Today road and rail traffic have taken over from the canal, but it remains open. It is part of the New York State Barge Canal system.

ERIE, LAKE *See* Great Lakes

ESKIMOS

The Eskimos are not related to the American Indians. They are descendants of people who crossed the BERING STRAIT and spread across the Arctic and subarctic regions of North America. They did this between 5,500 and 3,000 years ago. "Eskimo" is an Algonquian name that means "raw meat eaters." Eskimos prefer the name *Inuit* ("the people").

There are a number of different groups of Eskimos within three main large groups: the Alaskan, the Central, and the Greenland Eskimos. The Eskimos have a hunting and fishing style of life that is suited to their cold environment. They can make houses, called igloos, very quickly out of the ice and snow. For hunting in snow they use snowmobiles or special sleds. And for traveling on the rivers they use kayaks (completely covered except for a hole where the rider sits) and umiaks (larger open boats). Today many Eskimos live in settlements with buildings made of wood.

The Erie Canal remains an active commercial waterway. More than 5 million tons of cargo are still shipped through the canal each year.

▲ Eskimo girls make the most of the short summer months in Inuit Kangirsuk, northern Quebec.

◄ Fewer and fewer Eskimos live in the traditional way, ice fishing and hunting according to the season.

Although some Eskimos still live by hunting and trapping, most Canadian and Alaskan Eskimos now live in towns and settlements. The exploitation of oil and natural gas in northern areas has vitally changed their way of life, not always for the better. However, the arts and handicrafts of the Eskimos are becoming more widely known.

▶ *Ethnic differences seem unimportant when children get to know each other at school.*

ETHNIC GROUPS

Largest Ethnic Groups in the U.S. (by ancestral region and country)

American
American Indian

African
Black Americans

European
Germans
Italians
British
Irish
Austrians/Hungarians
Soviets
Swedes

Asians
Filipinos
Chinese
Koreans
Japanese
Vietnamese
Turks
Indians

Latin Americans
Mexicans
Puerto Ricans
Cubans
Dominicans
Colombians
Haitians

An ethnic group is any group of people who have certain things in common that set them apart from the larger society in which they live. For example, these people, or their ancestors, might have come from the same country. Or they may speak the same language, be of the same race, or practice the same religion.

The United States is especially rich in the number of different ethnic groups that make up its population. The people of American ethnic groups have come from almost every other country in the world.

People in the same ethnic group often tend to live in the same areas. This gives them a sense of belonging in their new land. Others try to become part of the larger society. But even when they do this, they like to hold on to their ethnic identity in some way, so that they can continue to share their common heritage. Special groups teach and preserve the cultural legacy of different ethnic groups. American life is rich in festivals and other events that reflect this ethnic variety.

There are many reasons why people of different ethnic groups have migrated to the United States. They have come to find religious freedom, to escape from wars, and to build better lives for themselves and their families. BLACK AMERICANS, however, were forced to come here—as slaves. And Native Americans—the American INDIANS, ESKIMOS, and ALEUTS—were here long before the Europeans. Ethnic groups have become a strong presence in all areas of American society.

EVERETT, Edward

Edward Everett (1794–1865) was an important politician and an outstanding orator in the 1800s. Between 1825 and 1854 he had a distinguished career as a congressman, governor of Massachusetts, U.S. minister to Great Britain, secretary of state under President Millard FILLMORE, and Massachusetts senator. He was also president of Harvard College. Everett delivered a brilliant speech at Gettysburg the day that Abraham LINCOLN made his famous GETTYSBURG ADDRESS.

EVERGLADES

The Everglades is a huge swamp that covers 4,000 square miles (10,000 km²) of southern FLORIDA. Much of it consists of glades, or prairies of sawgrass, a grass-like plant. The swampy water flows very slowly from Lake Okeechobee in the north to Florida Bay in the south. Many low islands, or hammocks, are covered with mangroves and other tropical trees. The animal life includes snakes, turtles, alligators, and many kinds of mammals and birds. The northern part of the Everglades has been drained and is used for farming. The Everglades National Park is in the southern part.

Edward Everett gave his speech at Gettysburg immediately before Abraham Lincoln delivered his famous Gettysburg Address. Everett was so amazed at Lincoln's ability to say so much in so few words that he declared then and there that Lincoln's speech would live for generations, while his own would be forgotten.

▼ *The Florida Everglades extend from Lake Okeechobee south to the Florida Keys.*

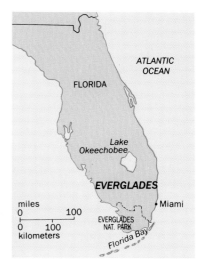

◄ *The anhinga, a bird of prey related to the cormorant, is native to the sluggish waters of the Everglades. It feeds on frogs, small fish, and even baby alligators.*

EXPLORATION OF NORTH AMERICA

The first Europeans to explore North America were probably the Vikings. Around the year 1000, the Viking Leif ERICSSON probably started a colony on the northern tip of Newfoundland, in an area called Vinland.

It was the Spanish, however, who began intensive exploration of the Americas at the beginning of the 1500s. They were searching mainly for gold and for a short route to the Far East. Some of them, such as Hernando DE SOTO and PONCE DE LEON, explored Florida; others, including Francisco CORONADO, traveled through Mexico into what is now the southwestern United States.

French exploration was centered mainly in the North, and the main attraction was the fur trade. French-Canadian traders and trappers had journeyed far into the GREAT LAKES region by the early 1600s. Later in the century the French explored the whole length of the Mississippi River and founded settlements in that region. Later explorers, thinking they were in unchartered territory, would often find French-Canadian fur trappers already trading there.

British victory in the FRENCH AND INDIAN WAR (1755–1763) opened up the land west of the Appalachian Mountains to exploration and settlement by its colonists. Thus began a push westward that was to continue for the next hundred years or so.

A great stimulus to American exploration was the LOUISIANA PURCHASE in 1803, which doubled the size of the United States. LEWIS AND CLARK and Zebulon PIKE led expeditions which opened up the West. And in the 1840s, John Charles FREMONT explored the ROCKY MOUNTAINS and pushed into California and Oregon.

The earliest map showing the New World was drawn in 1500 by the Spanish explorer Juan de la Cosa who sailed with Christopher Columbus on his second voyage in 1493. In 1507, Martin Waldseemuller, a German mapmaker, drew the first map on which the word America appeared. He named it after the explorer Amerigo Vespucci.

◄ This map, drawn in Antwerp in 1570, was one of the first guides to the New World.

▼ Lewis and Clark used their Shoshoni interpreter, Sacagawea, to speak to the Indians they met on their mission.

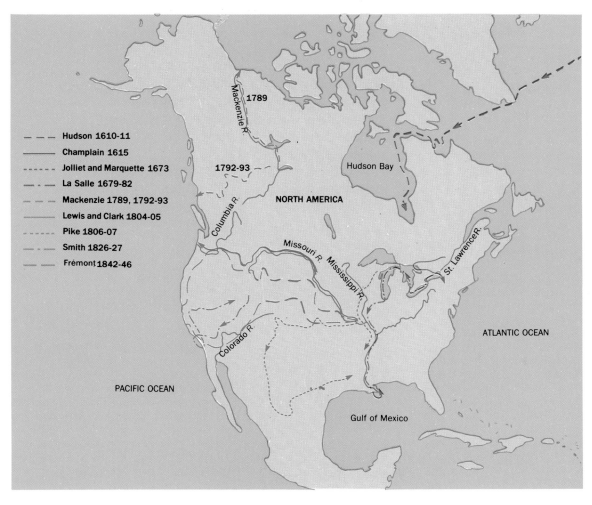

- - - Hudson 1610-11
——— Champlain 1615
- - - - - Jolliet and Marquette 1673
- · - · La Salle 1679-82
- - - Mackenzie 1789, 1792-93
——— Lewis and Clark 1804-05
· · · · · Pike 1806-07
- · · - Smith 1826-27
- - Frémont 1842-46

Mackenzie R.

1789

1792-93

Columbia R.

Hudson Bay

NORTH AMERICA

Missouri R.

Mississippi R.

St. Lawrence R.

Colorado R.

ATLANTIC OCEAN

PACIFIC OCEAN

Gulf of Mexico

▲ *Some of the exploration routes that opened up the North American interior.*

▼ *Zebulon Pike's explorations stimulated American settlement in the Southwest.*

A Chronology of North American Exploration

1535 Jacques Cartier sails up the St. Lawrence River.

1539–1542 Hernando de Soto explores the Southeast and discovers the Mississippi River.

1603–1616 Samuel de Champlain explores the eastern coast of North America. He sails up the St. Lawrence River as far west as Lake Huron.

1609–1611 Henry Hudson explores Hudson Bay, the Hudson River, and Hudson Strait.

1673 Jacques Marquette and Louis Jolliet explore the area of the northern Mississippi river.

1679–1682 Sieur de la Salle and Henri de Tonti explore the Great Lakes and follow the Mississippi to the Gulf of Mexico.

1789–1793 Sir Alexander Mackenzie follows the Mackenzie River to the Arctic Ocean and explores western Canada.

1804–1806 Meriwether Lewis and William Clark cross the Rocky Mountains and reach the Pacific Ocean.

1805–1807 Zebulon Pike explores the Midwest, Rocky Mountain region, and the Southwest.

1842–1846 John Charles Fremont explores the West.

FAIRBANKS, Douglas

Douglas Fairbanks (1883–1939) was a leading motion picture actor and producer from the silent screen era. Romantic and athletic, Fairbanks was well suited to the swashbuckling leading men he portrayed. His first motion picture was *The Lamb* (1915). In 1919, Fairbanks founded the United Artists Studio with Mary PICKFORD (his wife from 1920–1935), Charlie CHAPLIN, and the director D. W. Griffith. Douglas Fairbanks, Jr., his son by his first wife, played similar roles in 1930s and 1940s.

▶ Douglas Fairbanks never had fencing lessons, but he became famous by portraying masters of swordplay.

▼ During the Civil War, Admiral Farragut got the nickname "Old Salamander" for navigating ships past the forts at New Orleans and Mobile.

FARRAGUT, David

David Farragut (1801–1870) was an admiral in the U.S. Navy. He fought in the WAR OF 1812 and the MEXICAN WAR (1846–1848). During the CIVIL WAR he fought for the Union side even though he came from the South. In 1862 he sailed his ships past Confederate fortifications to capture New Orleans. He then sailed up the Mississippi River to attack the Confederate forces at Vicksburg, Mississippi. In 1864, Farragut led a fleet into Mobile Bay, Alabama, forcing that Confederate port to close down. During the battle, an officer spotted some mines, which were then called torpedoes. Farragut's defiant cry, "Damn the torpedoes! Full speed ahead!" made him a hero of the Union navy.

FASHION

Until well into the 20th century, the United States looked to the designers of Paris for the fashionable "look" of the year. But even in the 1800s there were some purely American ideas that set popular trends. Bloomers, the loose, gathered pants worn under short skirts, were named after the social reformer Amelia Bloomer. In the 1890s the illustrator Charles Dana Gibson created a distinctive female look. From 1890 to about 1910, women everywhere copied the "Gibson Girl" look with its long neckline and upswept hair.

The single biggest contribution of the United States has been not a style, but a fabric—denim. Levi Strauss first created a garment using denim and copper studs in 1850. This became widely used by workers who needed tough clothing, such as farmers and cowboys. But a clothing revolution started in the 1960s that carried on into the 1980s. Denim became high fashion. It fitted in well with the new "unisex" look. It was used for pants, jumpsuits, jackets, dresses, suits, and hats. And denim was not just American; it was world fashion.

▲ Fashion models display the works of leading designers such as Donna Karan at each spring's fashion shows.

Long pants for men arrived in the United States around the year 1820. The fashion had begun with the peasants who came to power during the French Revolution. The first wearers of long pants in the United States were seen as "revolutionary" as a result.

1780

1860

1900

1920

1960

◄ Over the past 200 years, everyday American fashions for men and women have become simpler. Styles were often based on what was fashionable in Europe at the time. Gradually American fashion developed its own characteristics.

▲ Denim clothes are a popular choice for all ages. It is durable, comfortable, and fashionable.

▼ The agreements reached by the Fathers of Confederation were legally binding in Canada until the Constitution Act replaced them in 1982.

Americans like to be comfortable in their clothing, whether it is for business, entertaining, or relaxing. The clothing designs of Halston, Oscar de la Renta, and Anne Klein dominated in the 1960s and 1970s. Today the strong styles of Calvin Klein, Ralph Lauren, Donna Karan, and Norma Kamali influence U.S. fashion.

FATHERS OF CONFEDERATION

The Fathers of Confederation were the "founding fathers" of Canada. By the early 1860s, the British colonies in Canada had been given a large measure of self-government. But some of their leaders, including John MACDONALD, of Upper Canada (Ontario), and George Etienne Cartier, of Lower Canada (Quebec), felt that the colonies would be stronger if they were confederated, or united.

In September 1864, 23 representatives from Upper and Lower Canada, Nova Scotia, New Brunswick, Newfoundland, and Prince Edward Island (P.E.I.) met in Charlottetown, P.E.I. They agreed to confederation. The following month they met again in Quebec City and drew up proposals for the new government. The British government favored the plan, and on July 1, 1867, Parliament passed the BRITISH NORTH AMERICA ACT, creating the Dominion of Canada.

FAULKNER, William

William Faulkner (1897–1962) was a famous writer. He was born in New Albany, Mississippi, and spent most of his life in that state. He wrote short stories and novels. His fame stems from the novels that were set in the imaginary Yoknapatawpha County (based on Oxford, Mississippi, where he lived). In these novels, Faulkner dealt with the values and morals of southern society. He wrote about race and prejudice, crime and violence, love and concern, honor and pride. Faulkner won the Nobel Prize for literature in 1949 and the Pulitzer Prize in 1955 and 1963. *The Sound and the Fury*, *The Reivers*, *Absalom, Absalom!*, and *Go Down, Moses* are among his greatest works. He also wrote many film screenplays.

▲ *William Faulkner came from a wealthy background. Many family friends were shocked by the controversial themes of his novels and short stories.*

FEDERAL BUREAU OF INVESTIGATION

The Federal Bureau of Investigation (FBI) is the chief law-enforcement arm of the United States Department of Justice. Its 9,600 special agents investigate bank robberies, hijackings, kidnappings, and other federal crimes. They also work closely with state law-enforcement agencies. Other FBI duties include tracking organized crime gangs such as the Mafia and investigating people it thinks are a risk to the country's security. In the past, the FBI has tracked down many enemy agents operating within the United States. The FBI also investigates drug dealing, terrorism, and white collar crime such as financial fraud.

The FBI was founded in 1908, though it got its name only in 1932. Its headquarters are in Washington, D.C., and its director is appointed by the president.

▼ *FBI agents wear a badge that features the American eagle and the scales and sword of justice.*

FEDERALISTS

The Federalists were those people who vigorously supported the adoption of the new Constitution, with its federal form of government. They included Alexander HAMILTON, James MADISON, and John JAY. During George WASHINGTON's government, a split occurred between those who believed in a strong central government and those who believed that the states and the individual should retain as many rights as possible. Those who believed in a strong federal government formed the Federalist Party under Alexander Hamilton.

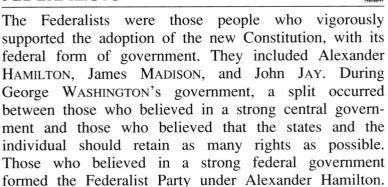

The Federalist is the title given to 85 essays published in 1787–1788 in various New York newspapers to convince voters to support ratification of the new Constitution of the United States. These essays were published in book form in 1788. It is believed that Alexander Hamilton wrote 51 of the essays, Madison 29, and John Jay 5. The essays are still a classic example of an analysis of federalism and free government.

It was the first political party in the United States. Among the policies it favored were the creation of a central bank, a system of tariffs and excise (indirect) taxes, and neutrality in the war between Britain and France that broke out in 1793. The Federalists achieved the election of John ADAMS in 1796, but by 1800 they had been overtaken by the new Democratic-Republican (later DEMOCRATIC) Party, led by Thomas JEFFERSON. By 1815, the Federalist Party had disintegrated. But the Federalists had done a great deal to strengthen the central government of the United States and give it its present form.

FEDERAL RESERVE *See* Banking

FEDERAL TRADE COMMISSION *See* Trade

FERBER, Edna

Edna Ferber (1885–1968) was a famous writer. She was born in Kalamazoo, Michigan, and raised in Wisconsin. She started work as a journalist when she was 17, but soon started writing successful novels and plays. These were largely about American life in the 19th century. Ferber claimed that her books were intended as social criticisms as well as entertainment. She won the Pulitzer Prize for fiction in 1925 for *So Big*. A number of her books, including *Cimarron*, *Giant*, *Ice Palace*, and *Show Boat*, were made into movies. She wrote a number of plays with George S. Kaufman. Some of these, such as *Dinner at Eight* and *Stage Door* were also made into films.

▼ *James Dean starred in the 1956 movie version of* Giant, *Edna Ferber's tale of 20th-century Texas.*

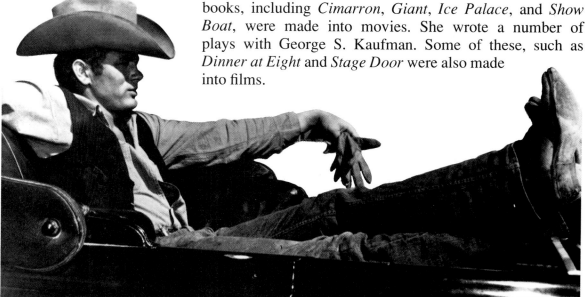

FERMI, Enrico

In 1934, Enrico Fermi (1901–1954) became the first person to split the atom. At that time, however, he did not know just what he had done. The process of splitting an atom is called *nuclear fission*. Born in Italy, Fermi settled in the United States in 1938. That same year he was awarded the Nobel Prize for physics for his work in the United States. In 1939, Fermi became a professor of physics at Columbia University, but he moved to the University of Chicago in 1942. That same year he produced a nuclear chain reaction. This led to both the atomic bomb—which Fermi helped develop during World War II—and nuclear power plants. After World War II, Fermi began research on high-energy particles. The Fermi National Accelerator Laboratory, in Batavia, Illinois, is named after him. So, too, is fermium, an artificially made radioactive element.

The chemical element fermium was named after Enrico Fermi. It was first discovered in the debris from the first H-bomb explosion. It is a radioactive element and has to be made artificially. The total amount of fermium that has been made since it was discovered in 1952 is less than one-millionth of a gram.

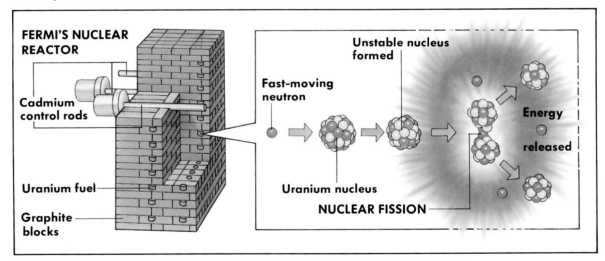

FIELD, Marshall

Marshall Field (1834–1906) was a U.S. businessman who founded the world-famous Chicago department store Marshall Field and Company. He introduced sales methods, such as marking prices on goods and allowing customers to exchange merchandise if they were dissatisfied. On his death, Field left money to create Chicago's Field Museum of Natural History, and he provided land for the new University of Chicago. Field's grandson, Marshall Field III, set up the family publishing business, which included the *Chicago Sun-Times*. The Field Corporation was established by Marshall Field V.

▲ Nuclear fission provides the energy for both nuclear power and atomic weapons. A neutron splits the nucleus of a uranium atom, giving off energy and releasing more neutrons. Each neutron can go on to split another uranium nucleus, which in turn gives off more heat and releases more neutrons in a chain reaction.

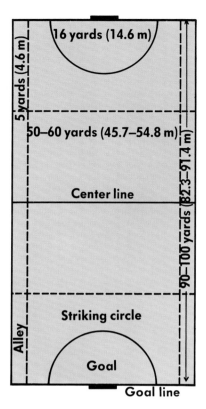

16 yards (14.6 m)

5 yards (4.6 m)

50–60 yards (45.7–54.8 m)

90–100 yards (82.3–91.4 m)

Center line

Alley

Striking circle

Goal

Goal line

▲ *Field hockey teams have 11 members. Goals can only be scored from within the striking circle and are worth one point.*

FIELD HOCKEY

Field hockey is a team sport. In the United States, it is usually played by girls. Each team tries to knock a ball into the opposing team's goal by using a stick with a curved end. Early in the 20th century the game was brought to the United States from Great Britain by Constance Applebee. The United States Field Hockey Association (for women) and the Field Hockey Association of America (for men) were formed in the 1920s.

Men and women play according to the same rules. Men first played field hockey in the Olympics in 1908; women have played in the Olympics only since 1980.

FIELDS, W. C.

W. C. Fields (1879–1946) was one of the great movie comedians. His real name was William Claude Dukenfield. Fields's strange way of speaking out of the side of his mouth is widely imitated by comedians even today. Fields was born in Philadelphia. When asked his opinion of things he found boring, he would say, "On the whole, I'd rather be in Philadelphia." This line became one of his trademarks. He was also known for his strong dislike for children and animals and made this part of his comic roles. *My Little Chickadee* and *The Bank Dick* are two of his best-known films. He also wrote movie scripts using made-up names such as Mahatma Kane Jeeves and Otis T. Cricklecobis.

W. C. Fields ran away from home at the age of 11 and within three years had begun a stage juggling act. He was well known for his tricks with a corkscrew-shaped billiard cue!

▶ *W. C. Fields and Mae West teamed up in* My Little Chickadee, *one of the most successful movies of 1940.*

Millard Fillmore was the 13th president of the United States. He became president in 1850, when the issue of slavery was dividing the country. Fillmore had been elected vice president on the Whig ticket with Zachary TAYLOR. When Taylor died in office, Fillmore became president. At that time, the Compromise of 1850 was being debated in Congress. This concerned whether slavery should be allowed in the lands won from Mexico in the MEXICAN WAR (1846–1848).

Even though he did not approve of slavery, Fillmore was in favor of the compromise. He felt slavery had to be permitted until it could be abolished without leading to civil war. He got the compromise passed very quickly. California was admitted to the Union as a free state (in which slavery was against the law), and the slave trade was abolished in Washington, D.C. The new territories of New Mexico and Utah were created; they both banned slavery. The boundary of Texas was also settled.

▼ Slavery was the subject of fierce Senate debates in the late 1840s. As vice president, Millard Fillmore was also president of the Senate at that time.

The other main section of the compromise was the Fugitive Slave Law. Under this law, people could be jailed or fined if they helped runaway slaves. Also, runaway slaves were to be returned to their owners without trial. The compromise postponed the Civil War by about ten years. But Fillmore's strict enforcement of the Fugitive Slave Law made him very unpopular in the North, where the ABOLITIONIST movement was strong.

Fillmore's major achievement was opening up Japanese ports to U.S. trade. In 1853 he sent Commodore Matthew PERRY and a U.S. fleet on this historic mission to negotiate trading terms with Japan.

Millard Fillmore
Born: January 7, 1800, in Locke, New York
Education: Received little formal education; legal training
Political party: Whig
Term of office: 1850–1853
Married: 1826 to Abigail Powers
Died: March 8, 1874, in Buffalo, New York

▶ *These Los Angeles fire fighters wear helmets, goggles, gloves, and waterproof suits. This special equipment helps protect them from smoke, flames, and falling debris.*

The Worst Fires in U.S. History
1871 Chicago Fire: 17,450 buildings destroyed; 250 dead
1876 Brooklyn, New York: 295 dead
1894 Minnesota forest fire: 6 towns destroyed; 413 dead
1900 Hoboken, New Jersey: 326 dead
1903 Chicago: 602 dead
1918 Minnesota forest fire: 400 dead
1930 Columbus, Ohio: 320 dead
1942 Boston: 491 dead

▼ *Chemicals dumped by air tankers help check the progress of a forest fire in California's Sierra Nevada mountains. Each year about 3 million acres (1.3 million ha) of forest are destroyed by fire.*

FIRE FIGHTING

In 1679, Boston became the first city in the colonies to set up a paid group to fight fires. Today there are tens of thousands of fire-fighting companies all over the country. Fire fighters have to be prepared to deal with fires in many different and difficult circumstances — in cities and towns, in the country, and in forests. Some fire departments have paid crews; others are staffed by volunteers. (Women were first accepted as paid fire fighters in the 1970s.) They receive special training, including first aid.

Today fire departments spend much time on preven-

tion and education—trying to prevent fires from happening in the first place. They have inspectors who regularly check public buildings to make sure there are no fire hazards. Fire fighters also speak to public groups. They warn them of the danger of fire and tell them how they can prevent it. There are clear guidelines for behavior in case of a fire—what to do and how to get out of the building as quickly as possible. Schools have regular fire drills so pupils will know how to cope in a real emergency.

FIRESTONE, Harvey

Harvey Firestone (1868–1938) was a businessman and manufacturer. Firestone was active in the early days of the automobile industry. Born in Ohio, he set up the Firestone Tire and Rubber Company in Akron, Ohio, in 1900. Early in his life Firestone saw how useful rubber could be. He devoted most of his life to working with this substance—not only making tires, but also improving the rubber and discovering new uses. As rubber began to be used more widely, he and Henry FORD carried out research to find an artificially made substitute that would be as good.

▲ The first tires made by the Firestone Tire and Rubber Company were solid. The company pioneered later developments, such as tubeless and radial tires.

FISH

Fish are *vertebrates*, or animals with backbones, that live in the water. Every fish lives in the region that suits it best. About two thirds of all species of fish live in salt water, and one third in fresh water.

North America is rich in freshwater species of fish. Some of the freshwater fish, such as minnows and trout, prefer fast-flowing streams. Others, including carp and catfish, do better in warm, muddy rivers. Still others, such as bluegills, lake trout, white perch, and whitefish, live in lakes. Some fish are found in lakes, rivers, *and* streams. These include black bullheads, largemouth bass, muskellunge, northern pike, rainbow trout, and yellow perch.

Many fish migrate from one area to another. Some trout leave their lakes to spawn (lay eggs) in rivers. Many types of alewives, salmon, and white sturgeon swim from salt water to fresh water to spawn. The North American eel migrates in the other direction. It lives in fresh water and spawns in salt water.

Some Unusual Fish
Atlantic croakers make croaking noises (like frogs) at dawn and dusk.
Catfish, like other bottom-dwelling fish, use feelers to search for food.
Flying fish don't really fly; they glide, using their long, stiff fins as wings.
Goose fish can open their mouths wide enough to swallow some seabirds.
Pilot fish swim alongside sharks and feed on their leftovers.
Porcupine fish puff up their spiny skin like balloons when they are threatened or attacked.

▶ *Salmon brave waterfalls and hungry bears on their way upstream to spawn.*

▼ *Some freshwater fish, such as the walleye perch and largemouth bass, are common throughout North America. Others thrive in special environments: the northern pike in cold northern lakes and the coho salmon along the Pacific northwest coast.*

**Common shiner
6–8 in (15–20 cm)**

**Walleye perch
1–2 ft (30–80 cm)**

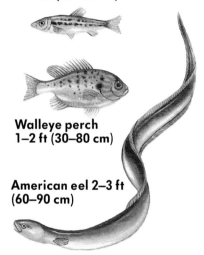

**American eel 2–3 ft
(60–90 cm)**

**Largemouth bass
1.5–2 ft (50–60 cm)**

**Rainbow trout 1–3 ft
(30–90 cm)**

Northern pike 2–4 ft (60 cm–1.2 m)

**Coho salmon 1–3 ft
(30–90 cm)**

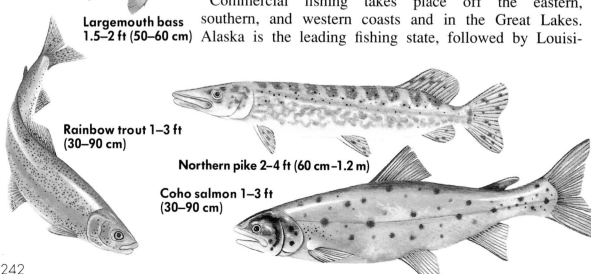

Some saltwater fish live only along the coasts and are referred to as coastal fish. Others live away from the coast, at various depths, and are known as oceanic fish. As with freshwater fish, certain saltwater fish migrate. For example, mackerel and many types of haddock migrate from coastal waters to deeper waters.

FISHING INDUSTRY

The United States fishing industry is involved in catching fish and shellfish so that they can be processed into food. The industry's catch in U.S. waters totaled 7.2 billion pounds in 1988 and was valued at $3.5 billion. About 360,000 people are employed by the industry. Of these, about 250,000 are fishermen who work on about 125,000 ships and boats.

Commercial fishing takes place off the eastern, southern, and western coasts and in the Great Lakes. Alaska is the leading fishing state, followed by Louisi-

ana and Virginia. In quantity, the most important fish caught is menhaden. In terms of value, however, salmon is the most important fish. Shrimp and crabs are the most valuable shellfish caught. Water pollution and overfishing are threats to the future of the industry. As a result, there are now restrictions on fishing in U.S. waters.

Fish and shellfish for human consumption are sold fresh, frozen, or canned. Only half the catch is eaten by people. Menhaden, for example, is used for its oils or as fertilizer or animal feed. And only half the fish eaten by Americans comes from the U.S. fishing fleet. The other half is imported.

Most Important Commercial Fish
1. Sockeye salmon
2. Halibut
3. Chinook salmon
4. Gulf menhaden
5. Sablefish
6. Pink salmon
7. Silver salmon
8. Yellowfin tuna
9. Pacific herring
10. Alaska pollock

FITZGERALD, F. Scott

F. Scott Fitzgerald (1896–1940) was a novelist and short-story writer. He wrote about the United States in the 1920s. Fitzgerald called this period the "Jazz Age." Others called it the "Roaring Twenties." It was a time of wild parties, drinking, and seemingly glamorous society. It was a time when wealthy people looked for excitement to ease the boredom in their lives. Fitzgerald wrote about these people in such books as *The Beautiful and Damned* and *The Great Gatsby*. In fact, he and his wife Zelda lived their own lives like the characters in his books. But they, like other people, and like some of his fictional characters, found that a life of pleasure-seeking could be very empty. His wife became mentally ill, and he became an alcoholic. Fitzgerald's last novel, *The Last Tycoon*, was about Hollywood. It was published in 1941, the year after he died.

▼ *F. Scott Fitzgerald once observed that "the rich are different." But he later learned that money alone could not make people happy.*

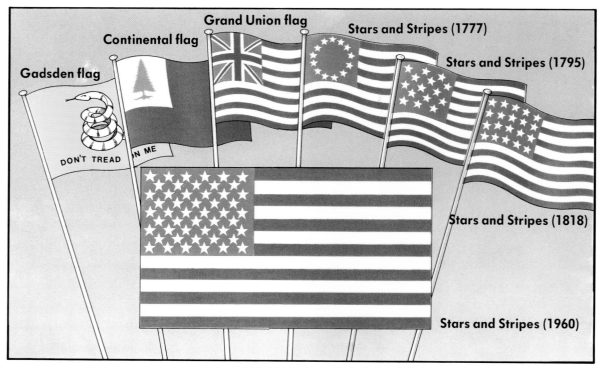

Gadsden flag

Continental flag

Grand Union flag

Stars and Stripes (1777)

Stars and Stripes (1795)

Stars and Stripes (1818)

Stars and Stripes (1960)

DON'T TREAD ON ME

▲ *Rattlesnake and pine tree symbols on the first American flags were signs of anger and strength. The stripes, symbols of the original 13 colonies, shared space with the British Union flag on the first national flag. In 1777 the Continental Congress replaced this flag with the first version of the Stars and Stripes.*

The American flag that inspired Francis Scott Key to write *The Star-Spangled Banner* had 15 stripes and 15 stars. Vermont and Kentucky had just joined the Union, so two stars and two stripes had been added to the original 13. Altogether the Stars and Stripes has been through 27 different versions.

FLAG

Popularly known as the "Stars and Stripes" or "Old Glory," the flag of the United States has changed many times, but the basic elements have remained the same.

In June 1777, after the DECLARATION OF INDEPENDENCE, the CONTINENTAL CONGRESS decided what the flag of the new country would look like. It had 13 stripes in alternating red and white, to stand for the 13 states. Also representing the states were 13 white stars on a blue background. The Congress said these represented "a new constellation." In other words, the new country in the world was like a new group of stars in the sky.

The colors were the same as those chosen in 1782 for the GREAT SEAL of the United States, in which red stood for hardiness and courage, white for purity and innocence, and blue for vigilance, perseverance, and justice, representing the qualities of the new nation.

As new states joined the Union, more stars were added, in different arrangements. The flag was changed to include 15 stripes when the first two new states joined. But since 1818 it has had 13 stripes. These represent the first 13 states. Since 1960 the flag has had 50 stars, for the 50 states of the Union. Before that no star had been added since 1912.

FLANAGAN, Edward J.

Father Edward Flanagan (1886–1948) was a Roman Catholic priest who founded Boys Town near Omaha, Nebraska. Born in Ballymoe, Ireland, he later was a priest in Nebraska. There he started taking in homeless and delinquent boys in 1917. In 1921 he bought a large farm and built living, study, and training areas. He called this community Boys Town. In 1979, Boys Town began to take in girls. About 560 children live in Boys Town. But through other programs, including foster care and hospital care, Boys Town assists more than 13,000 children a year.

FLOOD

The first pioneers called America "the land of a thousand rivers." We know now that there are even more rivers and that they can be killers when they flood. In 1889, for example, the Johnstown, Pennsylvania, flood caused the deaths of 2,200 people when a dam broke.

Beginning in the late 1920s, Congress set up a nationwide system of flood defenses. In Louisiana, where the land around the Mississippi River is the lowest, a network of channels, reservoirs, and levees (raised banks) was built. In California's Central Valley dams were built to protect against floods as well as to provide water for irrigation and hydroelectric power.

The Worst Floods in U.S. History
1889 Johnstown, Pennsylvania: 2,200 dead
1900 Galveston, Texas: 5,000 dead
1903 Heppner, Oregon: 325 dead
1913 Ohio, Indiana: 732 dead
1915 Galveston, Texas: 275 dead
1928 Saugus, California: 450 dead
1928 Lake Okeechobee, Florida: 2,000 dead
1972 Rapid City, South Dakota: 236 dead

▼ *The James River overflowed and flooded thousands of acres in Richmond, Virginia, in 1985. Parts of the city were cut off by flood waters.*

Mockingbird

Orange
blossom

Palmetto palm

Florida's nickname is the Sunshine State. Its blue skies, high temperatures, and almost year-round sun have made it a favorite vacation area for over 40 million Americans every year. Millions of senior citizens have retired there. In fact, Florida's population is growing faster than that of almost every other state. Its economy is developing rapidly, too. Agriculture remains one of its most important businesses—especially the cultivation of oranges and grapefruits. But many high-tech industries have also been established in the state recently. Electronic engineering, especially of computers, is increasingly important to Florida.

Except for Hawaii, Florida is the most southerly state. On a map it looks like a finger of land that juts out from the southeast corner of the United States. It extends almost 450 miles (725 km) from north to south. The Atlantic Ocean is to the east and the warm waters of the Gulf of Mexico are to the west. The state has many natural attractions, such as sandy beaches, the strange swamps of the EVERGLADES National Park, and the little islands that make up the Florida Keys. It also offers a host of man-made attractions, including sophisticated resorts, Walt Disney World, and Sea World in Orlando. The largest city is JACKSONVILLE; the capital is Tallahassee, located in the northern part of the state.

The first Europeans to settle Florida were Spaniards, in the 1500s. In 1763, Florida became a British colony, but in 1783 it was regained by Spain. It became an American territory in 1822 and a state in 1845.

▲ Specially trained guides conduct airboat tours of the Everglades.

► Modern hotels line the Strand at Miami Beach. This strip of land constitutes some of the most expensive real estate in the United States.

▲ *The Florida Keys, a string of islands, stretches south into the Gulf of Mexico. Many of the smaller keys make up the Great White Heron National Wildlife Refuge.*

Places of Interest

● St. Augustine was founded in 1565 and is the oldest city in the United States. Many colonial houses have been restored.

● Walt Disney World in Orlando offers an amusement park, a recreational center, a fairy-tale castle, and the futuristic Epcot Center as some of its many attractions.

● Marineland, near St. Augustine, was the world's first oceanarium. It includes more than 100 kinds of marine creatures – all living in natural surroundings.

● Everglades National Park is one of several national parks in Florida. The Everglades are home to many interesting and rare species of animals, birds, and plants.

Florida
Capital: Tallahassee
Area: 54,153 sq mi (140,256 km²). Rank: 22nd
Population: 13,003,362 (1990). Rank: 4th
Statehood: Mar. 3, 1845
Principal rivers: St. Johns, St. Marys, Suwannee, Apalachicola
Highest point: A hilltop in Walton County, 345 ft (105 m)
Motto: "In God We Trust."
Song: "Swanee River"

247

FOLK ART, AMERICAN

▼ Common household items from the 18th and 19th centuries (below) have become collector's items as folk art. In 1990 a 19th-century metal weather vane was sold for more than $100,000 in New York. Naive (or Primitive) art (right) was considered worthless until modern painters came to appreciate its bold simplicity.

Earthenware plate

Tole ware

Weathervane

Folk art is the art of ordinary people—people who are not professional painters, sculptors, furniture makers, or the like. North American folk art includes the work of people of European and African ancestry. Indian folk art, such as totems and beadwork, is usually considered separately. Useful objects can be folk art, but the decorative element must be the foremost consideration. Folk art is still being made. A 20th-century example is the Watts Tower in Los Angeles, which is made of found objects such as broken bottles. As early as the 1670s, folk artists, who were usually untrained and anonymous, were painting portraits of merchant families and other well-to-do middle-class people. Other popular subjects included landscapes, everyday (genre) scenes, and historical and religious subjects. These works are examples of what is called naive or primitive art.

The first American folk sculptors carved images on gravestones, but most later carvers worked in wood. They made ship carvings, weather vanes, and trade signs such as life-size Indians for tobacco dealers. In the Southwest, some Hispanic wood carvers made impressive *bultos* (holy figures). New

England seamen made some objects from the teeth and bones of whales—work that is known as scrimshaw.

Some everyday pottery achieved the status of art. Examples include redware dishes in the Pennsylvania Dutch tradition and stoneware face jugs made by black potters. Some quilts and hooked rugs are examples of abstract art.

The Museum of American Folk Art and the Metropolitan Museum of Art, both in New York City, exhibit folk art.

Influences on American Folk Art
British: shop signs, boat figureheads, wood carving, needlecraft, leatherwork.
Dutch: portraits and biblical painting.
Scandinavian: wood carvings, furniture, household utensils, inlaid wood pictures.
German: Pennsylvania Dutch tole ware, quilting, barn signs, painted chests.
Hispanic: carved religious figures (*bultos*), altar paintings (*retablos*).
African: baskets, ceramics, musical instruments, ironwork, wood carving, gravestones.

Cigar-store figure

▲ Life-size wooden sculptures stood outside many cigar stores in the 1800s. They were symbols of the Indians who introduced the white settlers to tobacco.

◀ This North Carolina quilter is carrying on a 250-year-old tradition. These quilts are made of patchwork, a decorative way of using scraps of cloth so that nothing goes to waste.

Some Features of American Folk Art
Figureheads were elaborately carved wooden statues placed on the bows (fronts) of sailing ships.
Limners were traveling American folk artists who specialized in painting portraits.
Samplers were embroidered "diplomas" showing that a girl had mastered many needlework stitches.
Tole ware household utensils were made of sheet metal and painted with vivid colors.

▼ New England whalers made intricate carvings on their long voyages. The pictures, called scrimshaw, were often carved from whales' teeth.

▲ Superstitions are part of folklore. Long ago the Pennsylvania Dutch painted hex signs on their barns to ward off witches. Today they are used as good-luck symbols.

▼ Plains Indians valued storytelling, an important part of folklore. Tribal lore and customs passed from one generation to the next in long evening sessions.

FOLKLORE, American

The word "folklore" means "knowledge, or learning, of the people." But it is a special kind of knowledge—the kind that has been passed down by word of mouth from generation to generation. There are many kinds of folklore. There are folk songs and folk dances, folk tales and folk art. Fairy tales and nursery rhymes and myths and legends are also folklore. So, too, are many superstitions, children's games, and riddles.

One of the most popular types of folklore is the folk tale. Many American folk tales are really tall tales. They are about bigger-than-life cowboys, lumberjacks, miners, or other people. Folk tales are often based on real people, but they are more fiction than fact. For example, there probably was a lumberjack with a name like Paul BUNYAN, but the tall tales invented about him have turned him into a superhuman folk hero who could chop down entire forests by himself. The folk hero PECOS BILL was based on cowboys of the Old West. But he was entirely made up by a journalist in the 1920s. Many ballads have been written about John Henry, that "steel drivin' man" who could work faster than a steam drill. And in terms of boasting, few could match Mike Fink, who bragged that he was the fastest shot and best fighter along the entire Mississippi River. Davy CROCKETT, a real-life hero, has become one of America's best-loved folk heroes.

The poem *The Courtship of Miles Standish*, by Henry Wadsworth Longfellow, has become part of American folklore. According to the poem, the famous Pilgrim leader was too timid to ask Priscilla Mullens to marry him, and he sent his friend John Alden to ask on his behalf. This account was not true, but it helped preserve Standish's memory.

▼ The songs children sing while jumping rope and other street rhymes and songs are part of the folklore tradition.

Animal tales are another type of folklore. Black Americans brought many animal tales with them from Africa when they were forced into slavery in the Americas. In the late 1800s, Joel Chandler HARRIS made these tales popular when he wrote the Uncle Remus stories. These were humorous tales about animals, such as Brer Rabbit, that have human qualities.

The American INDIANS also have their folklore. Many of their folk tales, myths, and legends are about the origins of people. One tribe, the Algonquins, even has a story like the well-known Cinderella fairy tale. (See MYTHS AND LEGENDS.)

The Story of John Henry

The black laborer John Henry worked on a team digging the Big Bend railroad tunnel in West Virginia in the 1870s. The railroad workers used sledgehammers to dig the rock. When a steam drill was brought in to replace some workers, John Henry had a race with it. He won but died of exhaustion immediately afterward. This story of man against machine became the subject of many songs and ballads.

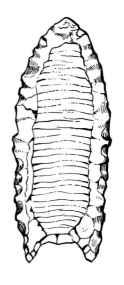

▲ *Pete Seeger has been collecting and singing folk songs since the 1930s. His music covers many themes, from songs of protest to traditional melodies.*

▼ *Scientists were able to date the Folsom culture by dating the bones of mammoths that lay near a Folsom spearhead. The notches on the spearhead exactly matched the grooves on the mammoth bones.*

FOLK MUSIC

Like other types of FOLKLORE, folk music usually originates among rural people. The songs are passed on orally long before they are written down. Some folk songs, called ballads, tell a story. Many of these were brought to North America by settlers from Great Britain and Ireland.

Other kinds of folk songs include lullabies, work songs, and religious songs. The hymn "Amazing Grace" and the lovely Appalachian Christmas carol "I Wonder as I Wander" are native North American folk songs. Among the best loved of all folk songs are black American spirituals, such as "Deep River" and "Steal Away."

Work songs have often helped to keep people's spirits up during long hours of toil and to help them work rhythmically. On sailing ships, teams of sailors performed many tasks to the strong beat of sea chanteys. The songs of American cowboys, such as "Red River Valley" and "Git Along, Little Dogie" are a distinctively American form of folk music.

Folk music has remained popular in the 20th century. American folk singers and composers have beocme internationally known for dealing with social issues through their music. Pete Seeger, who began performing in the 1930s, has influenced many other musicians, including Bob Dylan, Joan Baez, and Arlo Guthrie.

FOLSOM CULTURE

The Folsom culture is the name given to some prehistoric people who lived in North America about 10,000 years ago. Evidence of these people was first found at Folsom, New Mexico, in 1926. The Folsom culture came after the Clovis culture. These people hunted large game such as mammoths. The Folsom were also hunters, and many of their spearheads have been found. Although there was still some large game, the Folsom seem to have hunted smaller game such as the long-horned bison, now extinct (no longer existing).

The main Folsom site is Lindenmeier in Colorado. It shows that the Folsom were more advanced than the Clovis. Their spearheads were smaller and more carefully made. They also made different kinds of tools, such as special needles for sewing and possibly basket making, and scrapers used to prepare animal skins.